The Church: First Thirty Years

Exposition of Acts

Martin Murphy

Published by: Theocentric Publishing Group
1069A Main Street
Chipley, FL 32428

http://www.theocentricpublishing.com

Library of Congress Control Number: 2013947580

ISBN 9780985618179

To churches dedicated to the expansion of the kingdom of God on earth according to the biblical mandates for the mission and ministry of the church.

Also to all the faithful pastors committed to church growth consistent with the teaching of the full counsel of God.

Introduction

My exposition of the book of Acts began in 1999. I can trace my interest in this project to a few years before 1999 when I acquired the four-volume set of *The Collected Writings of James Henley Thornwell*, and his *Life and Letters*. He lived and ministered during the middle of the 19th century. I was aghast at the condition of the church during his life. So much of what he said reminded me of the church at the beginning of the 21st century. For example, he wrote his colleague, Dr. Breckinridge on January 27, 1841, because he was distressed over the condition of the church. A couple of sentences will reveal the resemblance to the current situation. "It is not to be disguised, that our Church is becoming deplorably secular. She has degenerated from a spiritual body into a mere petty corporation…We are doing God's work by human wisdom and human policy; and what renders the evil still more alarming, is that so few are aware to the real state of the case" (*Life and Letters of James Henley Thornwell*, page 224). My exposition of the book of Acts is more of a principled application, than an academic commentary.

My conversion to Christianity was not an emotional surge that compelled me to walk down the aisle of a building, commonly and mistakenly referred to as the church. During a brief hospital stay in 1982, I read the gospel of John. Then I re-read it and mused over the content. It became obvious that the way to have a favorable relationship with God was through Jesus Christ. My first challenge after believing that Christ was the only way to have an eternal favorable relationship with God, was finding a church. I had previous experience with a few churches, which is one reason I never examined Scripture long enough to believe that I could have a favorable relationship with God. Churches were on every corner and each one believed their doctrine of Scripture was right. It did not take a doctorate in theology to figure out the reason they did not meet together. They could not get along socially or they disagreed on biblical doctrine. Neither of those are sufficient reasons to divide the body of Christ. After going to one church, (later I would learn that phrase was an absolute logical impossibility), for about one year I asked one of the leaders to have an in-depth study of the book of Acts. His immediate response was, "a study of the book of Acts may cause doctrinal division in the church." Within two years that church split over where the building should be located. For my entire Christian life, I wanted to understand the nature, purpose, mission and ministry of the church. My research and study of the book of Acts helped me understand the nature, purpose, mission, and ministry of the church. I hope others will benefit from my work.

This book traces the early development of the church based on the book of Acts. It is not an academic commentary. It is an exposition of the book of Acts with special attention to the growth of the early church. The biblical text listed at the beginning of each chapter should be read before reading the exposition. It examines the first generation of the church and reveals principles for each succeeding generation of the church. Church growth will be the subject of special attention. The church consists of all the professing Christians in this world (Colossians 1:18; 1 Corinthians 1:2). The church is not a building, a social organization, or a place. The word "church" as it is found in Scripture has been grossly misunderstood for twenty centuries. If Christians do not understand the nature, purpose, mission, and ministry of the church, they will never understand the often-used terminology "church growth". Over the past thirty years, the church growth movement, with all its sophisticated plans gradually absconded the truth about God ordained church growth and replaced it with the god of church growth. The last chapter will explain the difference between the *God* of church growth and the *god* of church growth. The first thirty years of the church ought to be a flagship for the last thirty years of the church.

Table of Contents

1. The Old Church in a New Age

Acts 1:1-5

The opening words of the book of Acts will remind the reader that Acts is a continuation of Luke's inspired, infallible history of "all that Jesus began both to do and teach" (Acts 1:1). The first account or the former account refers to the gospel of Luke. Luke's account of the life and ministry of Jesus brought to completion God's covenant promise to send a Messiah to save God's people from their sin. Luke summarizes the good news of God's promise in the gospel of Luke. "Thus it is written, and thus it was necessary for the Christ to suffer and to rise from the dead the third day, and that repentance and remission of sins should be preached in His name to all nations, beginning at Jerusalem. And you are witnesses of these things. Behold, I send the Promise of My Father upon you; but tarry in the city of Jerusalem until you are endued with power from on high" (Luke 24:46-48).

From Adam to the most recent convert on earth, forgiveness is a wondrous gift from God. Forgiveness is a necessary condition for peace. If a person does not have peace with God, he or she will never have peace, ultimate peace, with other fellow human beings. Forgiveness for the believer is the result of God's redeeming grace. The result of God's saving grace is repentance and forgiveness. Repentance involves a turn from unbelief to faith and along with forgiveness is an expression of trust and thanksgiving for God's saving grace. The Bible is an inspired historical record of God's saving grace. The work and ministry of God's saving grace must be understood in terms of the past, present, and future in a historical context.

God promised to save His people after the best representatives of the human race sinned against God. Then throughout the Old Testament God gave types and figures so His people would have hope and confidence in the coming Messiah. The Messiah's appearance was a *kairotic* event (see page 4 for definition of *kairotic*) and fulfilled all the past promises of God. Yet there remained the future for all God's people and so today, that which was at one time present is now past and the future remains for God's children.

Luke, in a very unique way, left the church with the inspired history of all that Jesus began to both do and teach. Christians cannot avoid the inevitable centrality of Jesus Christ in all of human history. Please understand the emphasis on *all* of human history. A complete record of human history is not possible except in the mind of God who is the author and director of human history. It is impossible to know every action of every individual and the effect of that action on human history. A brief illustration may help. Let's say a man lives in a deep jungle and contracts a disease from an animal that is not common among human beings. Then the man through contact with the outside world passes the disease along. Then it spreads widely among humans. No one, except God, will ever know the widespread effect of that one event and how it affected the lives of people unknown to recorded history. Nevertheless, every event within the context of the spread of that disease is considered history. This question will further clarify the dilemma of knowing history.   Do you know what your great-great-great-grandfather accomplished chronologically throughout his life? If you do not know all the historical developments in his life, you have a limited knowledge of his life history. His life may not be counted by the historians as significant history, but his life is certainly a part of history. Every person, past and present, has a place in human history, even if it is not recorded.

Although some of the events of history are passed on to future generations, many of them have long been forgotten.

For instance, a few years ago someone loaned me a little book entitled *Government by Decree*. It is a history of the development of Presidential Executive Orders. After reading the history of Presidential Executive Orders, I realized that it has been a tool for good, but has also decreed evil sinister actions. My ignorance of the history of such an important part of our nation greatly distressed me. On another occasion a friend sent me an out of print book entitled *Samuel Davies: Apostle of Dissent in Colonial Virginia*. After I read the first few pages, it became obvious to me that I was grossly ignorant of an important figure in American Christianity. Given the fact that I had studied Davies' life for a graduate theology course, it made me aware of how little I knew about the history of Christianity in our country.

The most common remark I hear about history is, "I do not care about the past, I'm interested in the future." The great philosopher Aristotle said, "If you would understand anything, observe its beginning and its development." The great Roman poet and statesman Cicero has a fit word for the occasion. Cicero said, "not to know what has happened in the past is to remain forever a child." Christians should pay attention to Cicero because his comment is universally true. The history and recorded development of the church is necessary for Christians to understand their responsibility in the mission of the church.

God gave Christians an inspired history. The entire Bible is the history of HIS STORY. The book of Acts is HIS STORY that helps Christians today understand the growth of His church. More specifically, it is the inspired, infallible history of the God of church growth.

Some particular churches and denominations are immature because of their lack of understanding the history of the church. An immature church is a childish church. By way of analogy, children may be troublemakers, especially children who never grow up. There is sufficient evidence to say, in a general sense, the church is grown, but it is childish in its behavior. For example, there is much disdain for biblical confessional standards in the evangelical churches at the beginning of the 21st century. It is a sign of childish behavior. The juvenile behavior is most obvious when Christians reduce the Word of God to opinion, so that the Bible is a meaningless book of moral propositions. These and many others are the marks of a childish church.

In recent history, a cultural crisis has developed in America. The cultural battles are fought in the western world in general, but particularly in the United States. The cultural crisis includes, but is not limited to religion, family, education, the media, arts, and entertainment.

The church has reached a *kairotic* moment in history. Since time is associated with history we identify historical events as chronological or *kairotic*. Chronological history refers to a beginning followed by a sequence of events and then comes the end of history. The Greek noun *kairos* or the adjective *kairotic* is used in the New Testament, but it is rarely used by Christians today. However, it ought to be in the vocabulary of every Christian. For the sake of clarity, I will use the definition from a theological dictionary. A *kairotic* event or *kairotic* moment "refers to a specific event in time or a particular point in time which has great significance for the rest of time. In the history of salvation, the incarnation of Christ would be a *kairotic* moment" (*Theological Terms in Layman Language*, by Martin Murphy).

A few years ago, Dr. Os Guinness, a prominent sociologist and think tank guru from England wrote a book entitled *The American Hour.* Dr. Guinness made a noble attempt to call Americans to critically challenge and re-examine the cultural milieu from a kairotic perspective.

The one factor that will keep American Christians from this kairotic challenge will be the failure to re-examine the chronological history of the church, beginning with the history of the book of Acts. The next failure of the American church that will prevent a kairotic moment is neglecting the study of the history of Christianity and its development in the western world. Christians have either forgotten or ignored the influence of Jesus Christ on human history.

The examination of the church and its relation to the culture will fade into the postmodern fog if the church ignores the history of church growth. I specifically mention the postmodern culture, because it revived and canonized revisionist history. Professor Gene Veith rightly describes revisionist history in these terms. "Revisionist historians reinterpret past events according to contemporary concerns, seeing history through the lens of feminism, multiculturalism, and post Marxist politics." Sadly, Christian historians are falling into the revisionist trap. Since the Word of God is inspired history, it is not tainted with revisionism. It is sinless history.

Christians ought to be sensitive and discerning of the history that will shape their thinking and that it will be devolved to the next generation. At the same time, Christians must be passionate and aggressive in the attempt to recover biblical Christianity by understanding and applying the inspired history from Holy Scripture. The book of Acts is an inspired history that is both descriptive and normative. The history of God's people is either descriptive or normative history. Descriptive history refers to the events and words recorded in Scripture regardless of the evil words, intentions, and actions. David's sin against Bathsheba is descriptive history, but it is not normal according to the Bible. Normative history describes the authority for believing the truth and obeying the Word of God. An example of normative history is the Ten Commandments.

It will be my purpose in this book to examine all that Jesus began to both do and teach according to Luke's account in the book of Acts. Some of it will be descriptive history and some of it will be normative.

This study from the book of Acts will challenge the church to become more like a church. It will challenge the church to fulfill its purpose, mission, and ministry. The book of Acts will reveal the God of church growth. The church will be challenged to abandon the god of the church growth movement. The god of the church growth movement is modernity and all her children. I devoted the last chapter (46) to the god of the church growth movement.

I hope every Christian will experience a *kairotic* moment in history as they study the book of Acts. The time is now to recover our past, so we will have a vision for the future. The book of Acts, written by Luke, explains how the work of Jesus brought the church to maturity in His absence by the powerful work of the Holy Spirit. This book is the inspired history of the old church entering a new age.

Every Christian generation should carefully examine the inspired, infallible history found in the book of Acts. The book of Acts will bring the gospel account that Luke recorded under inspiration of the Holy Spirit into our personal lives as well as the life of the church.

There is special emphasis on the visible church throughout the book of Acts. In the opening words, we see the beginning of that emphasis because the apostles represented the visible church. As the Lord prepared for His ascension into heaven, He gathered the visible church together. The purpose of the gathering was to instruct the church and call its members to obedience.

Why should the church listen and obey? Luke answers the question. "He (Jesus Christ) also presented Himself alive after His suffering by many infallible proofs, being seen by them during forty days and speaking of the things pertaining to the kingdom of God" (Acts 1:3). Jesus Christ was a real historical person and the events of His life are provable.

The many convincing (infallible) proofs mentioned by Luke are not enumerated, but the history of our Lord recorded in the gospel of Luke does enumerate them. The miracles of Christ are sufficient convincing proofs that Christ is who He says He is.

The inspired history also records the appearance of Jesus at least ten times between His resurrection and His ascension. During the time between His resurrection and ascension, Jesus spoke of the things pertaining to the kingdom of God. Luke speaks of the kingdom of God more than thirty times in the gospel account, but only a few times in the book of Acts. Luke never mentions the church in gospel account, but mentions it many times in the book of Acts. Luke made those distinctions because of the transition from the old to the new. The kingdom of God refers to the rule of God. In the Old Testament, God ruled over His people through the nation of Israel. In the New Testament, we find that God rules over His people through His church by the power of the Holy Spirit according to His Word.

It seems the church has forgotten who she is. The church is called the body of Christ. It seems as if the body of Christ has forgotten that the Lord adds to the church daily.

When Paul went into the synagogues to preach he reasoned and persuaded them about the kingdom of God. After they were converted, they found their place in the church, because the church is the gathering place for the saints. In the final analysis, the kingdom of God is a picture of the church, the true church, both visible and invisible.

There is a true church and there is a false church. The difference between the true church and the false church is the absence or presence of God's Holy Spirit. Jesus said, "you shall be baptized with the Holy Spirit not many days from now" (Acts 1:5). The baptism of the Holy Spirit means that God gives new life to the soul. The sinful soul becomes saturated with the power of the Holy Spirit enabling the new creature in Christ to believe the gospel and observe all things that Christ commands. The evidence of the presence of the Holy Spirit is a changed life. The Holy Spirit changed the lives of the disciples and they represented the church. The Holy Spirit gives new life to the church.

It is time to either discover or re-discover what it means to be a church. This exposition from the book of Acts will help you re-live the history of the church as it is found in the Word of God. It will be a time of re-examination, challenge, and reformation for God's people.

Christians ought to invite their family and friends to be baptized with the Holy Spirit and be part of the history of the church. The inspired history of the church will reveal two concepts that we should adopt as a church. The militant church and the hospitable church are those two concepts. Those who are baptized with the Holy Spirit should gather with a militant purpose. Then they must set up a hospital to take care of the injured by preaching forgiveness and reconciliation. The militant church engages in Reformation and Revival. The church as a hospital must be ready for the ministry of forgiveness and reconciliation. This is the *kairotic* moment in the history of the church to take the old church into a new age!

2. Power for a Mission

Acts 1:6-8

A well known minister in a prominent Presbyterian Church in Philadelphia once remarked, "I am convinced the great problem in America today is that people are not thinking" (Dr. James Boice, July 1994). He was correct then, but now logical discourse is almost extinct in the western world. People in America may be thinking, but their thinking is a mixture of ungodly and anti-Christian worldviews. These ungodly worldviews have penetrated the church. Christians have sadly purchased a place among the unbelievers when it comes to sound rational thinking.

At the root of these ungodly worldviews is the quest for power. It is the desire for power over the physical and material world. The two primary means to obtain secular power is with words and war. Sometimes church leaders use crafty cunning charming words as aids to church growth. There are occasions that churches engage in war, figuratively speaking, against each other to gain power.

God's people must cling to the Word of God with a desire for spiritual power. The result will be spiritual growth. They must hold the Word of God dear to the heart, as well as the mind. The soul of man will be renewed by spiritual power so that the mind will be reformed by the Word of God.

Read the words of the inspired apostle Paul and decide for yourself.

And He Himself gave some to be apostles, some prophets, some evangelists, and some pastors and teachers, for the equipping of the saints for the work of ministry, for the edifying of the body of Christ, till we all come to the unity of the faith and of the knowledge of the Son of God, to a perfect man, to the measure of the stature of the fullness of Christ; that we should no longer be children, tossed to and fro and carried about with every wind of doctrine, by the trickery of men, in the cunning craftiness of deceitful plotting, but, speaking the truth in love, may grow up in all things into Him who is the head – Christ from whom the whole body, joined and knit together by what every joint supplies, according to the effective working by which every part does its share, causes growth of the body for the edifying of itself in love. (Ephesians 4:11-16)

The Lord created the church by His power. Then He provides the means and the people so the church will accomplish its mission and ministry. When individual Christians grow up in Christ Jesus, the result is the unity of the faith. The church is held together by the proper working of each individual part. However the history of the church in America reflects a hundred years of derision, division, and delirium.

Christians must ask some hard and probing questions and seek answers from the Word of God.

What happened to the Word of God?

What happened to the spiritual growth?

Where was the Holy Spirit during this tumultuous period?

These are difficult questions, but Christians must ask them for the sake of the future of the church.

The great Roman poet and statesman Cicero said, "Not to know what has happened in the past is to remain forever a child." Christians should be interested in the past if

they expect Christians in the future to think biblically, logi-
cally, and coherently.

Many churches have split over matters of secular
concern. Some congregations chase the pastor away without
any forethought or consideration. Then some pastors treat
congregations like goats rather than sheep. Something is
seriously wrong. What might have prevented the sad state of
affairs in the church? Maybe if Jesus Christ had appeared in
the flesh? Would the appearance of Christ have made a
difference? The Word of God answers both of those
questions.

There was a certain rich man who was clothed in
purple and fine linen and fared sumptuously every
day. But there was a certain beggar named Lazarus,
full of sores, who was laid at his gate, desiring to be
fed with the crumbs which fell from the rich man's
table. Moreover the dogs came and licked his sores.
So it was that the beggar died, and was carried by the
angels to Abraham's bosom. The rich man also died
and was buried. And being in torments in Hades, he
lifted up his eyes and saw Abraham afar off, and
Lazarus in his bosom. Then he cried and said,
"Father Abraham, have mercy on me, and send
Lazarus that he may dip the tip of his finger in water
and cool my tongue; for I am tormented in this
flame." But Abraham said, "Son, remember that in
your lifetime you received your good things, and
likewise Lazarus evil things; but now he is comforted
and you are tormented. And besides all this, between
us and you there is a great gulf fixed, so that those
who want to pass from here to you cannot, nor can
those from there pass to us." Then he said, "I beg you
therefore, father, that you would send him to my
father's house, for I have five brothers, that he may

testify to them, lest they also come to this place of torment." Abraham said to him, "They have Moses and the prophets; let them hear them." And he said, "No, father Abraham; but if one goes to them from the dead, they will repent." But he said to him, "If they do not hear Moses and the prophets, neither will they be persuaded though one rise from the dead." (Luke 16:19-31)

"They would not be persuaded if someone rises from the dead." If the Lord Jesus Christ appeared in bodily form today, would it make a difference in the state of the Christian religion and nation? To put it in the form of a rhetorical question, would the ungodly worldviews change?

The disciples standing on the Mount of Olives were aware that they were in the presence of the risen Lord Jesus Christ. The disciples had evidence of the risen Lord Jesus before their eyes. With all the evidence before them were the disciples persuaded that everything Jesus had told them was eternally true? Apparently not! "When they had come together, they asked Him, saying 'Lord, will You at this time restore the kingdom to Israel'" (Acts 1:6). Had the disciples forgotten what Jesus said or was their godly worldview mixed up with ungodly worldviews?

Pilate, the Roman judge at the trial of Jesus, asked Jesus a question and Jesus gave him an answer. "Then Pilate entered the Praetorium again, called Jesus, and said to Him, 'Are You the King of the Jews?'" (John 18:33). "Jesus answered, 'My kingdom is not of this world. If My kingdom were of this world, My servants would fight, so that I should not be delivered to the Jews; but now My kingdom is not from here'" (John 18:36). So the apostles did know that Jesus did not intend to "restore the kingdom to Israel" to the Jews.

Jesus was not a pacifist, a pessimist, or an eternal optimist. Jesus said, "My kingdom is not of this realm" to show His disciples that earthly powers are temporary powers. In another parable, Jesus explained that His disciples are called to faithfulness. They were not called to be power brokers anticipating an earthly kingdom. "And while they were listening to these things, He went on to tell a parable, because He was near Jerusalem, and they supposed that the kingdom of God was going to appear immediately" (Luke 19:11).

The disciples of Christ were not thinking clearly even after witnessing the miracles of Christ, raising men from the dead and Christ Himself being raised from the dead and appearing in a glorified body. They were thinking, but their minds were muddled. The invasion of ungodly worldviews will confuse the mind and persuade the weak!

The disciples were willing to trade the promises of God for secular power. When the promises of God are set aside, the evil ugly head of power hungry men will emerge. A passion for the wrong kind of power will always cloud the mind and motivate the heart to act wickedly to accomplish the desired end. When the disciples asked the Lord Jesus about the restoration of Israel, they apparently had forgotten the awesome resurrection day about forty days earlier. How quickly and easily Christians forget the matchless power of God.

The disciples wanted Jesus to liberate them from the pagan rule of the Romans. The disciples were weary of the oppression and wanted relief. The disciples were about to witness the ascension of Jesus Christ, the second person of the Trinity, and all they could think about was power. Power seeking people devote their lives and fortunes to become powerful. They want power so they can control others. They, like Nebuchadnezzar, think they are more powerful than God (Isaiah 47:10). Power hungry people hate God, because they are powerless before the almighty powerful God of the universe. Since unbelievers are aware of their limitations, they try to compensate for their lack of godly character by becoming control freaks. They do not have the power to create, so they desire power to control other people.

The disciples were interested in the wrong kind of power. Their interest was the same kind of interest that many church members have today. Let me paraphrase the question they had for Jesus just before He bodily left this world. "Lord will you at this time restore the kingdom and all its power to us Jews?" The same principle may be applied to Christians fighting for buildings, land, or money rather than fighting a spiritual battle for spiritual growth. Jesus rebuked His disciples because they were seeking the power of the world rather than the power of the Holy Spirit. "It is not for you to know times or seasons which the Father has put in His own authority" (Acts 1:7). Christians have a godly mission; therefore, they must have a passion for godly power. However the passion for power in the body of Christ in the 21st century is in a state of confusion. The passion for power, among professing Christians, is more widespread today than in the days Jesus was on earth during the 1st century.

Christians have uncritically adopted ungodly worldviews because of ungodly teaching. Mature clear thinking Christians will see the beauty, majesty, and import of these final words from the lips of the Lord Jesus Christ. Accompanied by the power of the Holy Spirit, these words are life changing. Jesus spoke these final words to His disciples! If you are a disciple of Jesus Christ listen carefully to His words. "You shall receive power when the Holy Spirit has come upon you; and you shall be witnesses to Me in Jerusalem, and in all Judea and Samaria, and to the end of the earth" (Acts 1:8). Christians have a mission to be witnesses for Christ. The mission will require godly power. The desire for godly power is a sign of the presence of the Holy Spirit. The Holy Spirit is the cause; the power is the effect. Christians are not able to generate this power. They cannot obtain this power with money. The most influential speaker alive cannot earn this power.

This power is a gift from God. The desire for godly power is from the Holy Spirit and comes only from God by His grace. It is not physical power. It is not the power of logic. It is not the power of eloquence. It is spiritual power and it belongs only to those who belong to God. God enables the elect with spiritual power, so they will be enabled to witness for Jesus Christ.

Christians are given spiritual power so they can resist their former master, the devil. It takes more than mere physical power to testify against the evil one. The Holy Spirit made the faith of the disciples unwavering. They were willing to die rather than deny the living Lord Jesus Christ.

Christians must understand the meaning of the words power and witness. The word "power" in our text comes from the Greek word *dunimis*. The English word "dynamite" comes from the Greek word *dunimis*. Dynamite represents power.

The word "witness" comes from the Greek word *martus*. The English word "martyr" comes from the Greek word *martus*. To be a witness for Christ is a serious matter, not to be taken lightly. The kind of spiritual power that God gives is explosive and unmoved to death. Human ability is infinitely powerless to change the hearts and lives of people, but the Holy Spirit of God is infinitely powerful to change the hearts and lives of people.

The church is in need of this spiritual power so God's people will have power for the mission, the kind of power that will make eternal changes, beginning in this world and throughout eternity.

The power of the Holy Spirit will cause the people of God to be witnesses in Jerusalem, Judea and Samaria, and even to the remotest part of the earth. These final words of the Lord were spoken near Jerusalem on the Mount of Olives just before the Lord ascended into heaven.

The missiologists interpret this verse as a mandate to go into the entire world to witness for Christ. The Lord was not merely referring to the missionary mandate. The Bible indicates the Disciples of Christ will give testimony of Him wherever they go. I will witness for Christ in my hometown, but if I end up in Tanzania, I will witness for Christ.

The two fundamental principles found in this text are these:

1) Christians must be witnesses for Christ - even to death.

2) Christians must not set limits on their witness - place, creed, color.

Both principles are worthless without the power of the Holy Spirit of God working to bring about His own glory.

If you were about to witness the ascension of the Lord Jesus Christ, which power would you seek? Or let's put it another way. If you were about to leave this world, would you sinfully seek the power of this world? Or would you seek the power of the Holy Spirit of God? Your passion for power will incline itself towards one of two positions.

1) Ungodly power in this world.

2) Godly power that transcends this world.

Choose carefully, because your decision will have eternal consequences.

3. The Amused Church

Acts 1:6-11

Every Spring there is a national holiday in the United States known as Easter. The church celebrates it with all kinds of pomp and plays. Preachers use the occasion to preach the death and resurrection of Jesus Christ. So much is said about the resurrection of Jesus Christ that His ascension almost becomes obscure. The ascension represents the departure of Christ relative to his physical presence. The doctrine of the ascension is as lofty as it is mysterious. The Word of God does reveal the importance of the doctrine. The ascension is a significant aspect of the exaltation of Jesus Christ and His enthronement at the right hand of the Father. Jesus Christ bodily ascended into heaven to fill everything in every way by His power and lordship.

Although the history of the bodily ascension of the Lord Jesus Christ is a matter of contention among professing Christians, this is not the time to prove the doctrine. Christians should trust the teaching of the Word of God. Jesus spoke of His ascension and the apostles' witnessed His ascension. The ascension is not a concept to be settled by physics. The ascension is a spiritual activity. If Christians rely on physics to explain the ascension, they will be clouded with confusion.

Although the evangelical church believes the Bible teaches that Jesus Christ bodily ascended into the spiritual dimension, commonly called heavenly places, many professing Christians do not believe. Every unbeliever and many professing believers do not believe Jesus Christ bodily ascended into heaven. They believe the story of the ascension is merely tradition that gradually found its way into the Bible.

The unbiblical view of the ascension is evident from many corners of the Protestant church. Unfortunately unbiblical views of the ascension occur, because of the amusements that keep the mind occupied. The question that motivated me to write on this subject ought to interest every Christian. "Is the church amused by the doctrine of the ascension?"

A few years ago Neil Postman wrote a book entitled *Amusing Ourselves to Death*. Mr. Postman examined the deep and broad effects of television culture and how "entertainment values" have corrupted the way we think. It is the fast moving imagery on television and the movie theater that entertains and amuses the human senses. Image is everything and rational discourse in the public arena has been absconded by the neo-aesthetic postmodern culture.

The sad news is that amusement has become the popular method of ministry even among those who call themselves Bible believing evangelicals. The emerging modernity of the 20th century fed the flames of the church growth movement so that amusement became a way of life for the ministry of the church. However, the church has and will continue to ask the question: What must Christians do in this present age? Dr. James Henley Thornwell, pastor and theologian during the 19th century wrote his friend Dr. Breckinridge about the condition of the church in 1846. Over 150 years ago he wrote these words.

> Our whole system of operations gives an undue influence to money. Where money is the great want, numbers must be sought; and where ambition for numbers prevails, doctrinal purity must be sacrificed. The root of the evil is in the secular spirit of all our ecclesiastical institutions. What we want is a spiritual body; a Church whose power lies in the truth, and the presence of the Holy Ghost. To unsecularize the

Church should be the unceasing aim of all who are anxious that the ways of Zion should flourish. (*The Life and Letters of James Henley Thornwell*, page 291).

One Presbyterian pastor wrote an article about amusement in one of his denominational churches. The headlines stated "Show Time at such and such church." The reporter writing the article called the Sunday service at one particular church "Entertainment Extravaganzas." His thesis was that the people were amused with the worship service.

To answer my previous question, the apostles were not amused with the ascension? The apostles representing the church of nearly 2000 years ago mused at the ascension of the Lord Jesus Christ. In contrast to that solemn occasion on the Mount of Olives, leaders in the contemporary church growth movement amuse God's people with the ascension of man-designed worship, man-centered doctrine, and man-made solutions to grow God's church.

Sometimes I find myself amused at the tragedy of this headlong leap into disaster, but my amusement quickly turns into contemplative musing. There is a radical difference between the terms amuse and muse. Amusement comes from the word amuse. Most people think of the word amuse in terms of entertainment, most often with a comical aspect. "He is so amusing" meaning his entertainment is funny. The word "muse" refers to meditation and most often a state of profound meditation. I hope God will be pleased to save His church from amusing itself to death.

Let me preface everything else I might say with a clarification. Entertainment is not a sin. What Christians do with entertainment may become a sin. Entertainment has consumed the hearts and lives of many if not most Americans. Christians have to be very cautious, because the sights and sounds of an unrealistic image amuse most

Americans and to a greater or lesser degree professing Christians. Ungodly amusement may replace godly musing. The disciples who witnessed the ascension of the Lord Jesus Christ were not amused. The apostles mused at the ascension of the Lord Jesus Christ. There must have been a cosmic melody to fall upon their ears as they heard the last words coming from the lips of the second person of the Trinity. But more significant is the description of their last view of the Lord Jesus Christ.

The Bible describes the awe and wonder of the disciples as they witnessed the ascension. Luke used different words to emphasize the spectacular, one time historical event of Jesus ascending to the right hand of God the Father.

They *watched* expresses a typical, reliable observation. (Acts 1:9)

They *looked steadfastly* indicates they strained their eyes. (Acts 1:10)

They were *gazing* up into heaven musing the ascension of Christ. (Acts 1:11)

This is a dramatic and scenic manifestation of the most unique person in human history, physically leaving the scene until His future appearance.

There are a couple of questions to muse. What was it like to actually see the Lord Jesus Christ, the second person of the Trinity, with a physical body disappear into a cloud? Can you imagine the profound effect it might have for one to witness such an event? Supernatural is about the best word to describe the ascension of Jesus Christ.

The doctrine of the ascension of the Lord Jesus Christ has received little attention in comparison to the doctrine of resurrection. Maybe one reason the doctrine of the ascension is low on the list of so-called important biblical doctrines is that it provokes deeper questions. Deeper questions require deeper inquiry and when people are busy with amusements, there is little time for musing the doctrine of the ascension.

The ascension certainly raised questions for the apostles. They were clouded with confusion. Confusion is not uncommon among sinners as the apostles were sinners, as all Christians are sinners. The apostles were clouded with confusion because they had not fully realized that Christ was the second person of the Trinity. They probably came closer to that realization than anyone, but they did not fully realize that Jesus Christ was God.

Matthew's account of the final appearance indicates they saw him (Christ) and they worshipped Him, but some doubted (Matthew 28:17). The Bible does not say why they doubted, but the Bible does say that many doubted that Jesus Christ was fully God and fully man at the same time.

Jesus Christ the second person of the Trinity has a divine and human nature. The two natures are "without conversion, composition, or confusion" (*Westminster Confession of Faith*, 8.2). The Godhead and the manhood are joined together into one person, the Lord Jesus Christ, without any alteration of the two natures. His God nature and His human nature are not mixed, but are two distinct natures.

A correct understanding of the doctrine of Jesus Christ is necessary for Jesus Christ our Savior to be Jesus Christ our Mediator. If Christ was only a man, He could not represent us before God. If He was only God, he could not experience our "common infirmities."

Some of the disciples doubted because understanding the idea of transcendent being is difficult. Christians today are clouded with confusion because they cannot think in terms of an independent Being called God. An independent being demands a transcendent metaphysical being. To contemplate and attempt to understand these concepts, will require serious musing. It requires too much effort, because Christians want to be amused. They conjure up pictures of a mild mannered Jewish Messiah with blonde hair and blue eyes; Unless the artist is continental, then the hair and skin of Jesus Christ are darkened to accommodate the culture.

The apostles were also clouded with confusion because they had not understood the ultimate purpose of the appearance of Jesus Christ. They thought He had come to restore the kingdom of Israel. How quick they had forgotten three years earlier John the Baptist said, "behold the Lamb of God who takes away the sin of the world" (John 1:29). Not much has changed. Christians still forget that ultimately, the kingdom of God is a spiritual kingdom.

Yes, we have physical bodies now and we are part of the kingdom of God, but in the end we will have glorified bodies in the New Heavens and the New Earth, which is spiritual.   God's people ought to mature spiritually and discover peace and harmony at the mention of the second person of the Trinity.

Deception is a source of amusement and confusion. Rather than being clouded with confusion, Christians must remember the mission of the church is to make disciples and teach the whole counsel of God. Amusement will retard the mission of the church, but godly musing will help Christians engage in the mission of the church.

The question that keeps coming to the surface is, "why do professing Christians often seem clouded with confusion in the same manner the apostles were clouded with confusion?" The answer to that question is not forthcoming quickly or easily. Maybe the Lord needs to send two men in white apparel and say to us, "why do you stand gazing into heaven?" I am sure someone may say "but they were awe struck with the Lord's departure." But remember the context. Just moments earlier the apostles had asked the question, "Lord will you at this time restore the kingdom to Israel?" It is for sinners to be amused, as it were, by the things they see or hear.

If Christians go about the work of rebuilding the church with human inventions for worship, man-centered doctrine, and man-made solutions for spiritual growth, they are clouded with confusion. The mission of the church will lack the God-centered biblical mandate given by the Lord Jesus Christ before His ascension into heaven (Matthew 28:18-20). For those who want this summarized in a philosophically succinct statement, it is this: Human experience is not the measure of objective reality. The way to measure objective reality is the Word of God.

Our watching, gazing, and looking should be with great expectation of God's powerful work among us. Christians will see clearly if they understand the Holy Spirit of God is their source of power. Then and only then will they be able to turn from the amusement of this world, so that they can muse of the things of the real and eternal dimension.

If Christians are clouded with confusion, their witness of Christ will be clouded with confusion. Speaking in a collective sense, our confidence is in the great High Priest and Intercessor who appeared in the presence of God for the church. Jesus Christ ascended into heaven. He is the Mediator, King and head of His church. The Christian hope is that Christ will return bodily to establish the New Heavens and the New Earth. The church should watch and look steadfastly, as the disciples did, for the fulfillment of His promise. Christians need to set aside amusements, so they may muse and meditate upon God with deep and enriching thoughts. There are many good reasons to muse about the Lord Jesus Christ. The most important reason is that your godly musing will cause you to see your Lord without any amusement.

4. Free From Complexity

Acts 1:12-14

The year is 33 A.D. Life is relatively simple. Wal-Mart does not exist. The food is basically the same day after day. People walk from one place to the other. Barter is the typical way to acquire needs for the family. There is not a building down the street called a "church." The Temple was destroyed about one hundred years ago, but the local synagogue conducts religious meetings.

People are talking about a man named Jesus and His little band of followers. News on the street is that He claimed to be God, but He was put to death for insurrection. So much had been said about this man named Jesus that some people dismissed the claims, because they were unbelievable. It has been reported that he not only healed the sick, but raised people from the dead. One thing is for certain; The religious leaders did not like Him. He must have been a complex person. The disciples of Christ watched Jesus perform many miracles. However, they experienced confusion, even though they witnessed His resurrection and His ascension into heaven.

Names and environmental issues may have changed since 33 A. D., but the principles are very much alive. The purpose, mission, and ministry of the church is vague for many professing Christians, but many professing Christians are very religious. They are clouded with confusion about the person and nature of the Lord Jesus Christ, which makes their lives more complex.

The resurrection and ultimately the ascension of the Jesus Christ should have been the high points in the lives of the disciples. After the Lord ascended into heaven, confusion appears to have overtaken the disciples. Just before Jesus ascended into heaven, they asked the question, "Lord will You at this time restore the kingdom to Israel?" (Acts 1:6).

The disciples wanted to remove all their perceived enemies who lived within the boundaries of Israel. The Jews were jealous for the property they inherited from their forefathers. They did not want Caesar or any foreign leader on their property.

Either the disciples had forgotten what the Lord had said moments earlier or they simply ignored the mission that Christ had given them. The Lord explained the mission of the church in terms that anybody could understand. He said, "you shall be My witnesses both in Jerusalem, and in all Judea and Samaria, and even to the remotest part of the earth." The piece of property they cherished was unrelated to the purpose, mission, and ministry of the church.

The disciples should have understood the purpose, mission, and ministry of the church. The purpose of the church is to worship and glorify God. The mission of the church is to make disciples of all the nations and teach the whole counsel of God (Matthew 28:19-20). The ministry of the church is to prepare the saints (the people of God) to understand the purpose and engage in the mission of the church. Jesus made the mission so simple and yet the disciples, and we like them, make it so complex.

After the Lord ascended into heaven, the disciples walked back to Jerusalem from the mount called Olives (Acts 1:12). Christians often overlook this little narrative as a routine historical comment. God does not make routine comments. When God says something Christians should ask themselves, "why did God say that?" Luke's version is, "they returned to Jerusalem from the mount called Olivet, which is near Jerusalem, a Sabbath day's journey" (Acts 1:12). The top of the Mount of Olives is about 200 feet higher than the city of Jerusalem. Apparently, the disciples had to go down to the city of Jerusalem. A Sabbath day's journey is approximately three fourths of a mile, which gave them time to contemplate what they had just experienced.

This is the second time the disciples had come down from a spiritual high, once at the transfiguration and now the ascension. Luke's account of the transfiguration of Jesus will help put this in proper context.

> Now it came to pass, about eight days after these sayings, that He took Peter, John, and James and went up on the mountain to pray. As He prayed, the appearance of His face was altered, and His robe became white and glistening. And behold, two men talked with Him, who were Moses and Elijah, who appeared in glory and spoke of His decease which He was about to accomplish at Jerusalem. But Peter and those with him were heavy with sleep; and when they were fully awake, they saw His glory and the two men who stood with Him. Then it happened, as they were parting from Him, that Peter said to Jesus, "Master, it is good for us to be here; and let us make three tabernacles: one for You, one for Moses, and one for Elijah"—not knowing what he said. While he was saying this, a cloud came and overshadowed them; and they were fearful as they entered the cloud. And a voice came out of the cloud, saying, "This is My beloved Son. Hear Him!" When the voice had ceased, Jesus was found alone. But they kept quiet, and told no one in those days any of the things they had seen. (Luke 9:28-36)

Peter and John were able to identify Moses and Elijah. The preponderance of these events ought to create a doxological hallelujah. Even after confessing that Christ was God and aware that Moses and Elijah retained their own personal character and identity, the disciples still had their eyes on this world and could not give attention to the metaphysical dimension. Peter wanted to keep Moses and Elijah in their glorious nature and Christ transfigured, so Peter could enjoy this miraculous event. Peter wanted to build a temporary shelter to keep them in time and space rather than allowing them to return to the proper place, which is the metaphysical dimension. Peter wanted to prolong the glory scene, because he did not realize what he was saying. Some Christians want to abuse God's wonderful providence by asking the Lord for something mystical and beyond the scope of the natural order of things. God placed Christians on earth to live and minister in this secular world until their time comes to go be with God forever. God gave Peter, John, and James a glimpse of glory and you too can have a glimpse of glory by the power of the Holy Spirit if you will believe and understand the nature and character of God.

Spiritual experiences may cause confusion, on the Mount of Transfiguration and the ascension of the Lord on the Mount of Olives. The confusion comes because sometimes Christians are not able to synchronize the perceived spiritual experience with objective truth.

We all have our spiritual highs. We remember them and cherish them, but we find ourselves again in the mundane day-to-day experiences. Christians, figuratively speaking, make that descent from the Mount of Olives, back down the hill to Jerusalem, but beware that the father of lies will charm them with confusion and complexity. The father of lies is the master of confusion. He turns that which is legitimately simple into illegitimate complexity. For instance, God is simple. Study the Bible and learn that God is a simple being. "God is simple" refers to the oneness of God. God is not a compound being. God is not complicated. God is simple and therefore God is absolutely free from complexity. The biblical and theological use of the word "simple" is radically different from the common use of the word "simple."

Although human beings are not essentially simple, they should aspire to be as free from complexity as possible. God's people above all people should desire the simple. Christians will find that life is not nearly as complex if they are in a vital relationship with Jesus Christ, but they will not be perfectly free of confusion and complexity. To know that you have the promise of eternal life in the favorable presence of God removes some of the complexity in this life. If you understand and believe the promises for eternal life, that is a spiritual experience. Spiritual experiences should uncomplicate life and should turn the complex into the simple. The next step is to bring that new found simplicity and freedom with us when we come down the mountain. The simple principle applies to the entire church. It is true that the church consists of many parts, thus it is complex. It is also true that the complex may be relatively simple or to put it another way Christians may experience freedom from complexity.

Jesus told His disciples not to leave Jerusalem because they would be baptized with the Holy Spirit. The Holy Spirit changed the lives of the twelve apostles in a very unique way, but the Holy Spirit also changes everyone that God calls to Himself. It is the work of the Holy Spirit that gives new life to the soul. Christians do not need the wind blowing through the building or fire on the tongue to experience the simple work of the Holy Spirit in the soul. If the Holy Spirit gives new life to the soul, it means He has given new life to the church. The principle is very simple. The people of God make up the church. Please do not turn the simple into the complex.

The disciples obeyed the Lord Jesus Christ, left the Mount of Olivet, and went down the mountain to Jerusalem. The Holy Spirit was able to do an extraordinary work on the Mount of Olives as well as Jerusalem. However, Jesus said go to Jerusalem to wait on the Holy Spirit. Christians will be surprised at the relief they find when they simply obey the Lord and cast all their cares upon Jesus, the author and finisher of their faith.

Sometimes Jesus says to do things that may not make sense. For instance, the Bible asserts that sinners are "justified by faith." "Therefore, having been justified by faith, we have peace with God through our Lord Jesus Christ, through whom also we have access by faith into this grace in which we stand, and rejoice in hope of the glory of God" (Romans 5:1-2). Justified refers to a right relationship with God and that right relationship is by faith. To put it another way, simply believe that Jesus Christ is the only way to have peace with God. Sinners that we are, we say to ourselves, "it sounds too simple." Sinners that we are, we love to dabble with the complex. Even so, obedience like that of the disciples will free your life of the complexity that sin brings your way.

The principle of oneness will overshadow the complexity that sin provokes. Luke, the inspired church historian, lists the apostles in one place with one mind (Acts 1:14). In the right sense, they were simple minded. They were simple minded in the sense that Paul explains in the Book of Ephesians. "There is one body and one Spirit, just as you were called in one hope of your calling; one Lord, one faith, one baptism; one God and Father of all, who is above all, and through all, and in you all" (Ephesians 4:4-6).

Simplicity is associated with unity, but complexity is associated with division. Even though Luke names every individual apostle, the Bible says they assembled collectively. They met at one place and they had one mind. They assembled together therefore, they were a local congregation of God's people. They were a local particular church. Every member of the local congregation has individual gifts and abilities, but their purpose, mission and ministry are one. In order to accomplish the mission and purpose of the church, their belief and their practice must be one.

Being an individual is not a sin, but individualism is a sin. Individualism is the world and life view that says, "I am and nobody else counts." Individualism says, "I'm going to have it my way or die trying." Some professing Christians have that attitude to a greater or lesser degree. The sin of individualism enslaves Christians to complexity. It is the simplicity of unity that frees Christians from complexity. Judas Iscariot is a good example of one that reflects the sin of individualism. Judas thought his agenda was more important than God's plan. We know what happened to Judas in the end.

Individualism is a worldview related to confusion, chaos, and complexity. The book of Judges describes one of the low points of the nation Israel: "every man did what was right in His own eyes" (Judges 17:6). On the contrary, the disciples, after a brief time of confusion on the Mount of Olives, did what was right in the eyes of their Lord and Savior. They returned to Jerusalem, every individual, but as one. "These all continued with one accord in prayer and supplication, with the women and Mary the mother of Jesus, and with His brothers" (Acts 1:14).

> NKJV - They were of one accord
> NAS - These all with one mind
> Literally - They were all continuing steadfastly with one passion (passion = together to death)

This was the normal pattern for the disciples. After the church had considerable growth, the disciples who were once confused and complex in their efforts, were "continuing daily with one accord" (Acts 2:46).

God expects unity among His people because it represents His simple character. Christians will benefit by remembering this important text from the book of Psalms.

Behold, how good and how pleasant it is For brethren to dwell together in unity! It is like the precious oil upon the head, Running down on the beard, The beard of Aaron, Running down on the edge of his garments. It is like the dew of Hermon, Descending upon the mountains of Zion; For there the LORD commanded the blessing Life forevermore. (Psalm 133:1-3)

Psalm 133 describes the unity Christians should experience and practice. The source that brings unity is like the holy anointing oil poured on the head of Aaron, running down his beard onto the collar of his robes. The simile is brilliant with symbols of the Holy Spirit turning the complex into the simple.

The ritual of anointing the High Priest was symbolic of how God's blessing comes to his people. Aaron was set apart to act as the representative of God for all Israel and become the mediator between God and the sinful people of Israel. The word picture describes the holy oil as *it comes from above*, down on Aarons head and descends over his garments. The sacred oil flowed upon Aaron's richly adorned garments, which contained the precious stones inscribed with the names of the twelve tribes of Israel. The whole body was consecrated in all its parts. The anointing comes from above, flowing to all the members so they all participate in the blessing.

The Psalmist also describes the blessing of unity in terms of nature and geography. The Psalmist says, "like the dew of Hermon coming down upon the mountains of Zion." Hermon is a mountain located adjacent to Lebanon and is noted for its majesty, size and beauty. Zion was lesser in size, but it was the location of the Temple at Jerusalem. The two mountains are nearly one hundred miles apart. The significance of Mt. Zion to Mt. Hermon in the mind of the Psalmist was its dew. When the air of the evening cooled the intense heat, the moisture condensed and fell upon the lower and dryer land. It was refreshing dew to the dry land in Palestine. Even though Hermon is 100 miles north of Jerusalem, there is a natural relationship in a supernatural way between the dew that falls on the lofty Hermon and the humbler Zion. The refreshing dew that belongs in another place is present in another place.

What can Christians learn from this beautiful word picture? The nature of Christian unity is like the dew that drenches the parched ground, a dew that refreshes and revives. This word picture should stimulate a simple spiritual experience. The dew from God's heavenly realm touches Christians as they have communion with the Lord Jesus Christ. God baptizes His people, not with a dunking in the creek, but with the dew that represents the descending of the Holy Spirit. He comes with His renewing and refreshing presence so the child of God may experience the unity that turns the complex into the simple.

Burdens, difficulties, doubts, and strife are complex in their nature. The only way to find relief is to find simple unity in your relationship with God and unity in your relationship with God's people.

It is simple. Believe Jesus Christ. Obey Jesus Christ and live a simple life. The disciples did and Christians today should endeavor to do likewise. They all continued with one accord in prayer and supplication. The following points summarize the doctrine described as "free from complexity" that plagues individual Christians as well as the church.

God has given his church a mission that is not complex or mixed.

Christians need to trust God's plan to be free from complexity.

Christians need to be obedient to be free from complexity.

Christians need to be diligent to be free from complexity.

Christians need to be united to be free from complexity.

5. Reformed by the Word of God

Acts 1:15-26

The war cry of the 16th century Reformation was "the church reformed is always reforming." Let me be quick to add that in the 16th century the terms protestant, reformed, and evangelical were very much in agreement with each other. It was not until the 18th century that the evangelical church began to denominate exponentially, which pleased the Roman Catholic Church. However, they are wrong to blame the sin of church division on biblical reformation. A pugnacious spirit is from the father of division, old Satan himself.

The movers and shakers in the church growth movement are quick to point out part of the truth in the reformed slogan, "The church reformed is always reforming." They say the church is "always reforming." It is the signal for change so the church will grow. Our forefathers left their descendents with this Latin phrase to describe the foundation for church growth. The Latin phrase, *Ecclesia reformata semper est reformanda*, reveals some interesting information relative to this subject. The word "Reformed" was originally in the passive, thus it means being reformed from a source other than itself. The Word of God was a resource for reforming the church. For example, Martin Luther studied the Bible, rather than church tradition, because the Bible would not err in doctrine. It was from the Word of God that Luther discovered justification was by faith alone, not by faith and works. It was the Word of God that set the standard for the reformation of the church. It was by the power of the Holy Spirit that the reformers understood the Word of God. If the church is passively reformed by the Word of God then the church is always reforming because every generation must discover the Word of God and all its doctrine.

There are many reasons the church needs to be reformed by the Word of God, but there are four to consider relative to the purpose, mission, and ministry of the church.

God's people need reformation because the hearts of God's people always need reform. The old sin nature always needs the enabling of the Holy Spirit to believe the Word of God.

God's people need reformation because of the hands of the evil one will try to convince the believer that the means of grace is not necessary.

God's people need reformation because sinful hearts and hands are inclined to abuse true worship and allow false worship to enter into the church.

God's people need reformation to understand the mission and ministry of the church.

Church leaders understand the word "reformation" in different ways. For instance, church growth movement leaders would probably use the word "reformation" as a synonym for the word "change". They would suggest change to contemporary worship to attract people. However, the Bible prescribes the way to worship that has been, is, and will be the standard. When Israel went to the temple to worship it was contemporary. If the church assembles to worship, it will always be a contemporary occasion. The classical meaning of the word "reformation" relative to the church goes further than just "change." Unfortunately the word reform and reformation reminds people of changes. Some people oppose changes. Some people like to change everything. Biblical reformation is not just about changes. Biblical reformation is essential to understand the nature and character of God. It is a process that will engage the believer to love the nature and character of God and give him or her a passion to glorify God with body and soul. The church that is not reforming will devolve its corruption to the next generation.

The 17th century Puritan, Francis Turretin, said the call to reformation is such that "a man is bound to purge his faith and worship of all the errors and superstitions by which it could be corrupted so that he may retain religion pure from every stain" (*Institutes of Elenctic Theology*, Vol. 3, p. 217). How is it possible for a man to purge his faith and worship of all errors and superstitions? Is it possible to remove all the corruption that comes with the sinful heart? Can Christians be pure from every stain? Just to think about it is quite a challenge! We can dismiss the idea of perfection in faith, practice and worship. What Turretin has in mind is the standard to which we judge all of life including faith and worship.

The disciples were in need of reformation immediately after Jesus ascended into heaven. The disciples were in a state of confusion and complexity. This is remarkable for the history of the church. The New Testament Church, still in its nascent stage, needed to be reformed. Peter the apostle was the spokesman for the reformation in the early church. Peter's first words after the Lord ascended called for reformation. Peter said, "Brethren, the Scripture had to be fulfilled" (Acts 1:16). The only way the church can experience reformation, is to take the Word of God seriously.

It appears that many professing Christians express disdain for the Word of God and hold to church tradition. Other professing Christians use the Bible for a "how to" book. It may be that professing Christians are amusing themselves to death with the television, sports, civic clubs, church, or who knows what, but more often than not the Word of God takes second place. Sometimes the Word of God does not just take second place, it is completely ignored.

If Christians ignore the Word of God, they cannot understand the glory of God's salvation for His people. Quite often the subject of reformation is exclusively applied to the doctrine of salvation.

If the sole purpose of reformation is to get people saved, then Christians have ignored the Word of God and forgotten their purpose is to glorify God in all of faith and practice. It begins with worship and extends to the mission and ministry of the church. The doctrine of salvation is very important, but Christians must glorify God in every thought and activity of life.

Reformation is like a water purifier. It keeps the church clean. Even business meetings in the church are subject to reformation according to the Word of God. The first business meeting in the New Testament church is a model for every church business meeting that would follow, but how far has the church lost sight of the Savior's business. The church is too busy trying to make rules rather than following the principles in the Word of God. The first business meeting in the church was conducted with sound doctrine, order, and prayer.

The business before the disciples was the selection of a new apostle, to replace the one who had just gone to hell. The manner in which they conducted the business of the church is the model for the church today. They acted like a church, not like a civic club or some other secular organization. The church assembled and was competent to conduct the business of the church. They did not consult a business or a religious organization outside the church to attend to its business. The names of the members present, about one hundred twenty, were sufficient for the church to carry on the business of the church. No one complained about the business before the church, because all continued with "one accord." They were sufficiently equipped by the Holy Spirit to conduct a business meeting for spiritual reasons. However, if a church meeting is not spiritual in nature, the church should not conduct it. Unfortunately, some professing Christians might act unbecoming of Christly character in a church business meeting. If such a person was not in a right relationship with the Lord, then that person may very well act with resolute contumacy. However, Christian people, being reformed by the Word of God will seek harmony and peace among the congregation of God's people.

Some of the churches that the apostle Paul started were not being reformed by the Word of God. The Corinthian church is a good example. The apostle Paul wrote the church to warn them about their disregard for the need for reformation.

> And I, brethren, could not speak to you as to spiritual people but as to carnal, as to babes in Christ. I fed you with milk and not with solid food; for until now you were not able to receive it, and even now you are still not able; for you are still carnal. For where there are envy, strife, and divisions among you, are you not carnal and behaving like mere men? For when one says, "I am of Paul," and another, "I am of Apollos," are you not carnal? Who then is Paul, and who is Apollos, but ministers through whom you believed, as the Lord gave to each one? I planted, Apollos watered, but God gave the increase. So then neither he who plants is anything, nor he who waters, but God who gives the increase. (1 Corinthians 3:1-7)

The church at Corinth was not being reformed by the Word of God. They were in a state of limbo. Jonathan Edwards made a comment during the reformation in the church at Northampton that the church today ought to muse. Edwards said, "At a time when God manifests himself in such a great work for his church, there is no such thing as being neuters" (*The Works of Jonathan Edwards*, Hickman ed., vol. 1, p. 380). Edwards is right! Christians cannot be neutral, because the Word of God is not neutral.

The church in Acts chapter one quickly became a reformed church after a brief time of confusion and complexity. They were being reformed by the Word of God. Peter's announcement at the first church business meeting indicates they were being reformed by the Word of God.

> Men and brethren, this Scripture had to be fulfilled, which the Holy Spirit spoke before by the mouth of David concerning Judas, who became a guide to those who arrested Jesus; for he was numbered with us and obtained a part in this ministry. (Acts 1:16-17)

Peter continues by quoting the Word of God. "For it is written in the book of Psalms: 'Let his dwelling place be desolate, and let no one live in it and let another take his office'" (Acts 1:20). "Fulfilled" does not merely refer to a prognosticating prophecy, as it is often preached. "Fulfilled" refers to Scripture that had to be obeyed so Scripture would be complete. To put it another way, the church had to be reformed by the Word of God.

Peter must have been studying the Scriptures and very likely the other disciples were studying with him.

> They studied the Scriptures, not Robert's rule of order.

> They studied the Scriptures, not the minute details of the secular law.

> They studied the Scriptures, not the political scene.

They studied the Scriptures, not the latest marketing schemes.

They studied the Scriptures, not management manuals.

They studied the Scriptures, because they wanted to be reformed by the Word of God.

They were not interested in conforming to the standards of this world.

They studied the Bible with great seriousness and with great depth. Peter quotes from Psalm sixty nine citing the curse upon those who rebel against God and His Word. The rebel that Peter has in mind is Judas Iscariot, the man who betrayed the Lord Jesus Christ. However, Judas is merely the representative of all those who rebel against God and do not have the spirit of God in them. The unconverted rebellious sinner has the horrors of death and judgment ever before his eyes. For Judas it was a horrible death, which the Bible describes as one who fell headlong bursting open, and his insides spilling out. The reward Judas got for his wickedness was marked by a violent death. (See Acts 1:18-19). Peter had studied the Word of God. Peter could relate the events of the death of Judas to the Word of God, because Peter was being reformed by the Word of God.

Peter's personal reformation set him apart as a leader and spokesman for the church. He was a man qualified to lead the church in every way including leading business meetings. The presence of one hundred twenty members of the New Testament church may have sounded like a democratic ecclesiology. The meeting was opened to everyone, but the business was conducted by the elders, with Peter as the moderator. Would you like to have been present for the first business meeting in the church? The order and harmony is as nearly perfect as you will find in any meeting since that day. If Christians are being reformed by the Word of God, they should desire to reform church business meetings in keeping with the Word of God.

The main business of the church at that first business meeting was to select someone to replace Judas. The qualifications for that office being immediately inspired by God were twofold. First, the candidate must have accompanied the apostles during the entire ministry of Jesus. Second, the candidate must have been a witness of the resurrection of Christ (Acts 1:21-22).

The principle for the replacement of the apostle also applies to those who seek the office of elder in the church today. Peter's principle, inspired by God, was that the new apostle should be intimately acquainted with the Lord. To be intimately acquainted with the Lord means to trust Him and know Him; the only way to know Him intimately is to study His Word. No man should be called into the Lord's service until the Holy Spirit has equipped him for the work. I cringe when I hear people say "let's promote such and such man to the office of deacon" or "let's promote a deacon to an elder." When I hear people say such things I know they have not been reformed by the Word of God. The selection of deacons and elders ought to be according to the full counsel of God.

In the case of the first business meeting in the church, there were two qualified men. Both men were equally qualified. It was the voice of God speaking through the Scriptures that made the business of selecting a new apostle so easy. The Word of God does not say, but the context speaks loud and clear that the one not selected did not get upset about the election. They were of one mind, therefore there was no feuding and fighting in the church meeting. They were not confused, because they were being reformed by the Word of God.

Being reformed by the Word of God will touch every part of the soul - the mind, emotions, and will. When a child of God discovers the truth from the Word of God, that person is reformed. The reformation of the soul will affect him or her intellectually. It will have an effect on his or her decisions and there will be an outward manifestation of his or her love for truth. If there is a love for truth then there must be a love for one another in the church. When God's people have been reformed by the Word of God, they will stick close to His Word throughout their lives. The joy of the redeemed sinner is being reformed by the Word of God! Are you being reformed by the Word of God?

6. Manifestation of God's Presence

Acts 2:1-13

Manifestation is probably not the most familiar word in the English language. It should be used often by Christians. Manifestation means "to make visible or clear." Speaking figuratively, understanding the presence of God ought to be clear for Christians to muse and ponder. Understanding the presence of God the Holy Spirit on the first Pentecost after the ascension of Christ will be either muddled or manifest.

The church, its beginning and its purpose, mission, and ministry is manifest in the Word of God. The church is a term primarily used in the New Testament to describe God's people. His people are in a special relationship with Him because of His abundant grace.

Some professing evangelical Christians, claim that God worked throughout human history trying to save His people. They believe God tried to save Adam and Eve, but that failed. Then God used plan B, but it was a failure and by the time Noah came on the scene wickedness prevailed. The Bible asserts the Lord, "was sorry that He had made man on the earth" (Genesis 6:6). It is alleged that God tried to save man throughout human history using different plans such as the Mosaic law and the Davidic kingdom. After all failed, God sent His Son to die and that ushered in the church age. Nothing could be further from the truth. God's people are one people throughout human history.

The apostle Paul explains that God chose "us" (His people) before the foundation of the world (Ephesians 1:4). The Bible makes the doctrine exceedingly manifest. "The Lord knows those who are His" (2 Timothy 2:19). The church is the assembly of God's redeemed people.

The church on earth is the visible church, but it is not definitive of all those redeemed by Jesus Christ. The invisible church consists of God's people from the beginning of time to the consummation. Although the church is manifest in time and space, the church is spiritual in its nature.

The assembly of God's people in the Old Testament was superficially different than the church in the New Testament, but substantially, both are the same. The superficial aspect is the outward manifestation or the appearance of God's grace. The sacrifices in the Old Testament are outward manifestations of God's grace. In the New Testament baptism and the Lord's Supper are outward manifestations of God's grace. By superficial, I mean the things Christians experience in their senses. The essential substance of the outward manifestation is invisible, because God has chosen not to reveal His full glory.

It is the manifestation of God's Spirit in Acts chapter two that causes many to believe the church began on the first Pentecost after the resurrection of our Lord. The manifestation of God's Spirit is fundamental to the Christian religion. Understanding the significance of Pentecost is essential to understand this great event. It was a religious festival of the nation of Israel. All males twelve years and older were required to attend. After the Jews were dispersed among the nations in 586 B. C. many of them stayed in the foreign lands even after the rebuilding of the temple. Over a period of five centuries they took up the foreign customs and language, but when Pentecost came many would remember their religious roots and return to Jerusalem. Luke's inspired record reveals that Jews "from every nation under heaven" were in Jerusalem for Pentecost (Acts 2:5).

The manifestation of God's Spirit did not begin at Pentecost nearly 2000 years ago. The manifestation of God's Spirit was evident when He (God's Spirit) moved over the face of the waters (Genesis 1:1). The Holy Spirit is evident by controlling the course of nature and history (Psalm 104:27-30). The Holy Spirit revealed God's truth and God's will for His Old Testament church (Micah 3:8). Throughout the Bible, the Spirit of God came upon one person or the other. Gideon, Samuel, David, Zechariah, and Isaiah are a few who experienced a mighty work of the Holy Spirit. In the Old Testament the Holy Spirit created, controlled, revealed, quickened, and enabled the Old Testament church to fulfill God's plan.

The same Spirit of God came upon the disciples in Acts chapter two. Even though it was the same Spirit of God, it came upon the disciples collectively, which is different than empowering the Old Testament individuals. The Holy Spirit came upon them in the form of visible sensible means. The Spirit came upon their ears. "There came a sound from heaven as of a mighty rushing wind" (Acts 2:2). The Bible says "as of a mighty rushing wind" or "like (similar to) a mighty rushing wind." The wind is an appropriate symbol for the Holy Spirit because it is invisible and mysterious to the naked eye. Wind is also a symbol of power and refreshment. The Holy Spirit also appeared to their eyes, as Scripture reveals, "there appeared to them divided tongues, as of fire" (Acts 2:3).

The supernatural appearances to the ears and eyes of the early disciples were ad hoc. That means the manifestation of the Holy Spirit on the day of Pentecost happened only one time. Those manifestations or appearances came, as the Holy Spirit always comes, with purpose.

The Holy Spirit of God acted upon those early disciples in such a way that their spiritual natures were filled with divine thoughts and divinely inspired wills and emotions. The disciples may have remembered the promise of Jesus as it is recorded in Matthew's gospel. Jesus promised persecution, but He also promised the presence of the Holy Spirit to enable them to speak before the courts (Matthew 10:20).

The Holy Spirit took possession of the disciples so that they could think God's thoughts, act out of God's will, and have the sympathetic affections like our Lord. It was a marvelous and miraculous event.

There is no hint in the Bible that the Spirit would appear today the same way it appeared to those early disciples. They had seen the Lord Jesus Christ heal lepers, raise the dead, and reverse the actions of nature. They did not need the Spirit of God to convince them of the nature and character of God. They did need this special work of the Holy Spirit to fulfill God's purpose in their lives at that particular time. They were designated to witness for the sake of the Lord Jesus Christ.   Some of them were God's instruments for writing the Word of God. The disciples were filled with the Holy Spirit to perform miraculous events to validate, with authority, the duty to write the Word of God. When the Word of God was complete, the special powers given to the disciples were no longer necessary. He had fulfilled His purpose that began on the day of Pentecost. Since the Bible is complete, there is no further need for the Holy Spirit to empower Christians for the same reason that He empowered the early disciples.

The purpose of the Holy Spirit coming upon subsequent generations up until this very day is for the purpose of changing the heart to believe the gospel and live according to God's Word. The Spirit of God now works in the hearts of His people so they will be able to believe the Word of God. The Holy Spirit also enables His people to worship God in a way pleasing to Him. God's people need the Holy Spirit to be witnesses of God's grace and enable them to live a holy life in a sinful world.

When the Spirit of God changes your heart you will be a different person. That does not mean that you will be a

Peter clone or a Paul clone. It does not mean that you have to speak with other tongues. Your native language is sufficient to worship, praise, and serve God. The early disciples were endowed with the special power of speaking foreign languages without any special training.

The sad state of understanding the work of the Holy Spirit in the present dispensation is evident by the emphasis on the physical body rather than the spiritual soul. The work of the Holy Spirit is necessary for physical needs, but more necessary for spiritual needs.

Christians may say, "I live the gospel." It is true to say, "no one will see Christ in your life, because Christ was not a sinner." The normal mode to communicate the gospel is through the means of human language. There is a great need for intelligent human discourse in this anti-intellectual age. I distinguish between scholarship and intellect.

Anyone can be a scholar without much effort. Being an intellect requires hard work. A scholar is simply someone who learns from another person and believes on the basis of another person's knowledge. Intellectual ability requires the use of rational and logical tools to discover the truth of any proposition.

Christians carry the responsibility for intelligent human discourse. Particularly applicable is the communication of the gospel. Let me re-state that a different way. Christians are responsible for communicating the gospel intelligently. Some of the words spoken by the apostles were divinely inspired words, unlike the words of other disciples.

The divine inspiration of the Holy Spirit was necessary for the church to have the Word of God. The sermon you hear from your pastor on Sunday may sound wonderful. It may feed your hungry soul, but the sermon is not inspired. The sermon of Peter on the day of Pentecost was divinely inspired. The words of the disciples were divinely inspired for the purpose of communicating the gospel intelligently and in written form, which we call the Bible. The disciples were enabled to speak foreign languages without any formal training.

God used the disciples to communicate God's truth to the visiting Jews in Jerusalem. For instance a Hebrew speaking Jew was enabled to speak the Egyptian language or Greek or Latin. Since we do not have the mind of God, we should not inquire into God's motive for giving a gift to the first disciples that He has not given to us. There is no record of Christians being enabled by the Holy Spirit to duplicate the event that took place on Pentecost nearly 2000 years ago.

Christians may learn a new language by long, systematic hard work. However important the original language of the Bible may be, the native language is all that is necessary to understand the gospel.

This unusual work of the Holy Spirit found in Acts chapter two reveals a church with spiritual power. The church was so amazed and perplexed that they said to one another "whatever could this mean" (Acts 2:12). Had they forgotten what Jesus said just before He ascended into heaven? Jesus said, "You shall receive power when the Holy Spirit comes upon you" The church collectively had spiritual power.

The early disciples needed extraordinary spiritual power, but now the disciples of Christ need the ordinary work of the Holy Spirit to be witnesses of God's grace. The true people of God, the true church on earth will believe and be faithful by the power of the Holy Spirit. The early church was a flagship for the remainder of church history.

The early church was faithful.

They were all in one place (complete congregation).

They were with one accord (complete and in agreement).

They were devoted to prayer (to glorify God).

They were patient (God was the center of life).

Is the modern church following the same spiritual principles used by the early church? If and when the modern church does, there will be evidence of spiritual power. Spiritual power coupled with spiritual truth will exhibit a vigorous desire to be witnesses for Jesus Christ.

The evidence of the Spirit of God in the church will cause some people to say, "What could this mean? Others will say, "they are full of new wine." The mysteries produced by the power of the Holy Spirit are obnoxious to unbelievers. Derision is a sign of unbelief.

Confusion and derision must not stop us. The power of the Holy Spirit is your shield when taunting and ridicule comes your way.

The Holy Spirit gave the Word of God to the church. The Holy Spirit is the person that will enable the church to give a divine explanation of God's saving grace according to His Word.

7.   Good News for the Church

Acts 2:14-36

The day of Pentecost, following the ascension of the Lord Jesus Christ into heaven (here after referred to as Pentecost), was an exciting day. The day of Pentecost mentioned in Acts chapter two is remarkable for many reasons. It was a religious celebration for the Jews. It was like main street USA the day before Christmas. There were throngs of people. A large crowd had gathered to hear the good news of the Messiah coming to redeem His people (Acts 2:42).

Can you imagine, Peter a poor uneducated fisherman standing to preach about the most significant and influential person and event to occur in human history? How could an unlearned fisherman give a metaphysical discourse on God coming to save His people? Not having finished seminary, he would not have a silver tongue or the finished rhetoric of the Greek culture. Yet without all the formal training he was a man of courage and obedience. He was not afraid to stand before a large crowd of people to tell them the truth of God's gospel. However, Peter was not standing alone. The Bible says he stood with the other eleven apostles. Peter simply obeyed the command of the Lord Jesus Christ, "be My witness" (Acts 1:8). A Growing church needs the gospel.

The gospel is the subject of much discussion among Christians. The word gospel, found in the New Testament refers to the good news of God's saving grace. John the Baptist preached the gospel or the good news of the kingdom. The Lord Jesus came preaching the good news. The apostles continued to preach the good news.

The message of the gospel is the announcement of God's salvation to sinners, because sinners cannot save themselves. Pentecost stands out as the beginning of the New Testament gospel preaching. Pentecost is often misunderstood as the beginning of the proclamation of God's saving grace. That proclamation began as soon as Adam and Eve sinned. Pentecost was the beginning of the announcement that the age of fulfillment was a present reality.

Peter's sermon begins with an appeal to common sense and general revelation. Some among the large crowd of people said, "They [the Apostles] are full of new wine" implying they were drunk. However, common sense would indicate that they were not drunk since it was only 9 A.M. in the morning. The apostles were mocked for speaking foreign languages without any special training. They were ridiculed for the apparent supernatural work of the Holy Spirit. However, Peter used common sense (general revelation) to dispel their false accusations.

Peter's answer is that of a master apologist. Then Peter answered the charges of the critics with special revelation. Peter quoted from the Word of God, specifically the prophet Joel (Acts 2:17-21). Peter used God's Word to be the witness of the events on the day of Pentecost. The promise of the coming of the Spirit had been promised by the prophet Joel many centuries before the appearance of Jesus Christ. Peter's sermon simply revealed the presence of Christ through the power of the Holy Spirit.

There is no end to the profound expressions of God's gospel found in Peter's sermon on the day of Pentecost. The work of the Holy Spirit and witness of the Word of God should capture the attention of all Christians. Without the Holy Spirit and the Word of God, the gospel will not be clear to anyone. With the powerful work of the Holy Spirit and the presence of the Word of God it will be clear and believable. Peter's appeal to the Word of God is a plea for the modern day church to be reformed by the Word of God. Quoting from the Word of God Peter said, "In the last days, God says"...and then proceeds to quote the Word of God (Acts 2:17-21). This text may be taken several different ways, but either way it is a reference to the reformation of the church.

Some theologians believe the "last days" is a reference to the destruction of the temple in Jerusalem in 70 A. D. Others believe it is a reference to the perfect restoration of the church, ultimately the new heavens and new earth. I believe the "last days" in Peter's sermon refers to the concept known as "the already, but not yet." The Hebrew idiom "in the last days" often refers to the present historical situation in which the words were spoken, but there was also the expectation of the future.

Peter's application was that the kingdom of God is now before us, but the kingdom of God is not in its final estate. The fullness of time, whether that fullness was under the Old Testament, New Testament, or for today, that fullness will find the church always reforming, only to be perfectly restored after the final judgment.

Scripture is abundant with evidence that God will reform His church. The enabling power for reformation comes from the Holy Spirit. Peter quoting the Word of God said, "I (God) will pour out my Spirit on all flesh" (Acts 2:17). The Spirit of God is the agent of conversion. It is the Holy Spirit that changes unbelieving hearts so they will be able to believe. The Spirit not only changes the souls of men, it is the Spirit of God that bestows a variety of gifts to His church.

God poured out His Spirit on the day of Pentecost and it reflected the fullness of time for the church in that day. Now God pours out His Spirit in this age which reflects the fullness of time for the church today. God will pour forth His Spirit upon all flesh or all men, but it does not mean that all men will be saved in the end.

There is no reason to be confused about the salvation of God's people. "And it shall come to pass that whoever calls on the name of the Lord shall be saved" (Acts 2:21).

The Bible does not say that all men will be saved. It says that all (Jew or Gentile) who believe will be saved. The Psalmist preached this same gospel in Psalm 65:2 where the Psalmist said, "To You [God] all flesh will come" all flesh referring to Jews and Gentiles.

God's gospel has always been the same good news expressed in various ways. Before Abram was circumcised and before Abram received the sign and seal of the covenant, "he believed in the Lord; and the Lord reckoned it to him as righteousness" (Genesis 15:6). There you have God's gospel thousands of years before Christ died on the cross.

The people who heard the gospel on the day on Pentecost in Acts chapter two heard the same gospel with more fullness than God's people under the Old Covenant. The promised Messiah in Joel, was the exalted Mediator on the day of Pentecost. The message of God's gospel was clothed differently in the Old Testament than it was in the New Testament, but the essence of the message was the same in the Old Testament as well as the New Testament.

Central to the gospel message and salvation is faith. The Bible plainly says that anyone who believes on the Lord Jesus Christ will be saved. The sinfulness of confusion and the lack of understanding the Word of God are the primary reasons for the misinterpretation and misrepresentation of "justification by faith alone." The Bible never teaches that anyone who says they believe will be saved. There may be a vast chasm between a person *saying* "I believe" and a person *actually* believing.

I can say there is a cat hanging from the ceiling, but there may not be a cat hanging from the ceiling and further-more I may not be able to persuade a cat to hang from the ceiling. A person may say, "I believe in Jesus Christ" but that same person may not actually believe Jesus Christ is the second person of the Trinity.

The word "believe" may mean something different to the minds of different people. Belief may mean an assent to truth. In other words the Muslims believe that God sent Jesus Christ as a prophet of God. Even though Muslims believe in Jesus, they do not believe that Jesus Christ is the second person of the Trinity.

Christians must carefully examine that portion of Peter's inspired sermon that promises, "everyone who calls on the name of the Lord shall be saved" (Acts 2:21). We know that one must not only call on the Lord, but one must believe to be saved. So how do we reconcile all saved against some being saved? Someone may say, "I'm saved" but that does not necessarily mean that one is saved, because one may not believe what one says.

For example, the Pharisees believed they were the elect of God and is evident by what Jesus said about how the Pharisees "sit in Moses' seat" (Matthew 23:2). The Lord Jesus Christ had something else to say to those arrogant religious leaders. "But woe to you, scribes and Pharisees, hypocrites, because you shut off the kingdom of heaven from men; for you do not enter in yourselves, nor do you allow those who are entering to go in" (Matthew 23:13).

Just because the Pharisee believed he was a teacher of God's people, did not mean that he had a place in the kingdom of God. To a large extent the evangelical church has been deluded with the concept that one must believe even if one does not know why one believes. It is called blind faith. Even some of the Pharisees believed in Jesus as the Messiah, but they did not understand fully what Jesus had done to save their souls. There were, "certain ones of the sect of the Pharisees who had believed, stood up, saying, 'It is necessary to circumcise them, and to direct them to observe the Law of Moses'" (Acts 15:5). Some of the Pharisees believed that Jesus Christ was the Messiah, but they did not understand the nature, character, and ministry of the Messiah. To put it another way, they believed, but they did not believe the right doctrine.

The misunderstanding at the church assembly recorded in Acts 15 led to a great schism in the church. However, their misunderstanding did not change the essence of the gospel. The Gospel of God does not change.

The sermon Peter preached on the day of Pentecost is a sermon about the saving grace of Jesus Christ. It is a sermon about the salvation of His people. Peter's arguments in his sermon conclude with a majestic statement. "Therefore let all the house of Israel know for certain that God has made Him both Lord and Christ - this Jesus whom you crucified" (Acts 2:36). The house of Israel is merely an expression referring to the church. The church consists of those who trust Jesus Christ for eternal life and Peter says they must know for certain who Christ is.

A person can say, "I believe" a thousand times, but that person must know why he or she believes and what he or she believes. Peter challenged the "Men of Israel" to believe what they actually knew about Jesus Christ.

> Men of Israel, hear these words: Jesus of Nazareth, a Man attested by God to you by miracles, wonders, and signs which God did through Him in your midst, as you yourselves also know — Him, being delivered by the determined purpose and foreknowledge of God, you have taken by lawless hands, have crucified, and put to death; whom God raised up, having loosed the pains of death, because it was not possible that He should be held by it. (Acts 2:22-24)

It is good news for the church that Jesus was attested by God with miracles, wonders, and signs. The word "attested" is a synonym for the word "approved". The Savior does not need to meet the approval of men. God showed approval by giving Jesus Christ supernatural power, even power over the grave.

God, in His infinite wisdom, grace, and love predestined the death of Jesus Christ. God's plan of salvation does not violate the necessary principle called justice. For that reason God predestined a sinless man to die for sinful men. The gospel will be empty unless we know that God raised Jesus Christ putting an end to the agony of death. Know for certain that God will save His people, which is good news for the church.

8. Prosperity and Hope for the Church

Acts 2:37-47

How may the prosperity and future hope of the church be secured? You will find a full and complete answer in the whole counsel of God. However, the Book of Acts is a good place to begin the inquiry. Biblical mission and ministry is the answer to the prosperity and future hope of the church.

The modern evangelical church has fallen on hard times. Its ministry is no longer effective and its ministers are no longer respected as honorable men called to speak for the dignity and glory of God. Courage and conviction is not popular in the contemporary church. The war cry for the church today is healing and peace at all cost. The majority of the Protestant church says doctrine divides, but service unites.

It was during the life and ministry of Nehemiah that the Old Testament church set out to rebuild the walls at Jerusalem. The new wall would strengthen and fortify the ministry at Jerusalem. Christians are called to rebuild the evangelical church that has been in decline for more than one hundred and fifty years. The faith, worship and life of the church must be restored according to the standards set by the Lord Jesus Christ.

The restoration of the church is a spiritual enterprise which requires the power of the Holy Spirit to secure the prosperity and future hope of the church. The Holy Spirit enables God's people to understand the truth of God's Word. Therefore, it is the responsibility and duty of the church to teach the truth from the Word of God. The early church was a teaching church and truth was its object. Peter's Pentecost sermon reveals distinctive features relative to teaching the truth.

Teaching truth means teaching what some people call the hard doctrines of the Bible. For instance, The Bible states that Christ was "delivered by the determined purpose and foreknowledge of God" (Acts 2:23). The Greek text could be translated, "*having been fixed by the counsel of God*." This is a reference to predestination. It is one of the alleged hard doctrines in Scripture but, Peter was not afraid to teach the alleged hard doctrine.

God's truth is evangelistic. "Then Peter said to them, 'Repent, and let every one of you be baptized in the name of Jesus Christ for the remission of sins; and you shall receive the gift of the Holy Spirit'" (Acts 2:38). The good news of salvation is a gift from God, a truth to be cherished. The evangelistic message tells the truth about the forgiveness of sins.

God's truth is also full of promise. "For the promise is to you and to your children, and to all who are afar off, as many as the Lord our God will call" (Acts 2:39). God's promises are for every generation of God's people. God said to Abram, "I will make you a great nation...I will bless you..." (Genesis 12:1-3). The promise is to all who belong to Jesus Christ. The promise to the children has been and still is abused in the church. The abuse is relative to the doctrine of baptism. Baptism is not something you do. The word baptize is a passive verb. Baptism is something that happens to the person. The person being baptized is not taking the action. Furthermore, the promise of God's grace extends to God's covenant people, regardless of their age.

There is no mention of nursery facilities when Peter preached the sermon on the day of Pentecost. In fact, children have been part of the covenant community from the earliest days in Israel.

These are the words of the covenant which the Lord commanded Moses to make with the children of

Israel…All of you stand today before the Lord your
God: your leaders and your tribes and your elders and
your officers, all the men of Israel, your little ones
and your wives…also the stranger who is in your
camp. (Deuteronomy 29:1,10-11)

The promise of God's grace is a familial principle. Paul
alludes to the covenant family in his letter to the Corinthians.

For the unbelieving husband is sanctified through his
wife, and the unbelieving wife is sanctified through
her believing husband; for otherwise your children are
unclean, but now they are holy. (1 Corinthians 7:14)

The church is in great disrepair. Covenant believers
baptism and covenant infant baptism are two of the neglected
doctrines.   The argument in support of covenant infant
baptism is based upon the essential unity and continuity of the
covenant of grace administered to Abraham, unfolded in the
ministry Moses and David. The covenant of grace appears to
its fullest development in the new covenant, which is fulfilled
in Jesus Christ.

The Bible reveals some implications that arise out of
disobedience to God's command to apply the sign of the
covenant to the children of believing parents. Christians who
are Reformed in their doctrine and theology recognize that
baptism points to what Christ has done, not what man has
done.   However, the danger is to believe the error that
baptism brings about regeneration (born again). It is a very
grave danger. The water has no power, except to make a
baby cry when applied to his or her head.

The spiritual certainty of the effect of baptism resides
entirely in the pledge of God's faithfulness. The spiritual
certainty is found only in the grace of God. When you
present yourself for baptism as a believer it means you

believe that God is faithful in His promises. To baptize your children means you believe that God is faithful in His promises.

The primary way to restore the ministry of the church is to teach like Peter taught so that the truth of God's promises are not hidden from spiritual eyes and ears. People are confused enough. Christians are looking for substance or to put it another way they are looking for truth and they will find it in the Word of God. Then the church must proclaim the truth.

Proclaiming God's truth was instrumental for the early church to secure the prosperity and future hope of the church. "And with many other words he testified and exhorted them, saying, "Be saved from this perverse generation" (Acts 2:40). Peter spoke serious words to them. He warned them declaring solemnly the truth with many different words. The truth is so important it may take many other words to describe it. Peter's warning was to believe the truth of the gospel and to flee those things which lead professing Christians away from Jesus Christ.

The command was "be saved from this perverse generation." Later in Peter's letter to the churches he issued a warning about false prophets and teachers.

> But there were also false prophets among the people, even as there will be false teachers among you, who will secretly bring in destructive heresies, even denying the Lord who bought them, and bring on themselves swift destruction. And many will follow their destructive ways, because of whom the way of truth will be blasphemed." (2 Peter 2:1-2)

Although Christians demonstrate charity among the brethren and seek unity in the visible church, they must be bold against the poison darts of heresy. The church must proclaim the truth. The truth about faith, worship and life is normative in any age.

It is not possible to believe the metaphysical assertions about God, Jesus Christ, and the Holy Spirit, without accepting the truth set forth about them in the Word of God. The Holy Spirit must accompany the word of truth to secure the prosperity and future hope of the church. "Then those who gladly received his word were baptized; and that day about three thousand souls were added to them" (Acts 2:41). This text must be understood in its historical dimension and correlate it to other parts of Scripture which are more definitive of the doctrine mentioned in it.

"The Lord changed the hearts of many" refers to the work of the Holy Spirit enabling the soul (often called the heart) to believe the truth of the gospel. According to the Bible "about three thousand were added" to the church. The changed hearts were obedient; those who accepted his message were baptized.

God gave His church the Word of God so God's truth, by the power of the Holy Spirit, would give hope to those who see nothing but despair in this world. Preaching God's truth, accompanied by the power of the Holy Spirit, changes the way a person believes and thinks. He or she will have a God-centered view of life and existence. To have faith in an object, is the same as believing in an object. The word faith is generally used as a noun. The word believe is generally used it as a verb. For instance, to have faith in Christ is to believe in Christ.

The true and living God instructs His people to worship Him according to His doctrine in the Word of God. When Christians look at life with faith in God and proper worship to God, hope is the joy they experience.

The church continued, "steadfastly in the Apostles' doctrine and fellowship, in the breaking of bread, and in prayers" (Acts 2:42). John Calvin explains:

> ...They did constantly give themselves to those exer-
> cises which serve to the confirmation of faith; to wit,
> that they studied continually to profit by hearing the
> apostles; that they gave themselves much to prayer;
> that they did use fellowship and breaking of bread
> very much. (*John Calvin's Commentary, Book of
> Acts*, http://www.ccel.org/ccel/calvin/calcom36.ix.viii
> .html)

The church made it a habit to continue in the Apostles' teaching. People must hear and understand the gospel in
order to believe. Many well-meaning professing Christians
teach by their experiences of life. However, life experiences
must be tested by the Word of God. For instance, those early
disciples were not busy looking for another miracle. They did
not pray for another tongues experience. They were busy
studying and learning the Word of God. "The Apostles'
doctrine" refers to the full counsel of God.

Fellowship refers to the common life of the church.
The early Christians found joy and happiness in sharing with
each other. They were generous and kind to each other. The
life of the individual Christian finds its place in the
community of the church.

The breaking of bread has been interpreted by some as
a common meal, while others believe it refers to communion.
The church ought to share in common meals together and take
communion regularly with solemnity and joy.

The praying church will stay on course. Notice from
the text the emphasis is on multiple prayers. Prayer is not
begging for things. Prayer is closing out other thoughts and
focusing on the nature and character of God. Christians who
pray will delight in God's glory, majesty, dignity, love,
justice, holiness, truth, wisdom, power, goodness,
excellencies, perfections, and mercy.

The spiritual condition of the church depends on the spiritual condition of the individual members of the church. If there are evil, envious, greedy and cruel people in the church, the spiritual condition of the church is on a low ebb and must be restored. If the members of the church are filled with love, joy, peace, kindness, and goodness then the church is shining as a light in a dark world. Christians will experience the prosperity of the church and rejoice in the hope for the church.

9. Principles for Church Growth

Acts 3:1-26

The apostles ministered during a time of transition from the Old Covenant to the New Covenant. The teaching, worship, and life of God's covenant people changed, not in substance, but in form and appearance. The apostles were the divine instruments of establishing normative principles for living in the kingdom of God under the New Covenant. The apostles were filled with the Holy Spirit with an overflow and God used them as instruments or the means for performing many supernatural miracles. But they were men - mere men. They had diseases, sickness, and felt the pain and misery of this world just as we do. They had the ability to know and discern the truth from a lie. They were called to be disciples in a corrupt world. However, all covenant believers are disciples of Jesus Christ. The early disciples were obedient and Christians today are called to be obedient. The disciples of Christ in every generation must understand and engage in the purpose, mission and ministry of the church. Christians, in every era, must engage in the culture and communities they live, work, and play with the intention to advance the kingdom of God.

The Book of Acts ought to be examined to discover the inspired eternal principles that produced the church in the first century and apply those principles to the contemporary church. Then God will add to the number as it pleases Him. Underlying all the reasons for the tremendous church growth throughout the history of the church are fundamental divine principles for church growth

The disciples of the nascent church of the Lord Jesus Christ understood those divine principles that God used and still uses for church growth. Christians must embrace those principles to the glory of God. To embrace the divine principles will ensure the right practice.

In chapter three of the Book of Acts, there are two providential events. First, a supernatural miracle and then a sermon by the apostle Peter. To put this in its proper context, a brief summary of events will be necessary. Peter and John, along with other Jews were going to the mid afternoon prayer meeting at the Temple. On their way they come upon a chronically disabled beggar. Peter did not have any money for the beggar but Peter knew that Jesus Christ could heal the disabled man and the man was healed.

The cause and effect principle is worthy of attention. What was the cause that produced the supernatural miraculous healing of the disabled beggar? Peter said, "in the name of Jesus Christ the Nazarene, walk" (Acts 3:6). The Lord Jesus Christ was the first cause of the supernatural miracle. The normal natural process of second causes were unnecessary, except for the helping hand of Peter in getting the man to his feet. The biblical text has no ambiguity. "And His name, through faith in His name, has made this man strong, whom you see and know. Yes, the faith which comes through Him has given him this perfect soundness in the presence of you all" (Acts 3:16). Jesus Christ was the cause or to put it another way, the author of the healing. Simple Bible doctrine teaches that humans cannot cause or produce supernatural miracles.

Everything in creation, including the human race, is dependent on God. Human beings, including Christian human beings, are not endowed with the power to create anything. Even though the Holy Spirit of God changed the man, both body and soul, Peter still took his hand and helped him to his feet. God uses means and instruments to bring about the glory due His name.

After the healing, the man expressed his faith in the name of the one who healed him. So many people today believe that there is healing power in faith. Faith does not and cannot produce anything. Faith does not have the power to create. Just as regeneration of the soul, by the power of the Holy Spirit precedes faith, so the power of God as the cause of healing also precedes visible manifestation of the healing.

Acts 3:16 is often misunderstood and there are several reasons for the misunderstanding. First, Christians may not study words carefully. Second, they often fail to consider the law of causality; that for every effect there must be a *sufficient* cause. The disabled man was healed; that was the effect. The cause was Jesus Christ, but the people did not realize what Christ had done. The people mistakenly attributed the entire event to the Peter's alleged power to heal.

Christians may see effects, such as little or no interest in serious Bible study. When you see such a few people in worship, you see the effect. Christians tend to look more at outward circumstances, than inward change. If the Holy Spirit changes the heart, the believer should act differently, just like the disabled man walking about and praising God (Acts 3:8).

The first principle for divine church growth is a change of heart, which is the soul. The symbol of Peter healing the disabled man should remind Christians of a restored soul because of the work of Christ and the application of it to their lives. Obviously, the people were astonished at the miracle, but Peter did not say, "if you think that is a miracle, watch this" only to perform another miracle more impressive than the healing of the disabled man.

Peter seized the occasion to preach a sermon. Peter applied a principle that is a duty of all Christians. Peter said, "we are witnesses" (Acts 3:15). Witnesses of what? The immediate context is that Peter and the other disciples were witnesses of the life, death, resurrection and ascension of the Lord Jesus Christ. Today Christians are witnesses, not based on their human experiences, but by virtue of the Word of God.

Peter's life was changed because of what Jesus Christ had done. The disabled man's life was changed. Both Peter and the disabled man were the recipients of a supernatural work of God. It is just as much a miracle that God changes the heart of a rebellious sinner, as the miracle of healing the body. It is more of a miracle when God changes an unbelieving heart. The healed body will eventually die, but the restored soul will live forever.

The second divine principle necessary for the growth of the church is to seize every occasion for the purpose of being a witness of what Christ has done in the life of the Christian. I've often heard professing Christians say, "but I don't have dynamic story to tell about my conversion." Or to put it another way they are saying, "I don't have much of a witness." On the contrary, every Christian can be a witness without a super-duper testimony. Christians today do not need to witness a supernatural external miraculous event to be a witness of God's grace.

The most dynamic Christian witness is to say with integrity, "Repent therefore and be converted, that your sins may be blotted out, so times of refreshing may come from the presence of the Lord" (Acts 3:19). It is refreshing to believe that God will give a sinner a new heart. It is refreshing when the power of the Holy Spirit causes the new heart to recognize sin. It is refreshing to repent of sin and be converted by the power of the Holy Spirit. Peter explained, "that your sins may be blotted out" (Acts 3:19). The picture is that of a chalkboard that can be wiped clean. Apparently Peter's plural use of the word sin means that Christians are not only forgiven of the guilt they inherited, but particular sins committed by the saved sinner.

There is a relative analogy in the healing of the disabled man to the pardon by God that wipes sin away. If

God wipes away sin, why do so many professing Christians rewrite them on the slate. When God blots out your sin, your response should be faith, repentance, and reconciliation. You can be a witness of God's forgiveness, if God has forgiven you. True forgiveness wipes away the guilt. If there is no guilt, there must be reconciliation. When Christians demonstrate true forgiveness and reconciliation, they have given a very good reason for unbelievers to believe and repent.

Another reason for Christians to share the saving grace of Jesus Christ is the hope of rest and restitution. Peter said, "repent therefore and be converted, that your sins may be blotted out, so that times of refreshing may come from the presence of the Lord" (Acts 3:19). While theologians argue over the precise meaning of the phrase "times of refreshing" Dr. William Larkin's commentary explains with clarity. He describes it as, "the immediate relief that the people can expect, since salvation is now accomplished...(*The IVP New Testament Commentary Series, Acts*, by William J. Larkin Jr., pg. 69). There is a "time of refreshing" for all of God's people in every generation. Christians need refreshing because they tend to live by a set pattern. They have a set routine. They find comfort with uniform habits. Many people work on jobs even when there is no sense of accomplishment. Some people find life dull and unexciting. Some Christians find worship, mission and ministry stale and boring. What they need is a time of refreshing. The language of this text denotes that refreshing is by divine authority. Christians refreshed by the power of the Holy Spirit will be a witness of God's generous grace.

The word "refreshed" found in this text is used in conjunction with agricultural metaphors. Rain is said to be a time of refreshing. Likewise religious revivals are often times of refreshing. Revival is a biblical concept generally ignored by churches today. The typical revival meeting is merely a pep rally. However, true revival, preceded by being reformed by the Word of God is refreshing to the soul. Even though the soul is refreshed, revival is an outward expression of an inward change. Reformation brings inward change and revival brings outward expression. Revival is also an expression of religious energy. Revival is a picture of the beauty of life.

The conceptual idea of revival may be found in a natural illustration. The natural illustration is the change of season in the spring of the year. The dormant trees and shrubs express a fresh beauty and vigor of life. Flowers bring forth sweet odors. The spring rain refreshes the ground and it seems as if the whole world is energized with new life.

The divine principles for church growth are numerous, but two are necessary for the others to be effective. The first principle is, believing that Jesus Christ is able to change the heart. If Christ by the power of the Holy Spirit, changes the heart, then the second principle will follow from the first. Christians will seize every occasion to witness of God's forgiveness. The centerpiece of church growth is to trust and obey.

10. Persecution by Religious Hypocrites

Acts 4:1-12

The church was growing but several of the older members were not happy with what they perceived to be a takeover by newcomers. They thought it was necessary to persecute the new comers and the leader of this new gospel. It all began with the growth of the church in Jerusalem around 33 A.D. Persecution is normal for Christians. The Word of God is rather straightforward with the subject of Christian persecution by religious hypocrites. "Yes, and all who desire to live godly in Christ Jesus will suffer persecution" (2 Timothy 3:12). Jesus said, "Blessed are you when they revile and persecute you, and say all kinds of evil against you falsely for My sake" (Matthew 5:11).

God's children have been persecuted from the beginning. The Lord Jesus Christ was persecuted to the point of death. The apostle Paul suffered persecution for his devout service in the gospel. Persecution may be physical torment, harassment, aggravation, or verbal assaults. Sometimes persecution may result in death. The first recorded persecution in the New Testament church came from the hands of the religious hypocrites in Israel. Peter and John were seized by the religious leaders and placed in custody.

It has been said that the Jewish rulers were persecuting Peter and John because of the healing of the lame man described in Acts Chapter three. The healing was the instrument that gave occasion for the persecution. Peter and John experienced persecution for several reasons. Peter and John were teaching the people and they were preaching the resurrection of the dead in Jesus' name.

The office of teaching belonged to the Jewish religious leaders. According to Jewish religious laws, only the Jewish religious leaders were permitted to teach the people. All unauthorized teachers were perceived as usurping the authority of Jewish religious leaders. Authority is the means for power. Religious people are passionate about authority, because they are passionate about power.

These same Jewish religious leaders hated Jesus because they recognized His authority. Those same religious leaders hated Jesus and had Him killed. It makes sense that if Jesus taught with authority and then passed that authority to the apostles, then the apostles were a threat to the Jews. Although the culture is different today and the religious scene has changed, the struggle for authority and power has not changed.

Peter and John were not merely teaching a new ethic or a philosophy of success, they were teaching the resurrection of the dead. The Sadducees did not believe in the resurrection of the dead, so to teach the resurrection of the dead was contrary to their tradition. The Pharisees believed in the resurrection of the dead, so why were they disturbed with the teaching of Peter and John? Peter and John were preaching that God had raised the Lord Jesus Christ from the dead. Having killed the Lord Jesus Christ, those religious leaders did not want to hear that Christ had been raised from the dead. Maybe they were fearful that Christ was alive. They feared the loss of their authority, so they coveted their hypocritical offices. Things have not changed much in the past 2000 years. Religious people still persecute the Lord Jesus Christ, because they hate the Lord. They hate the Lord Jesus Christ because their father is the devil. Jesus, speaking to the Jewish religious leaders said, "You are of your father the devil, and the desires of your father you want to do" (John 8:44).

The Lord Jesus Christ is no longer present in His flesh, so the opponents of Christ go for the throat of those who minister in the name of Jesus Christ. The opponents of those who minister in the name of Jesus Christ are a strange lot. There are at least ten named parties opposed to the preaching and teaching of Peter and John. (Acts 4:1-6).

Verse one:
1) The priests – Levites – in charge of religious life
2) The captain of the temple guard – in charge of temple – He was second in command
3) The Sadducees – the upper class, wealthy, powerful

Verse five:
1) The rulers – position of authority – perhaps in government
2) The elders – older men of influence
3) The teachers of the law - scribes

Verse six:
1) Annas - represents the individual priests
2) Caiaphas
3) John
4) Alexander

The opponents to the gospel and the church of Jesus Christ are many, but most of them fit into three categories. Religious leaders are the most frequent and aggressive opponents to the true gospel. Sometimes civil government officials are the cruel opponents of Christianity. Skeptics are the most arrogant of the opponents of the true gospel. These enemies of the church conspired to crush the young church in the Book of Acts. They are still opposed to the growth of the true church. The Holy Spirit of God distinguishes godly church leaders from the crafty-minded charlatans who occupy seats of leadership in the church. The religious hypocrisy that opposes the church today is as rampant as it has ever been.

The religious leaders who oppose the true gospel use the only power available to them, the power of this world.

The abuse of power is the result of sin. It naturally follows that the greater the abuse, the greater the sin. The power of the world depends on physical strength to suppress those who minister in the name of Jesus Christ (Acts 4:3). After physical restraint, the world intimidates the servant of Christ (Acts 4:7).

While the world operates with this kind of intimidation, Christians must take a stand with resolve to witness the grace of the Lord Jesus Christ. Fear and timidity is not the witness Christ expects of His children. Christians have the greatest message known to humanity. They must not be afraid of any harm that will come to them if they are witnesses of God's grace.

The world thinks it can stop the work of God by intimidation and threats. If that does not work, the world will exert more force, which may include physical harm and maybe death. However, not even death will stop God's truth.

Tertullian was one of the early church fathers who was not afraid of persecution and martyrdom if necessary for the sake of the gospel.   A paraphrase of his comment to a Roman governor was, "The blood of the martyrs is the seed of the church" (*The Apology*).

The worldly forces against the people of God are incomparable to the force of God. God's force, which is freely given to God's people, is the Holy Spirit. The Bible indicates that as Peter began to speak he was "filled with the Holy Spirit" (Acts 4:8). When people are filled with the Holy Spirit, they will proclaim the truth of God. Peter did and so should Christians in the modern church. While Peter was standing in the midst of these vicious opponents of Jesus Christ, Peter was not afraid to speak the truth. Peter said they were guilty of crucifying Jesus. Peter told them that they may have killed Jesus, but Jesus rose from the dead.

The inescapable truth that all men need to hear is that Jesus Christ is the one and only way of salvation. "Nor is there salvation in any other, for there is no other name under heaven given among men by which we must be saved" (Acts 4:12). Peter knew that one statement may cost him his life, but he was not afraid. Peter took the risk because he knew it was the truth. The power of the Holy Spirit is essential to enable Christians to witness the truth. The Holy Spirit proved His power by healing the crippled man. The Holy Spirit will also prove His power when Christians are persecuted for the sake of Jesus Christ.

The only weapon that ungodly opponents have is brutish temporary power. They may use the power of money to persecute the church. They may use the power of civil government to persecute the church. They may use the power of deception. In the final analysis, all worldly power is temporary.

Persecution may come from unexpected sources. It may be a husband or a wife. It may be a parent or a child. It may be from the people at the workplace. Christians must remain faithful to the whole counsel of God. God's people are redeemed to give a testimony of God's saving grace, to make disciples and teach the full counsel of God.

11. Religious Resistance

Acts 4:13-31

Christians often disenfranchise themselves from church growth that took place during the first thirty years of the New Testament Church. The claim is, "I don't have the power of the apostles." That kind of attitude denigrates the work of the Holy Spirit to mere pietistic gratification. Christians today do not have the power to speak or act under inspiration from God like the apostles. There is no evidence that anyone since the death of the last apostle has the unique powers that were given to the apostles.

Christians in every generation must exercise themselves in the manifestation of witnessing God's grace. A witness is one that tells the truth about what he or she has seen or heard. Grace in this context is evidence that God has favored the witness with the blessing of God.

The most common way to witness is by speaking. Peter and John were brought before the leaders of Jerusalem and they spoke to the leaders about God's grace. When they were put on the witness stand, they maintained a distinctively fearless witness. "But Peter and John answered and said to them, "Whether it is right in the sight of God to listen to you more than to God, you judge. For we cannot but speak the things which we have seen and heard" (Acts 4:19-20). The religious leaders in Jerusalem were disturbed because the speech of the apostles was commanding the attention of about five thousand men.

The problem facing those civil and religious leaders was "What shall we do to these men?" (Acts 4:16). The leaders did not know how to handle the authority issue. The authority for teaching and preaching rested in the hands of the religious leaders. Peter and John taught and preached with authority evidenced by the healing of the lame man (Acts 3:2-10).   The leaders could not deny the divine authority associated with the teaching and preaching of Peter and John. The leaders responded by warning them not to speak to anyone in the name of Jesus Christ.   It was a threat to intimidate the disciples and create fear of human authority. The leaders probably thought that Peter and John would take heed to the warning. The disciples of Christ did not have the blessing of the religious leaders in Jerusalem.

The Jewish religious and civil leaders were educated, so surely they knew what was best for the ignorant and unlearned men. The disciples were perceived as uneducated and untrained men. Uneducated is not the best reading. They were literally unlettered men.   To put it another way they were educated, but not with a formal degree from the approved authorities. The implication is that Peter and John did not attend the rabbinic schools of the day. The modern equivalent would be the lack of a degree from a prestigious seminary. The apostles were not associated with the popular religious groups. The modern day equivalent is that they were not associated with a popular denomination.   The Jewish religious leaders did not understand that Peter and John had attended the best seminary the world had ever known. They had been with the Lord Jesus Christ for three years. The Lord not only taught them the true gospel, but the apostles were equipped by the power of the Holy Spirit with authority to write the Word of God, attested by supernatural miracles.

It seemed remarkable to the religious and civil leaders at Jerusalem that these two fishermen showed no fear as they stood before the rich and powerful. It seemed odd to the leaders in Jerusalem that Peter and John would give a powerful believable testimony of the resurrection of the Lord Jesus Christ.   The disciples were capable of intelligent communication. We live in a dispensation of unintelligible speech. The once cherished pursuit for truth has been replaced by politically correct language.

The academic discipline commonly known as rhetoric, has lost favor in the eyes of most educational institutions. There are many reasons for the demise of rhetoric. There was a time in this country when universities required its students to take rhetoric. The substitute in modern universities is speech 101. Rhetoric is the ability to use language effectively. Speech is the ability to express ones thought and emotions by sounds and gestures. There is a great chasm separating rhetoric from speech. Rhetoric requires the right use of words so truth propositions will cut to the heart of the subject. Speech is more subjective. It is the ability to say something that will convince someone to believe the words of the speaker. Peter and John were rhetoricians. Peter's remarks are evident of his rhetorical skills.

> Then Peter, filled with the Holy Spirit, said to them, "Rulers of the people and elders of Israel: If we this day are judged for a good deed done to a helpless man, by what means he has been made well, let it be known to you all, and to all the people of Israel, that by the name of Jesus Christ of Nazareth, whom you crucified, whom God raised from the dead, by Him this man stands here before you whole. This is the 'stone which was rejected by you builders, which has become the chief cornerstone.' Nor is there salvation in any other, for there is no other name under heaven given among men by which we must be saved." (Acts 4:8-12)

The logic is impeccable. The composition is without prejudice. The delivery is fearless. These Christian men were cutting to the hearts of a society of religious hypocrites. After the powerful speech by Peter the religious and civil leaders commanded the disciples not to speak at all or teach in the name of Jesus.

The politically incorrect rhetoric of the apostles was not popular but it effectively presented the truth. Some preachers have historically resisted the temptation to accommodate biblical truth, especially the fundamental principles of the gospel of Jesus Christ. Others allow the intimidation to suppress preaching and the proper use of rhetoric.

During Medieval Christianity there were Monks who declared that the world and its governments were so corrupt they could do nothing with them. They retreated from the sound teaching of Scripture that calls Christians to stand boldly and proclaim the truth as it is found in Scripture. American Christians have followed the teaching of the monastic's and retreated from the noble call given to them to be witnesses of God's grace.

It is easy to push God out of the picture in the face of secularism. This ungodly worldview dismisses theism. Like the religious leaders in Jerusalem, secularism today commands Christians not to speak nor teach in the name of Jesus. The intimidation has been successful. The religious and civil leaders of the past few generations have created a new generation of cowards. Christians are not only afraid to speak the things which they have learned and know to be true from the Word of God, they have bowed to every wind of doctrine in the religious world and given Caesar the right to demand those things which do not belong to him. Every Christian should fear God rather than man.

Peter and John stood before the religious and civil leaders in Jerusalem with courage and conviction. If civil leaders, religious leaders, or anyone else tries to intimidate Christians, they need to be ready to speak the truth for the sake of the gospel. Christians must be ready to say to those who oppose the gospel, "Whether it is right in the sight of

God to listen to you more than to God, you judge" (Acts 4:19).

Christians must face ungodly opposition and threats with resolve to fear God rather than men. They must not retreat into a monastic lifestyle. Throughout the history of the church some Christians have chosen not to contend with the government authorities or false religion. They would say, "the world is corrupt, we're outnumbered, so don't contend for the truth." Other professing Christians have compromised with civil and religious authorities to the point of departing from the true faith. Christians must not compromise or retreat from ungodly civil leaders and false religion. Peter and John told the governing authorities to judge whether it was right to preach the gospel. There is the final judgment and the Judge is a just Judge. Christians will not answer to any man in that judgment. Therefore, they must determine what is right in the eyes of God. It is right in the eyes of God to preach righteousness. It is right in the eyes of God to obey God against the wishes of any worldly force.

The judgment of the ungodly will ultimately stand before a higher Judge, the Lord Jesus Christ. The time and place to begin standing before God is in this secular world. God's children will prefer to stand before the righteous Judge of the universe. Such was the position assumed by Peter and John when the leaders in Jerusalem released them.

Peter and John along with other Christians lifted their voices in prayer (Acts 4:24-31). Christians today ought to pray in the same manner. Pray to the sovereign God of the universe. Remember, when men claim to be sovereign, they are but mere puppets. Men do not have the power to create and therefore they do have the right or authority to judge the God who created all things. Pray for wisdom as you stand against the evil in this world. Pray for boldness to speak the Word of God. The child of God must speak the truth of God's Word in the face of this present world. They did pray for boldness that the preaching may continue uninhibited by threats and fear. The apostles and disciples did not pray for their own safety. They prayed that the kingdom of God would advance by means of teaching and preaching the full counsel of God. God is still present and will give His people, emphasis on *His people*, the courage to be witnesses of Jesus Christ in Jerusalem, in Judea, in Samaria, and to the end of the earth.

12. The Community Church

Acts 4:32 – 5:11

If the Spirit of God changes your soul, then the Word of God should change your life. The change should affect your family, your work ethic, your social involvement, and many other benevolent associations, but above all you should have a desire to recover the Eden that was lost at the fall. Although it is not possible to live without sin in a sinful world, God's people must act differently than those who belong to the evil one.

Eden enjoyed unity in every respect. Sin entered and polarized all of creation. During the early days of the New Testament church there was the unique demonstration of unity in community. It is a model for the church today. The early church was truly a community church because there was unity in community.

The community church refers to any particular church that endeavors to fulfill the purpose, mission and ministry of the church. The purpose of the church is to worship God and all that the concept of biblical worship encompasses (John 4:24; Revelation 14:1-3). The mission of the church is to make disciples and teach the Word of God (Matthew 28:19-20). The ministry of the church is to equip the people of God for the works of service (Ephesians 4:11-16). The level of unity in the community church will depend of the level of maturity of individual Christians and their faithfulness to fulfill the purpose, mission, and ministry of the church.

Unity among the Christians at a local church or unity among local congregations does not presume conformity. Later in the book of Acts the church at Antioch will be introduced, but the church at Jerusalem did not insist on conforming to the church at Jerusalem. Likewise Antioch was not a flagship church. For instance, the church at Antioch did not require its missionaries, such as Barnabas, to precisely duplicate the church at Antioch as other churches were established churches in other regions.

The disciples of Christ went forth to evangelize and teach, not form an organization to be mimicked by others. Church unity was determined by the Word of God. Mark McAllister wrote a book for laymen, but well researched that explains the biblical concept of unity applied to the 21st century church (*Red Rover, Interlocking Arms Around the World to Fulfill Jesus' Prayer*, by Mark McAllister).

The early church was unique in its ministry to hold all things in common (Acts 4:32). More than unity, it represents service for the sake of the gospel. However, this particular "sharing" ministry was grounded in unity. Those who come to Christ come by the power of the same Holy Spirit.

The Bible teaches that the church exhibits community by holding to one calling, one faith, and one baptism (Ephesians 4:4-6). This oneness in doctrine is the unity that Christians desire for the church.

One of the notable characteristics of the early church is they were "of one heart and one soul" (Acts 4:32). One Greek philosopher has said that this phrase brings together the Greek ideal for friendship: "a single soul dwelling in two bodies" (*Acts*, by William J. Larkin, p. 82).

It should be no surprise to hear of this kind of unity because Luke has already mentioned that the disciples were with one mind (Acts 1:14; 2:46). The one heart and one soul concept has deep roots in the Old Testament. An example is the coronation of David as King of Israel.

> All these men of war, who could keep ranks, came to
> Hebron with a loyal heart, to make David king over
> all Israel; and all the rest of Israel were of one mind to
> make David king. And they were there with David

three days, eating and drinking, for their brethren had prepared for them. Moreover those who were near to them, from as far away as Issachar and Zebulun and Naphtali, were bringing food on donkeys and camels, on mules and oxen—provisions of flour and cakes of figs and cakes of raisins, wine and oil and oxen and sheep abundantly, for there was joy in Israel. (1 Chronicles 12:38:40)

The people of Israel were of one mind, one heart, and one soul because they served the same God and believed the Word of God was the final authority for faith and life. Although the people of God in the Old Testament were often alienated, when it came time to worship, they were united. "Behold, how good and how pleasant it is For brethren to dwell together in unity!" (Psalm 133:1).

It is difficult to imagine a church where there was no dissension and no division. Our experience simply does not comprehend the kind of unity we find among the believers in Jerusalem described in the book of Acts. Even so, the fountainhead of Christianity began with unity in the community. However, there never has been and there never will be a perfect church on earth, but there was and there should be representative unity among believers.

You might wonder if there is a secret to the unity demonstrated in the early church. No secret and the answer is really very simple. The act of believing brought the multitude together in one heart and one soul. The power to believe was given to them by the Holy Spirit. They believed the apostles' doctrine with one mind and will. Unity of love and purpose brought the early community of believers together.

Although God's people may not achieve perfect unity, they must believe with one heart and soul. Any conflict between Christians individually or churches collectively must be managed with charity and humility. However, doctrinal differences must not be ignored, because in due time they will raise their heads and cause division. Discernment and prudence is necessary to determine if the error is sufficient to divide the ranks.

The church is a community of believers called to demonstrate the evangelistic character of the church. It was with great power that the apostles "gave witness to the resurrection of the Lord Jesus" (Acts 4:33). The common mark that identifies and distinguishes Christianity from all other world religions is the resurrection of the Lord Jesus Christ. The early church was careful to hold dear the bodily resurrection of Jesus Christ. Many Protestant churches explicitly or implicitly deny the bodily physical resurrection of the Lord Jesus Christ. If you ask a preacher or theologian in one of those denominations if they believe in the resurrection of Christ they may say, "yes." However, some of those who say yes, may also say no to the bodily physical resurrection. They say yes to the spiritual resurrection of Christ, but no to the bodily resurrection of Christ. It is not possible to experience unity if the church ignores the basic doctrine in Scripture.

Another characteristic that brought unity to the community of those early Christians was their view of possessions. The Bible explains in descriptive history that "they had all things in common" (Acts 4:32). The early church could easily be identified because it was a caring community. The Word of God does establish normative patterns for giving, but this text does not establish the normative pattern for giving. Jerusalem was never a haven for economic security and the political unrest of that region would certainly have impoverished some of those early Christians. Sharing with one another was a witness of God's grace to the community church. If God has graced us, then we must be gracious to others.

Barnabas is a man that truly believed in the community church. He gave generously without reservation for the sake of the gospel (Acts 4:36-37). Ananias and Sapphira are an example of a couple that allegedly believed in the community church. They gave begrudgingly with reservation. They are examples of unfaithful professing Christians. The lies of Ananias and Sapphira show how quickly the community of believers may lose the unity. Therefore, God's direct and instantaneous punishment caused great fear to fall upon the church and all who heard of it.

The story about Barnabas, Ananias and Sapphira should remind Christians of the gospel of God's saving grace. If the love of God is in our hearts, it should be seen in our hands. The church must fear God, not man, as she lives in unity for the sake of the gospel.

13. Faithful Ministers

The religious leaders in Jerusalem instructed the disciples of Christ not to preach and teach in the name of Jesus. The disciples concluded that they ought to obey God rather than men. The religious leaders in Jerusalem feared the loss of power and ultimately the power to control religious life in their culture. It was an undeniable witness of God's power when the disciples healed the sick and preached to the large crowd of Jews. The religious leaders reacted with frustration. They wanted the disciples to move on and get out of Jerusalem.

I have heard pastors and laymen say, "the pastor at such and such church has done all he can do. It's time for him to move on." It is a nonsense comment. The pastor is an elder and his responsibility is to shepherd the church. The disciples were faithful ministers and the saving power of God was evident. The early church was devoted to the disciples' teaching. The church practiced a deep level of refreshing fellowship. The people prayed diligently for God's hand of blessing.

The contemporary church has turned into such a massive commercial enterprise that it has forgotten the sound teaching of the Word of God. Christian fellowship consists of a fried chicken dinner in a building called the "fellowship hall." Sometimes fellowship consists of small groups, meeting according to the demographics established by church leadership. Wednesday night is set aside for prayer meeting, but really consists of a Bible study. "Having church" has replaced worship.

The false notion that "ministry ends because of trouble and persecution" is unbiblical. The early disciples of

Jesus Christ were repeatedly condemned and persecuted. It is worthy to note that the primary source of trouble came from religious leaders, not unbelieving Gentiles.

It is sad but true that many Christians are taught that the book of Acts is dedicated to taking the gospel to the unbelieving Gentiles (un-churched). That is simply not true. There is a major emphasis on Gentile unbelievers in the ministry of the apostle Paul, but at least one third of the book is dedicated to reaching those first century Jews. The Jews already believed in God. They were attending Synagogue services.

According to the Word of God, "believers were increasingly added to the Lord, multitudes of both men and women" (Acts 5:14). The Holy Spirit changed the hearts of men and women so they could believe the gospel. This is the first time that women were mentioned as being added to the church. This may be in response to the unfaithfulness of Ananias and his wife Sapphira. Perhaps Luke wanted to point out the significance of faithful men and women in contrast to those unfaithful men and women like Ananias and Sapphira.

The church in Jerusalem was alive. The church rapidly expanded because of God's saving grace and the faithful ministry of God's people. Many Christians attribute the rapid expansion of the early church to the miraculous healings. It is that mentality that provokes many professing Christians to literally worship alleged faith healers. The miraculous healings in the early church simply showed the multitude that the Apostles were acting with authority. Today Christians do not need the miracles to demonstrate God's authority because they have the Word of God, which attests the truth of God's power over all things. The Bible often refers to the disciples speaking with authority and power. It was their faithfulness and obedience that made them known among the people.

Faithfulness and devotion to the Word of God is a mark of faithful ministers. The Jewish religious leaders put the faithful disciples in prison (Acts 5:17-18). While they were in jail, the angel of the Lord instructed the disciples to "stand in the temple and speak to the people" (Acts 5:19-20). A faithful minister will continue to preach the Word of God even in the face of trouble and persecution.

An angel of the Lord set the faithful disciples free and they went back to the Temple to teach the Word of God. They were brought before the religious leaders. "And when they had brought them, they set them before the council. And the high priest asked them, saying, 'Did we not strictly command you not to teach in this name? And look, you have filled Jerusalem with your doctrine, and intend to bring this Man's blood on us!'" (Acts 5:27-28). The religious Jewish leaders opposed the faithful ministers of the gospel. The rapid growth of the Christian Church distressed those in charge of religious and political life. The same thing happens today in many churches when a dead church comes alive with godly people; there will be an uprising from the ungodly against the new converts and godly leaders. The Jewish religious leaders in Jerusalem expected the Messiah to accommodate their man-made religion. The name of Jesus represented the saving grace of God, contrary to the works salvation of the religious leaders.

Jesus represented the authority of God and the old-line religious leaders and politicians did not like anybody stepping into their playing field. Anyhow, Jesus was just a young upstart rabbi who was going against the tradition of the old line church. Jesus Christ is always a threat those who do not belong to Him, because He is the image of the invisible God. As long as God is invisible and metaphysical, He does not seem to be a threat to the unbeliever. Jesus Christ is the second person of the Trinity, with full and final authority. He becomes the object of hostility by unsaved ungodly religious people. Today those who would like to kill Jesus are not able to get to Him, but they can get to those faithful ministers who obey Jesus. For that reason Jesus said, "If they persecuted Me, they will also persecute you; if they kept My word, they will keep yours also" (John 15:20). Paul also says, "And indeed, all who desire to live godly in Christ Jesus will be persecuted" (1 Timothy 3:12).

Some of the Jewish religious leaders in Jerusalem did not believe in the bodily resurrection. The resurrection of Jesus Christ proved He was God. If He was God then he had ultimate authority. Natural man does not like authority. Natural man says, "I am, and there is no one else besides me" (Isaiah 47:10). However, God says, "I am the Lord and there is no other" (Isaiah 45:5).   It was the cosmic clash of authority. Who is in charge?

The religious leaders in Jerusalem were jealous. They were jealous of Jesus and His ability to reveal their wicked ways. They were jealous of the unlearned fishermen speaking with authority and attracting a multitude of men and women. The abundance of jealousy among professing Christians is a clear sign of unrest and dissension in the church. When the religious leaders come to the pastor and say it is time to leave, what must he do? The Word of God has the answer for faithful ministers. "We ought to obey God rather than men" (Acts 5:29). The word "ought" implies debt. The word can be traced to the word "owe" as in someone owes someone else some money.

Faithful ministers owe it to God by divine imperative to preach and teach like Peter preached and taught when the religious leaders confronted him. Peter's response was short, but it cut to the bone. Peter's sermon had four points.

1. The crucifixion (Peter accuses those present with murder).
2. The resurrection (God raised Jesus from the dead).
3. The ascension (God exalted Jesus to his own right hand as Prince and Savior).

4. Faithful ministers were witnesses.

This is the centrality of the gospel message that unbelievers need to hear.

In spite of the opposition a faithful minister will count it a privilege to suffer for the sake of Jesus Christ. In spite of the opposition a faithful minister will follow the example of the faithful ministers in the early church. "And daily in the temple, and in every house, they did not cease teaching and preaching Jesus as the Christ" (Acts 5:42).

The Holy Spirit is the source of power needed to enable faithful ministers to teach and preach the Word of God and experience a growing vitally alive church.

14. Servants in a Growing Church

Acts 6:1-7

The historical data that might help Christians better understand Luke's historical timeline of the church is non-existent. Luke said "now in those days" (Acts 6:1), but it is difficult to estimate the exact month and year. Luke said the disciples were increasing, but he does not mention a number. There is no way to determine the exact date of this occasion, but two years had probably past since the ascension of Christ and the church consisted of thousands of men, women, and children.

The ministry of the early church was unique in many ways. Ministry is a primary doctrine in the Bible, especially in the New Testament. The word minister derived from the Greek word *diakonos* is also translated into English as "servant." The ministry of the church requires servants. God calls some men to be servants by serving as elders or deacons. All Christians serve the Lord in one way or the other.

Until this time in the history of the church there was no mention of a complaint or disagreement among the followers of Christ. The early church had been a godly productive ministry, but now the church must resolve a conflict among the followers of Christ. Luke explains that "there arose a complaint against the Hebrews by the Hellenists, because their widows were neglected in the daily distribution" (Acts 6:1). The increase and growth apparently put a burden on the disciples. Their duty to preach and teach to the newly converted disciples did not leave time to tend to the daily distribution of food to some of the widows. According to Luke's inspired account, a complaint came from the Greek speaking Jews because their widows were being overlooked. Obviously Hebrew-speaking Jews did not distribute the food with equity. The early church was careful to provide for the needs of widows and orphans.

The apostles were appointed as ministers of the Word, but they also ministered to the physical needs of the people. Even if the disciples did not actually serve food, they were responsible to see that the food was distributed to those in need. The Apostles were busy preaching and teaching so they were unable to manage the distribution of food. God had called the apostles to serve the Word of God to those who were hungry for the Word of God.

The apostles resolved the conflict quickly without a division in the church. The apostles were deliberate and decisive. The peace of the church was important. It is the responsibility of every Christian to promote peace and harmony in the church. The church must remove all conflict without compromise so the ministry will find favor with God.

The apostles resolved the conflict by appointing deacons to care for the needs of the poor and the widows. The division of responsibility is biblical and redemptive. The Lord God Almighty determines who will be added to the church, the Lord Jesus Christ redeemed those who God has chosen, and it is the responsibility of the church to minister to their needs.

The ordination of deacons reveals the need for a plurality of church leadership. The Word of God instructs the church in a clear and simple way the manner in which a man should be chosen and installed in the office to serve as a deacon. The qualifications for a deacon are stated in general terms. They were "men of good reputation, full of the Holy Spirit and wisdom..." (Acts 6:3). It was the responsibility of the congregation to choose a man based on his Christian character and his spiritual maturity. It is the responsibility of the elders to ordain the deacons by the laying on of hands.

Some denominations in the contemporary church deviate from these simple principles. Too often they appoint men and women to serve as deacons because of their social standing in the community or financial resources. Unfortunately, men who are short on Christian character and spiritual maturity will not like to serve in a servant role. They may think of themselves as too important to serve like a servant. The instruction of a master would be repulsive to a man who thinks he is important. They will not like having an all-powerful ruler like the Lord Jesus Christ instructing them.

There is a division of the servant's responsibility in the church. The elders are responsible for the ministry of the Word and sacraments. The deacons are responsible for the ministry of mercy and benevolence. They handle the collection and distribution of financial resources. The deacon is not a subordinate office to the elder, but rather a helping office. The minister of the Word and Sacraments does not compete with the minister of money. They are both ministers of the Lord and both are needed for God's redemptive purposes.

The ministry of the church over the past 2000 years has taken a turn for the worse. In recent church history, the church growth movement has influenced the church to fulfill the ministry of the church with man-made ideas. Instead of biblical principles, the church has turned to unbiblical worldviews like managerialism and psychotherapy to minister to the church. They have become the definitive norm for church growth models for many evangelical leaders.

The Word of God and particularly the book of Acts is the norm as a model for church growth. The struggle over the church growth model has its root in the words of Jesus in Matthew 20:28: "the Son of Man did not come to be served, but to serve and give His life a ransom for many."

The words of the Lord Jesus Christ explain two theological concepts. One is service (ministry) and the other is the atonement (the doctrine of God's saving grace through the person of Jesus Christ). The contemporary church has a distaste for the biblical teaching on the atonement, but it must come to grips with the fact that "many are called, but few chosen" (Matthew 22:14). His atonement is limited to a specific number. The servants job is not to ponder who or how many, but to "make disciples of all nations...teaching them to observe all things" that Christ has commanded (Matthew 28:19-20).

The early church experienced unique growth. The Bible indicates, "the disciples were multiplying" (Acts 6:1). The early church experienced a large increase in disciples. God changed the hearts of men and women to believe the gospel. God was adding to the number each day. The contemporary church growth model acts as if the leaders and their programs are adding to the number. A growing church will experience problems, especially when God adds to the number each day. God is not a respecter of persons. God adds all kinds of converted sinners to the church. Fortunately, professing Christians have no control over who the Lord adds to the church, so they are left with the responsibility to minister to those who are added by the Lord.

The pastor or minister is not a narrowly defined office or person, in the New Testament. For instance, in the New Testament angels are referred to as ministers. Deacons were referred to as ministers. Likewise, pastors are called ministers. We should be very careful how we use the word minister. For instance, if you attended a social gathering in the another country and used the word minister, they probably would not think you intended to address a member of the clergy. In many European countries a minister is one who has been given authority by the state to administer or serve as an envoy to that state. God has called every Christian church member to minister and perform works of service in the kingdom of God. Unfortunately many saved sinners do not like to serve; they like to be served. It is the servant/master controversy that brings a growing church into conflict. It is most necessary to get a biblical picture of a servant and a biblical picture of a master. The picture of a servant and a master has been grossly distorted by contemporary sociologists. It is now quite common to hear sociologists talk about the "psychological trauma" of the progeny of those who served as slaves in past history. The Bible speaks to the sins of slavery such as brutality, disrespect, and mistreatment by the master. Likewise the Bible speaks to the sins of hatred, dishonor, and indolence on the part of the servant, but the Bible never calls the institution of slavery a sin.

> Let as many bondservants as are under the yoke count their own masters worthy of all honor, so that the name of God and His doctrine may not be blasphemed. And those who have believing masters, let them not despise them because they are brethren, but rather serve them because those who are benefited are believers and beloved. Teach and exhort these things. (1 Timothy 6:1-2)

The word "Master" is translated from a Greek word that is translated into English as "despot" (See Jude 4). It denotes a person having supreme authority over someone else. We often think of a despot as a wicked ruler who abuses others, but the Greek word *despotes* in the Bible refers to God the Son as a despot (See Luke 2:29). He has supreme authority and uses it for the glory of God. Jesus Christ is the ultimate sovereign Master, but He was also a servant. Until Christians come to a better understanding of what it means be a servant, that is a minister, the church will always be in a state of confusion and conflict. When God blesses the church and the church grows, there will certainly be conflicts as it was in the early church.

The Lord Jesus Christ redeemed His people while they were slaves of Satan. The new master, the Lord Jesus

Christ, reconciled God's children to Himself and gave them the ministry of reconciliation (2 Corinthians 5:18-19). The early church served faithfully and God blessed the church.

15. A Faithful Testimony

Throughout history records show that armies advance and conquer. History also reveals that conquering nations fall into ruin or subjugation to the rule of another. As long as sin remains the nations of this earth will rise and fall. The church is in the likeness of an army. In fact Jesus uses language to indicate the church is advancing and the Gates of Hell shall not prevail against the advancement. However there is a major difference between God's kingdom and the sinful nations on earth. The church represents the kingdom of God on earth, however the church on earth is not the fullness of the kingdom of God. The Kingdom of God includes all of God's creation and His kingdom will prevail throughout eternity.

The kingdom of God on earth has a cultural mandate. "Be fruitful and multiply; fill the earth and subdue it; have dominion over the fish of the sea, over the birds of the air, and over every living thing that moves on the earth" (Genesis 1:28). The cultural mandate is to subdue the earth. God gave the rational creature, man, the ability to rule over the earth. God will never tell anyone to do anything and not supply the necessary resources. Man did not have the authority to rule over God. However, man rebelled against God and lost control of the culture. Sin left unfulfilled man with a passion to be in control.

There are many metaphorical analogies that describe the church. For instance, the church is like a hospital. The saved sinner is in need of restoration and spiritual repair. Paul describes the metaphor in terms of, "this is the will of God, your sanctification" (1 Thessalonians 4:3). The military metaphors in Scripture used to describe the church are numerous. Paul refers to military metaphors in Ephesians six where Christians are commanded to put on the full armor of God.

The life and ministry of Stephen is one of a soldier in service for the Lord. The Lord equipped Stephen with grace and power. God's grace is God's favorable relation demonstrated by his love and mercy. The power of God comes from His authority, which he gives to His people, the church.

The contest for power is very real. The battle over who has the power is fought because of misunderstanding the source and purpose of the power. For unbelievers power means control and more specifically self-centered control. The motivation to acquire power comes from the sinful nature. The unbeliever's self-centered quest for power is for the purpose of manipulation to accomplish self-gratification. For believers power means God-centered control. God gives the believer power to engage in spiritual warfare.

Christians need power to apologize for Christianity which means they make a defense for their faith. Christians need power for the mission and ministry of the church. As defenders of the faith, Christian apologists must be ready to engage in battle against unbelief and heresy. Peter describes the job of an apologist as one who must be "ready to make a defense to everyone who asks you to give an account for the hope that is in you" (1 Peter 3:15). Stephen was ready to give a defense for his hope in Christ. Stephen had been accused of heresy.

The Greek speaking Jews said they had heard Stephen speak blasphemous words against Moses and against God (6:11). Stephen was ready to answer the false charges. His answer is a recapitulation of Jewish history. The call of Abraham, the life and abuse of Joseph, Moses and the taber-nacle were central to his answer (See Acts 7:1-36). The section that deals with Moses actually answers the charges made against Stephen that he had blasphemed against Moses (See Acts 7:17-43).

After recounting the life of Moses and thus acknowledging the ministry of Moses, Stephen brings the rebellion of the Old Testament congregation to their attention.

> This is he who was in the congregation in the wilderness with the Angel who spoke to him on Mount Sinai, and with our fathers, the one who received the living oracles to give to us, whom our fathers would not obey, but rejected. And in their hearts they turned back to Egypt. (Acts 7:38-39)

Stephen's reference to the living oracles is a reference to the law of God. It was the Jewish religious leaders who turned the living oracles into dead works (Acts 7:38-40). It was not Stephen who rejected the Law of Moses; it was the Jewish religious leaders.

Stephen probably questioned the manner in which the religious leaders interpreted the law. The Jews then and today should realize that the law of God was the means to lead them to Christ, which the apostle Paul articulates in his letter to the Galatians.

Today the evangelical church treats the law of God with great disdain by either dismissing it or by turning its precepts into a world and life view called moralism. The law is morally binding to God's people today just as it was in the day that it was given. Keeping the law is necessary for salvation. The Psalmist said, "The law of the Lord is perfect, converting the soul" (Psalm 19:7). However, sinful man cannot perfectly keep God's law. No one can escape the inevitable truth that the law of God never was and never will be the perfecter of the soul, except through the Lord Jesus Christ. The law of God is saving because the lawgiver became the lawkeeper for the sake of the lawbreaker. It is the fault of the church for not preaching and teaching the purpose of the law covenant given at Sinai. The law is saving only if it is kept to perfection. Christ kept the law perfectly for the sake of God's elect. The law is the means of sanctification only when Christians understand it and obey it.

The religious leaders in Jerusalem were unable to hear the truth in Stephen's speech because the law convicted them. If they were unbelievers, they probably were very angry to be called to the carpet. They did not like Stephen's testimony because they were unable to cope with the wisdom and the Spirit with which Stephen gave his defense for the faith. They not only accused Stephen of speaking blasphemous words against Moses, they also accused Stephen of speaking blasphemous words against God. Stephen answered the false charge bringing it to a conclusion with a quote from Isaiah (Isaiah 6:1-2).

Stephen explained that God does not dwell in houses made by human hands, which irritated the religious leaders (Acts 7:48). Christians may boast of their religious shrines, commonly known as a church. The religious Jewish leaders in Jerusalem worshipped the temple during the life of Jesus on earth. Christians have worshiped buildings for nearly 2000 years that are erroneously called churches.

Stephen was not silent. Christians must speak fearlessly, but accurately and carefully from the Word of God to set the church on the right course for the coming generations. Stephen knew the bitterness and hatred that the members of the Sanhedrin had stored up. They were religious leaders motivated by the dominion and control factor. Stephen knew he would die because the evil men would not be satisfied for anything less. Christians must defend the glorious truth of God's holy Word against the accusers of this age. Make it a matter of prayer each day asking God for grace, power, and wisdom accompanied by His Spirit for the apologetical ministry.

Stephen's evangelistic ministry is worthy of attention. It is true that Stephen did not mention the name of Jesus or the resurrection, but he was clearly on track to give these men the gospel. Stephen was preparing them to hear the good news of God's saving grace through the Lord Jesus Christ, but he never got to present the good news. They killed him before he announced the gospel. Today, in this country, stoning to death is not the popular method for shutting the mouths of Christians. Other tactics are used to close the mouths of Christians. They are silenced, not by stoning, but by seduction of a humanist worldview.

Unconverted people do not want to hear that they are sinners, but they must hear that they are sinners before they can hear the good news of God's saving grace. There is no reason to believe that Christians should treat sinners any different than Stephen treated those religious leaders in Jerusalem. Stephen told the religious leaders the truth about their sinful condition. "You stiff-necked and uncircumcised in heart and ears! You always resist the Holy Spirit; as your fathers did, so do you. Which of the prophets did your fathers not persecute? And they killed those who foretold the coming of the Just One…" (Acts 7:51-52). Sinners do not like to hear what they are really like. They want to whitewash the tomb.

Preaching the truth and powerfully applying it made the religious leaders very angry. The Bible reveals their anger: "they were cut to the heart and they gnashed at him with their teeth" (Acts 7:54). They hated Stephen and they hated Stephen's Lord and the Lord's Word. What happened to those religious men? Their religious shrine was destroyed before the death of all the apostles. The building they treasured the most was turned into rubble. Some old church buildings house the most liberal and most wicked doctrine contrary to Christianity.

The Lord Jesus Christ did not come to save a passive uninterested church. The Lord Jesus Christ came to save and equip the church so she may give a faithful testimony. The Lord secured salvation for saved sinners to give a faithful testimony and then see the glory of God.   It is called the beatific vision, which is the great hope of all believers, that they will see the manifestation of the glory of God. They should not have to wait until death to experience the beatific vision that Stephen experienced at his death.

> But he [Stephen], being full of the Holy Spirit, gazed into heaven and saw the glory of God, and Jesus standing at the right hand of God, and said, "Look! I see the heavens opened and the Son of Man standing at the right hand of God!" Then they cried out with a loud voice, stopped their ears, and ran at him with one accord; and they cast him out of the city and stoned him. And the witnesses laid down their clothes at the feet of a young man named Saul. (Acts 7:55-58)

The high court of Israel turned from a dignified court to a lynch mob. Those who oppose God's truth oppose God's people; therefore they oppose God's church.

God has set His church as guardians over His message in the law and the gospel. Christians must fight the good fight, stand firm against the arrows of the enemy and give witness of a victorious testimony until they see the Lord Jesus Christ, their advocate, standing at the right hand of God to receive them into their permanent home.

16. Preaching Provokes Persecution

Acts 7:51-8:8

Preaching the Word of God has never provoked any serious persecution in the United States. There are a few instances such as the great Jonathan Edwards. His persecution consisted of being removed as pastor. Many preachers have been disenfranchised from a local congregation because the congregation *allegedly* did not like the pastor's preaching ministry. Pastors have been harassed and eventually chased away because the religious leaders in a particular church did not like the pastor's ministry. The difference from the early church to the contemporary church is preachers like Stephen were murdered for preaching the Word of God.

Looking back a couple of years from the time of Stephen's death, Christians should remember the words of the Lord Jesus Christ just before He ascended into heaven. "You shall be my witnesses both in Jerusalem, and in all Judea and Samaria and even to the remotest part of the earth" (Acts 1:8). For several years the apostles and other disciples were primarily in Jerusalem and maybe a few surrounding towns preaching the gospel and teaching the whole counsel of God.

The immediate response of the religious leaders was to the shut the mouths of the apostles. They tried intimidation, threats, and even some jail time, but the apostles continued to preach and teach. After the religious leaders had taken all they could take they finally resorted to murder. So Stephen became the first martyr in the Christian church. If the Bible was silent about persecution in every other place, the event of Stephen's murder is sufficient to establish the doctrine of persecution. The doctrine of persecution teaches that the faithful, full orbed preaching of the Word of God provokes persecution. Consider the Old Testament prophets. They were persecuted because they preached the full counsel of God. Stephen asserts that all of the prophets were persecuted. "Which one of the prophets did your fathers not persecute?" (Acts 7:52). Time would fail for me to mention all the lives and stories of prophets persecuted for the preaching the judgments of God. Jeremiah is an example of a persecuted preacher.

> "The Lord said to me...whatever I command you, you shall speak." (Jeremiah 1:7)

> "The Lord said to me...I have put My words in your mouth." (Jeremiah 1:9)

> "The word of the Lord came to me, saying, Go and cry in the hearing of Jerusalem, saying Thus says the Lord." (Jeremiah 2:1)

> "Declare in Judah and proclaim in Jerusalem and say..." (Jeremiah 4:5)

Like Jeremiah, Ezekiel also preached, but with even a greater weight on his shoulder.

> Son of man, I have made you a watchman for the house of Israel; therefore hear a word from My mouth, and give them warning from Me: When I say to the wicked, 'You shall surely die,' and you give him no warning, nor speak to warn the wicked from his wicked way, to save his life, that same wicked man shall die in his iniquity; but his blood I will require at your hand. Yet, if you warn the wicked, and he does not turn from his wickedness, nor from his wicked way, he shall die in his iniquity; but you

have delivered your soul. Again, when a righteous man turns from his righteousness and commits iniquity, and I lay a stumbling block before him, he shall die; because you did not give him warning, he shall die in his sin, and his righteousness which he has done shall not be remembered; but his blood I will require at your hand. Nevertheless if you warn the righteous man that the righteous should not sin, and he does not sin, he shall surely live because he took warning; also you will have delivered your soul. (Ezekiel 3:17-21)

The prophets used the term "watchman" as an allegorical device to describe a prophet as a watchman for God. It was the duty of the watchman to announce to the people of God either good news or impending doom as the case may be. Preachers ought to make the same announcements. Jeremiah and Ezekiel were persecuted for their preaching just as Peter and Stephen were persecuted for their preaching.

When the religious leaders set out to kill Stephen, "Saul was in hearty agreement with putting him to death" (Acts 8:1). Saul was not merely agreeable with the persecution. The Word of God reveals the extent of Saul's persecution. "As for Saul, he made havoc of the church, entering every house, and dragging off men and women, committing them to prison" (Acts 8:3). Saul continued to make trouble and persecute the church. Saul certainly wanted to destroy the church.

It all started when Stephen preached a sermon reminding Saul and all his Jewish friends of their sins. Saul hated to hear the Word of God because he was a rebel against the authority of God. Saul simply followed the stream of opinion and the will of the majority. We have to ask ourselves the question, "Why is the persecution so severe against the preaching of the Word of God? The logical line of reasoning will lead to a deep morass of distasteful realities. Unconverted sinners do not like the truth. Preaching is an exercise of presenting the truth from the Word of God.

Dr. Dabney wisely told his students that the "only legitimate weapon of conviction is the truth" (*Lectures on Sacred Rhetoric*, by R. L. Dabney, p. 72). Dr. Dabney's wisdom still stands because truth is timeless objective reality. Something happens at the preaching the truth from the Word of God. If preaching is concerned with truth and truth is concerned with absolutes and absolutes are concerned with power and authority, then sinful man will have a distaste for truth. Therefore, unconverted sinners will have a distaste for preaching.

Dr. Dabney brings truth into the realm of intelligence and rationality. "Religion is an intelligent concern, and deals with man as a reasoning creature" (*Lectures on Sacred Rhetoric*, by R. L. Dabney, p. 118). A rational being is an intellectual being and an intellectual being engages in the enterprise of discerning truth.

Preaching brings people face to face with reality and therefore with the realties of heaven and hell. Children of Satan hate to hear about hell and know that heaven is out of reach. The result is that these God hating people will persecute those who preach the Word of God, which includes God's judgment and justice.

Preaching caused persecution and the persecution caused the church members from Jerusalem to scatter throughout the region. Although the church members scattered, the apostles remained in Jerusalem. It was a brave move on the part of the apostles. They knew they may be cast into prison or even worse they could have been stoned to death, but they would not leave Jerusalem.

They remained in Jerusalem to give the church a sense of order and stability. It is never wise to run from the opponent if you are right. The apostles were right to stand against the religious leaders in this battle for the truth of the gospel.

Does that mean that those who left Jerusalem were cowards? No! In the providence of God the persecution was merely an opportunity to carry the gospel to the places in which Jesus had already commanded. The Bible says those who were scattered went everywhere. The word "everywhere" is hyperbole. Hyperbole is a gross exaggeration to express the magnitude or significance of something. Everywhere means everywhere in that area of Judea and Samaria. The word "scattered" also needs some explanation. The word in this text conveys the idea of scattered in order to be planted.

Although persecution scattered the Christians, there were other factors to consider. They may have moved from Jerusalem because of job discrimination. They may have moved from Jerusalem because of property confiscation. Social ostracism may have driven them away, but in any event the providence of God scattered them. God may scatter you because of work, family, education, or personal convictions and it is there that you must consider yourself planted for the Lord Jesus Christ. The church should not be afraid of persecution. The more that Saul persecuted the church the more the church grew.

The church expanded over the past twenty centuries, because Christians went everywhere preaching the Word. "Therefore those who were scattered went everywhere preaching the Word. Then Philip went down to the city of Samaria and preached Christ to them" (Acts 8:4-5). The proclamation of the Word of God as a means of grace to God's people will always have Christ as the proper subject of preaching.

The truth of the gospel is not silent or passive. The gospel of Jesus Christ is not religious piety. The truth of the gospel is not a dormant contemplative spirit. The gospel is the grand truth of salvation. It is the instrument that overthrows the kingdom of Satan and establishes the kingdom of the Lord Jesus Christ. Preaching must be deliberate and direct. The Bible says Philip preached Christ "to them." The preaching was directed to those within the hearing of the Word of God.

The good result of preaching is that it brings joy. Preaching brings joy because it is the way that God has chosen to show His favor to His adopted children. Peter's closing words of chapter one of his first letter are also my closing words to you: "The word of the Lord endures forever. Now this is the word which by the gospel was preached to you" (1Peter 1:25). On earth, in heaven, or in hell the preaching of the Word of God will remain forever.

17. Counterfeit Christianity

Acts 8:9-25

Christians take the gospel to strange places. For instance, Philip the evangelist was taken to Samaria, which is a strange place for a Jew. Jews were not inclined to associate with Samaritans. The Samaritans were considered half-breed Jews and as such were considered ceremonially unclean.

When Jesus spoke with the woman at the well, the Samaritan woman was quick to say, "For Jews have no dealings with Samaritans" (John 4:9). Samaria was known for its idol worship (Jeremiah 23:13). Although Philip is a proper Greek name, Philip was a Jew and perhaps a devout Jew. Therefore, Philip would not be inclined to associate with Samaritans and their culture. However, the gospel crosses cultural lines. The gospel took Philip into a strange place and if you are faithful in your witness of the gospel truth, you will be taken into strange places.

I remember the testimony of a distinguished reformed scholar explaining how his gospel ministry started by preaching in homosexual bars in Houston, Texas. I was surprised to learn that such a distinguished scholar would be involved in such a ministry. During his testimony he said many came to Christ because he went to a place like Samaria, a place that seemed the least likely to receive the gospel.

Some historical background of Samaria is necessary to understand the context of Philip's ministry to the Samaritans. Samaria was a center of political intrigue. A cursory reading of Kings and Chronicles reveal the atrocities involved with the eventual downfall of the Northern Kingdom and its association with Samaria. Isaiah spoke of the pride and arrogance of the Samaritans (Isaiah 9:9). Hosea tells us that Samaria was a place of false worship (Hosea 8:6). Samaria was in social bankruptcy. Hosea said, "Samaria is held guilty, For she has rebelled against her God. They shall fall by the sword, their infants shall be dashed in pieces, and their women with child ripped open" (Hosea 13:16).

God may lead you into a place like Samaria. You have to decide to what extent your culture resembles the Samaria that Philip ministered in, under the providential hand of God. Think about the Samaritan culture. False teachers bewitched Samaria. The Samaritans were dazzled by what the saw and heard. Samaria was an economically rich society, but morally bankrupt.

In the 21st century church, false teachers charm the followers. Sophism has been renewed in the world of high tech communication. Sophism is the art of using deception to persuade someone that a false argument is true. The field of arts and sports dazzle the public. Images, not rational thought, set the agenda for cultural change. Famous celebrities, religious leaders, and athletes become social icons and try to change the culture with their sophisticated assertions. Materialism and consumerism, created by fiat money, diverts public attention away from rational reality.

Christians must all come to grips with truth. They must come to grips with the empirical delusion of entertainment. They must all come to grips with an economy built on the words of sophisticated arguments. The sooner we come to grips with our Samaria, the sooner we can come to grips with the Simons in our society.

Samaria was a sick society, which is evident by the people who were deluded, and deceived by a man possessed with satanic powers, a man named Simon. There are people like Simon in every society. Simon was a sophist. He was a master of deception. The Bible is not ambiguous in its description of Simon. Luke's descriptive history describes Simon and how the people reacted to him. "But there was a certain man called Simon, who previously practiced sorcery in the city and astonished the people of Samaria, claiming that he was someone great, to whom they all gave heed, from the least to the greatest, saying, "This man is the great power of God'" (Acts 8:9-10).

The Greek word for "great" is *megas* sometimes referred to as *mega*. Used as a prefix, the word *mega* is very popular. A civil engineer would use the word "megaton" to describe a million tons of material that needs to be moved to build a highway. An electrical engineer might use the term "megavolt" to describe one million volts. A statistician might use the term "megacity" to describe a city with a population of one million. The computer literate person may use the term megabyte to describe a large segment of data on a computer disk. The word *mega*, often used to describe a million units of something, was the kind of influence that Simon had in Samaria.

Throughout history, greatness has been associated with Simon the Samaritan. He had a mega-influence which in the eyes of natural man made Simon appear to be great. Great men, either good or bad, shape societies. Great men who rule over a culture very often have mega-influence in the society. It does not matter if it is the church or the culture; men like Simon will be called great by those whose hearts are of like mind.

Samaria is the place that reminds us of a sin sick society. Simon is the man that reminds us of a sin sick church. Theologians have long argued about the spiritual condition of Simon. There are those who believe that Simon was a believer, born again, but merely out of fellowship with God. Then there is an equal number who believe that Simon was not a believer and had no place in the Kingdom of God. The evidence from Scripture sides with the latter. If the argument is from silence, there is no argument.

It appears that the majority of the Samaritans respected Simon. Evidence indicates that Simon was ambitious. Following his ambition, he was a man who desired power. He thought that money could buy anything. Like many great men, Simon had an influential role in the history of the Church. The practice of Simony is attributed to Simon Magus of Samaria. Simony began early in the church when men would buy an office in the church. *The Apostolic Constitutions* compiled during the fourth century mentions the practice of Simony.

> If any bishop or even a presbyter or deacon, obtains his office through money, let him and the person who ordained him be deprived. And let him be entirely cut off from communion as Simon Magus was... (*The Apostolic Constitutions,* Sec. 8, *The Ecclesiastical Canons of the Same Holy Apostles*, Number 30).

Early church fathers wrote about Simon's subsequent activity as a charlatan. Simon was a counterfeit and his Christianity was counterfeit.

The practice of simony is indeed relevant to the contemporary church. Many men today buy their office in the church and then joke about it. I have heard pastors say they had to attend such and such seminary to get their card – sort of like buying a Union card. In essence, they are practicing Simony because a $50,000 seminary degree will assure them of an office in the church.

Do pastors seek the office for power and financial gain? It is a hard question, but only the individual can answer that question. The desire for power and influence motivated Simon to buy apostolic power. There is no reason to believe that Simon was a man of God gone astray. Why would anyone think that Simon was in a right relationship with God? The answer is easy. Simon said he believed the gospel therefore was baptized a member of the church. The average person would accept Simon's profession regardless of the emptiness of the practice that accompanies the profession. Luke records the event the way it happened; "Then Simon himself also believed" (Acts 8:13). The act of believing is the same as professing faith. It is not possible to read the heart of the alleged believer. Simon said he believed, however that does not necessarily mean that he truly believed. If the Holy Spirit did not change Simon's heart, he was still an unbeliever. However, he was baptized and Simon was admitted into the membership of the church. If unregenerate people are admitted into the membership of the church, it is possible for them to be ordained as elders in the church. An unregenerate elder is unable to fulfill his biblical responsibilities.

Local churches set standards to admit members to the church. Sometimes it is by profession of faith and baptism followed by rapid integration into every program sponsored by the church. If a man or woman stays busy enough in the church, no one will ever notice the lack of spiritual growth. Other local churches admit new members by profession and baptism accompanied by a rigorous course of study on theology, doctrine, and church government. New members very often become statistics. If membership is meaningless, the church will fall into a state of natural religion.

Simon's false profession becomes apparent when he asked the apostles for the power and offered to pay for the power. Simon wanted the kind of power that he saw in the apostles. Peter's response was to the point.

> But Peter said to him, "Your money perish with you, because you thought that the gift of God could be purchased with money! You have neither part nor portion in this matter, for your heart is not right in the sight of God. Repent therefore of this your wicked- ness, and pray God if perhaps the thought of your heart may be forgiven you. For I see that you are poi-

soned by bitterness and bound by iniquity. (Acts 8:20-23).

Peter identified the state of Simon's soul by the evidence of his nature. Simon was poisoned by bitterness and bound by iniquity. The poison of bitterness reflects the bitter spirit of someone who has no dependence on God for saving grace. Simon was disappointed that Peter would not go along with his sin. The bond of iniquity is a metaphor that describes enslavement to sin. There is no evidence of Simon's repentance.

The appearance of Christianity is not enough. Counterfeit Christianity does not bring peace and hope. The fruit of a Christian's profession will show evidence of a true profession in due time. A true Christian profession will result in knowledge and discernment of divine things leading to a new way of life.

We might live in Samaria or we might go to Samaria to proclaim the good news of God's saving grace, but the Simon church we must leave behind. The Lord Jesus is the way, the truth and the life. It is in Christ that the appearance of Christianity corresponds to the reality of Christianity.

A true Christian profession is great in every respect.

Great is the sweetness of salvation.
Great is the pardon of sin.
Great is the comfort found in the gospel.
Great is the rest for a weary soul.

18. The Right Knowledge of God

Acts 8:25-40

God's redemptive grace always touches the secular as well as the sacred. The Lord Jesus Christ gives Christians a worldview that neither disenfranchises them from this world, nor leaves them hopelessly destitute of any future hope for the advancement of His kingdom on earth. Philip was a man who saw the world with the lens of the gospel. Philip's optimism is so evident in his approach to life. He was willing to serve as a deacon or he was willing to serve as an evangelist. In any event, Philip was confident of his call in the kingdom of God. Samaria, strange as it was, did not intimidate Philip. He considered his call to Samaria a privilege. The people in Samaria did not intimidate Philip. Even the chief of the tricksters, Simon Magus, did not intimidate Philip. His preaching had a radical effect on the people of Samaria. The Bible says there was much rejoicing in that city. The Samaritans believed and they were baptized. Philip's preaching and teaching brought reformation and revival in Samaria. It must have been an exciting time for Philip.

After Peter and John went back to Jerusalem, Philip was the man of the hour. After all the work Philip put into the Samaritan revival and with marvelous results, God called Philip into the desert to preach. There is no way to know how Philip felt about the sudden change, but many pastors and evangelists in the modern American church would probably respond with disappointment.

Many preachers today would say something like this: "God I'll go down into the desert, but let me finish this work here. Lord you must be able to see how important I am to this work. Lord let me send someone else down into the desert. I need to stay here to make sure the revival continues."

Philip responded with humility and obedience. He went to the desert with the gospel (Acts 8:26-27). How did Philip know that going down to the desert was the right thing to do? An angel of the Lord spoke to Philip. Although Christians today do not have an audible word from the Lord, they have the written Word, which is complete and full of God's message. The salvation of Philip's soul created a passion to obey God. God saved Philip and Philip trusted God. Philip's immediate obedience indicates a certain knowledge he had about God. He knew that God was perfectly rational. God's plan is not based on an emotional whim. Philip did not question God, even though Philip had a thriving ministry in Samaria.

Christians trust God because they believe that God is the author of all knowledge and understanding. Although there are different degrees and different levels of knowing God, the knowledge of God is inescapable (Romans 1:19-21).

A desert ministry may not appear as favorable as the Samaritan revival, but Philip's immediate and unwavering obedience indicates he had a right knowledge of God. He had confidence that God is the sovereign Lord. Philip, knowing the Lord to be true, faithful, and holy, went into the desert and found one very religious and very pious man seeking a right knowledge of God. Even though religion is everywhere in our society and piety abounds, yet the ignorance of God's saving grace prevails in our society just as it did in the desert at Gaza nearly 2000 years ago.

The biblical account of Philip's ministry in the desert reveals how people seek a right knowledge of God.

> Now an angel of the Lord spoke to Philip, saying, "Arise and go toward the south along the road which goes down from Jerusalem to Gaza." This is desert. So he arose and went. And behold, a man of Ethiopia, a eunuch of great authority under Candace the queen

of the Ethiopians, who had charge of all her treasury, and had come to Jerusalem to worship, was returning. And sitting in his chariot, he was reading Isaiah the prophet. Then the Spirit said to Philip, "Go near and overtake this chariot." So Philip ran to him, and heard him reading the prophet Isaiah, and said, "Do you understand what you are reading? And he said, "How can I, unless someone guides me?" And he asked Philip to come up and sit with him. (Acts 8:26-31)

The Ethiopian had acquired some portion of the Word of God and was either reading it or having it read. Philip was brave enough to ask the question: "Do you understand what you are reading?" Christians ought to ask themselves the question, "Do I understand the Bible when I read it? The phrase "Do you understand what you are reading" may also be translated "Do you know what you know?"

There are millions of professing evangelical Christians in the United States. They are divided into scores of denominations and many of them do not agree on the interpretation of Scripture. Interpreting Scripture is not easy, but interpreting will have its consequences. Some people interpret Scripture to satisfy a theory they have relative to existence. Some people interpret Scripture to find fault in it. Sometimes the study of Scripture is merely intellectual and speculative gathering of knowledge. Some people spiritualize everything in Scripture and others literalize everything in Scripture. God has made provision for Christians to understand the Word of God. Knowledge of the Bible precedes an understanding of the Word of God. Then the Holy Spirit enables the believer to understand the Word of God (Isaiah 59:21).

It is possible to hear what God says in His Word, but not like it. Even so, continue to read it, study it, and pray for divine understanding. Seek the counsel of godly teachers. The Ethiopian Eunuch was in a desert, but God provided a teacher to help him understand the Word of God. Christians ought to have a passion for knowing God. The Psalmist did. "Open thou mine eyes, that I may behold wondrous things out of thy law" (Psalm 119:118). The Psalmist begged God to open his eyes. The Psalmist confessed his spiritual blindness. He wanted to see wondrous things. The wonderful stories of the creation, the deluge, and Israel's passing through the Red Sea were important. Wondrous things in God's law, reveals his respect for those distinguishing and wonderful excellencies, and marvelous manifestations of the divine perfections and glory, contained in the commands and doctrines of the Word.

Christians must possess knowledge of God's dispensation of salvation, covenant of mercy, and way of grace towards his people, as peculiar to the saints, and given only by God. The right knowledge of God is not burdensome. It reminds God's people of His redemptive love, saving grace, and generous provision. God finds pleasure when His children seek to understand His nature and character. "For I desire mercy and not sacrifice, and the knowledge of God more than burnt offerings" (Hosea 6:6). Our knowledge of God is pleasing to Him and it is like riches to us to know Him. "Oh, the depth of the riches both of the wisdom and knowledge of God" (Romans 11:33).

We live in perilous times. The man-made church growth gospel has replaced the true gospel message of God's justice and God's grace. The Word of God has become a tool of pragmatism to insure church growth. The wolves that appear in sheep's clothing assault the minds of Christians. These destructive worldviews and false teachings affect Christians, even though the local church may make every effort to be faithful to the Word of God.

Philip explained from the Word of God the right knowledge of God. "Then Philip opened his mouth, and beginning at this Scripture, preached Jesus to him" (Acts 8:35). The Ethiopian was baptized and rejoiced because he had a right knowledge of God. Believers will rejoice when they have a right knowledge of God. They will understand that Jesus, the suffering servant is the Savior. They will understand that Jesus paid the price for their sin. Philip understood and the Ethiopian understood because they had a right knowledge of God.

Christians should not forget that a few fishermen, relatively illiterate men, attained to the knowledge of eternal saving truth, while the scribes and Pharisees, men of vastly higher education and knowledge remained ignorant of God's saving grace. Ignorance of God's saving grace is no delight and comfort to the soul.

19. Saul Meets Jesus

Acts 9:1- 30

Saul of Tarsus is an important and significant person in the history of western civilization. Historians and religious leaders in every century inquired into the life of Saul. Later in the Book of Acts, Saul assumes his Roman name, Paul (Acts 13:9). Christians are particularly aware of Saul's life and ministry for many reasons. He wrote more in the New Testament than any other person. The apostle Saul expresses his self-designation in every letter he wrote to the New Testament churches. One good example of his self-designation is found in his letter to Titus. "Paul, a bond-servant of God, and an apostle of Jesus Christ, for the faith of those chosen of God and the knowledge of the truth…" (Titus 1:1). Paul called himself a slave and an apostle. As a slave Paul understood his humble place in this life. As an apostle he understood God's call on his life.

Before Saul's conversion to Christianity, he exhibited zeal for his religious views in terms of breathing threats and murder against the disciples of the Lord. Saul was a proud, arrogant, and ungodly man. Since Saul was not in a right and favorable relation with God, he acted like an unregenerate man.

Saul's life was distinctive in many ways. Saul was unique in that he held dual citizenship in the Roman Empire as well as the nation of Israel. He was born in Tarsus in the region of Cilicia during a very tumultuous time in the Roman Empire. Saul came from a well to do family since Roman citizenship was generally held only by the upper class. The Bible tells us that Saul was a Hebrew of Hebrews. It follows then that Saul must have lived by Jewish law. He began to study Scripture at an early age. At age thirteen a Jewish boy was admitted *bar mitzvah* or the son of the commandment. The *bar mitzvah* requires the full obligation of the law. Later Saul studied at the feet of Gamaliel, one of the most influential of the Jewish Rabbi's. Saul had a thorough education.

God used educated men in the most profound way in both the Old Testament and New Testament. Moses immediately comes to mind. The Bible tells us that Moses had the best education in his day and I might add it was a secular education (Acts 7:22). We learn from the Bible and deduce from the general teaching of Scripture that Saul probably had the best education in his day.

Even though Saul was educated by the best religious mind in Jerusalem at the time, Saul was in an unfavorable relation with the Lord. However, Saul was a very religious man. Prior to his conversion to Christianity, he was a religious Jew. After Saul's conversion to Christianity, he became a religious Christian.

At the beginning of the 21st century, people in the United States are very religious. Religion is the cause of many disputes, conflict, and war throughout the history of mankind. Religious zeal has motivated more crimes, more wars, and more destruction of human life than any aspect of human existence. A study of religion will not save anyone. Only the Holy Spirit can change the hearts of educated religious men.

God created every person with a religious passion. Saul alludes to this truth when he spoke to the unbelievers at Athens saying, "I perceive that in all things you are very religious" (Acts 17:22). The Athenians feared the demons or to smooth out the translation they feared the gods.

There is a radical distinction between religion and theology. The word religion is difficult to define. It often denotes a spiritual relation through worship to the god of ones choice. Religious activity is one of the diversions that occupy the minds of unbelievers. Theology is easy to define. Theology is a study of God. Knowing God is the goal of theology.

The unbelieving educated religious Saul failed to understand and believe the truth of the gospel. Therefore, he persecuted the followers of Jesus Christ. Saul's education kept him from the gospel because he was not able to believe the gospel. As an educated Jew it would be natural for Saul to reject Christianity as a false and dangerous cult. Saul's education would have prohibited polytheism (worship of more than one god). It would have been unthinkable for Saul to worship Jesus Christ and God. Therefore, Christianity was a false religion and an enemy of Saul's Judaism. Saul went to the high priest to get letters of approval from the high priest so the false Christian religion could be put to death (Acts 9.1).

Saul referred to the Christian religion as "the way" (Acts 9:2). The word "way" comes from a Greek word also translated "road" in the New Testament. The reason most people are on a road is to make a journey, therefore the word is sometimes translated journey. The Bible describes the human experience as a mere journey. We are just traveling though this life to get to the next life which will be the permanent location of our existence. Saul probably knew that Jesus was the way, truth and life and that would mean that Saul referred to the church in a pejorative sense. Saul was devoted to protect his religious interest in Judaism. Are Christians zealous to protect their religious interest in a pluralistic world?

Acts chapter nine describes the events of Saul's meeting with Jesus on the road to Damascus.

> As he journeyed he came near Damascus, and suddenly a light shone around him from heaven. Then he fell to the ground, and heard a voice saying

to him, "Saul, Saul, why are you persecuting Me?"
And he said, "Who are You, Lord?" Then the Lord
said, "I am Jesus, whom you are persecuting. It is
hard for you to kick against the goads." So he,
trembling and astonished, said, "Lord, what do You
want me to do?" Then the Lord said to him, "Arise
and go into the city, and you will be told what you
must do." (Acts 9:3-6)

Those few verses reveal the passion of Saul's religion, but he
was passionately wrong. The darkness of his religion met the
true Light. Saul's goal was to stop the spread of Christianity.
The Lord had other plans for Saul.

Since the word *goad* is not typically used in every day
language, Christians must learn the meaning of the phrase, "It
is hard to kick against the goads" (Acts 9:5). A goad was an
instrument used in the agricultural community. It was a sharp
stick used in prodding cattle. In the Old Testament the word
goad is used in Ecclesiastes in this way: "The words of the
wise are like goads..." (Ecclesiastes 12:11). A goad will
prick, wound, or incite someone to action. Therefore, kicking
against the goad multiplies the effect. The goad was a
metaphor for the pain Saul experienced in his zeal to
exterminate Christianity. God will naturally provoke men
for their own good. It is never wise to kick against the goad.

Saul had a zeal for God, but he had a mistaken view of
God's nature and character. When Saul met Jesus, it was a
kairotic event (See page 4 for the definition of *kairotic*).
Saul's conversion to Christianity by the power of the Holy
Spirit was the Light invading darkness. Immediately Saul
was ready to obey the Lord (Acts 9:6).

The integrity and unity of Saul's conversion was
evident by the theology that supported the experience. The
truth of the message associated with Saul's religious
experience was unmixed. It was pure theology. His theology

began with the gospel of Jesus Christ, pure and simple. Since the gospel is pure and simple, Christians should not call the gospel complex. The gospel is not entangled with a maze of confusion or contradiction. Saul did not complicate the gospel message nor did Saul complicate his place in the kingdom of God. Saul's religious experience provoked him to ask two theological questions. Who are you Lord and What shall I do, Lord?

Many Christians do not understand the nature and character of God, yet they are very zealous for their religious views. It was the Damascus road experience that re-oriented Saul's zeal and passion to proclaim the truth of the one true and living God. Saul's conversion to the Christian religion was a reformation. Saul's reformation came when the Lord changed his heart so he could believe the true nature and character of God. It was God's reversing power that began the reformation in Saul's life. God the Holy Spirit enabled Saul to believe on the Lord Jesus Christ and believe that the Lord Jesus Christ was God in the flesh. Saul's life was never the same, but his zeal and his passion never died, not even with his bodily death.

A godly man named Ananias confirmed Saul's religious experience by the laying on of hands and baptism (Acts 9:10-19). Saul's conversion was a simple meaningful religious experience in the sense that Saul had a clear understanding of his relationship with God, by the grace of the Lord Jesus Christ and by the power of the Holy Spirit. The Lord used Ananias to reveal the power of God and his Saving grace.

It does not matter which side you are on, the side of a spiritually immature Saul or the side of a courageous godly Ananias, you have a responsibility to answer as Ananias did, "here I am, Lord." It does not matter whether you are a Saul or an Ananias you need to hear the words of our Lord: "Arise and go" (Acts 9:6 and 9:11). If you are born again by the power of the Holy Spirit, you do not need to hear a voice from heaven. God has already spoken in His Word and He has spoken loud and clear, arise and go.

God sent Saul on a mission. "Immediately he preached the Christ in the synagogues, that He is the Son of God" (Acts 9:20). Saul taught that Christ is the Son of God. Saul was neither ashamed nor afraid to proclaim the truth as he had received it and his preaching was effective. "All those who heard him were confounded" (Acts 9:22). Saul's understanding of Jesus Christ the God-man overtook the Jews. Saul's theology captivated them. The Jews could not answer Saul's arguments. Saul was "proving that this Jesus is the Christ" (Acts 9:22).

There are two unfortunate extremes found in the contemporary church. Many professing Christians never prepare for the noble task to defending the truth of the gospel. Others are always preparing, but never defending the truth of the gospel. Religious experiences remain private, subjective and woefully short of proving that Jesus is the Christ.

Most religious experiences are complex from the standpoint of relationships with other people. Saul's religious experience did not help him win friends and influence people. In fact, the Jews were ready to kill him. Saul's former friends became his enemies. You should not be surprised when you proclaim the gospel and find your friends despising you for what you believe. The sad and most complex aspect of Saul's religious experience was when the Christians refused to accept him in their ranks.

If God has restored your soul and reformed your life use your religious zeal and passion to proclaim the truth of the one true and living God. The mission is to announce the saving grace of Jesus Christ. Tell everyone about your meeting with Jesus.

20. Peace and Faith in the Church

Acts 9:31-42

Every Christian should ask the question that many Bible scholars have asked, "What's happening at this juncture in the development of the church?" Saul was recently converted to Christianity. After Saul's conversion, he went to the Synagogues and preached Christ to the Jews. Saul "confounded the Jews who dwelt in Damascus, proving that this Jesus is the Christ" (Acts 9:22). The Jews attempted to kill Saul, so the disciples of Christ sent Saul to Tarsus (Acts 9:29-30).

Luke's inspired history of the first thirty years of the church continues with Peter as the protagonist after the strange interlude with the introduction of Saul. What do we make of this? How should Christians interpret this text? They must look at the larger context. When God says something He means what He says. For instance, the Lord said, "you shall be witnesses to Me in Jerusalem, and in all Judea and Samaria, and to the end of the earth" (Acts 1:8). In a few years the church spread from Jerusalem to Samaria in the north and to the Gaza desert in the south.

The apostles of Christ and other disciples of Christ began in Jerusalem with the message of the nature and character of God that had never been heard before. The nature and character of God had not changed, but the manifestation of God was more evident to the people of God. The second person of the Trinity, the living Lord Jesus Christ, took to himself a true body and a reasonable soul. The third person of the Trinity, the Holy Spirit of God, became evident in His work and actions. The Lord promised the disciples that they would "receive power when the Holy Spirit has come upon you" (Acts 1:8).

The transitions that take place in the book of Acts are fast and deliberately describe church growth. The history of the development of the church moves from one scene to another at the same time. The Bible student must be very careful not to twist the Word of God to mean something that it does not mean. There is a tendency for interpreters to apply the collective church to individual Christians. Although individual Christians make up the body of Christ, the individual does not constitute the collective body of Christ. Saul's persecution was against individuals in the church. After Saul's conversion the church collectively experienced peace. "Then the churches throughout all Judea, Galilee, and Samaria had peace and were edified. And walking in the fear of the Lord and in the comfort of the Holy Spirit, they were multiplied" (Acts 9:31). This juncture in the history of the early church is profound because it speaks of the condition of the church in a way that touches every Christian. The condition was peace.

This text reveals the nature and character of God in His relation to His people. God was the source of peace expressed by "the fear of the Lord" and the "comfort of the Holy Spirit." The early church was a witness for the world to see and believe that God was true to His Word.

Dr. William Larkin makes an astute observation from this portion of God's Word. "Is the Christian Church for real? When it fits the description of Acts 9:31, the watching world has evidence that the church is authentic and its message true" (*Acts*, by William J. Larkin, p. 148)

God's word is most persuading because God proves his Word by His actions. God healed the paralysis of Aeneas (Acts 9:32-35). God also raised Dorcas from the death bed. God performed these two miracles and Peter was a witness. This portion of God's Word must be understood in light of God's plan to save His people. Salvation requires faith in

God and produces peace in the believer. Therefore faith and peace are related to each other.

God healed Aeneas and raised Dorcas from the dead to establish God's authority over life and death. Many "turned to the Lord" (Acts 9:35) and "many believed on the Lord" (Acts 9:42). The "many" that believed saw the power of God. Peter did not have the power to heal or to restore life and neither does any other human being possess that power. Peter was a witness to God's power and Luke records the events so that everyone may believe God. It was faith in God, through the work of Jesus Christ, by the power of the Holy Spirit that gives Christians the proper fear of the Lord, comfort in the Holy Spirit and peace. "Then the churches throughout all Judea, Galilee, and Samaria had peace..." (Acts 9:31). However the Lord Jesus Christ said, "Do you suppose that I came to grant peace on earth? I tell you, not at all, but rather division" (Luke 12:51). Has God spoken a contradiction? Is not Christ the Prince of Peace? We know that the Bible teaches in great abundance that Jesus Christ gave peace to His people. "Peace I leave with you; My peace I give to you; not as the world gives, do I give to you. Let not your heart be troubled, nor let it be fearful" (John 14:27). The Christian will not have peace with the world. The unbeliever is never strengthened, does not fear the Lord, will not find comfort of the Holy Spirit; therefore, the unbeliever cannot have peace.

Can it be that churches have peace and division at the same time in the same relationship? No, it is not possible. However, it is possible to have peace sometimes and not at other times. It is possible to have peace in one area and not the other. Peace in a church or a group of churches ought to be the norm. However, Peace is conditional. Peace with God is essential if there will be peace in the church.

The first step to peace is a saving relationship to God. The second step is to have a soul growing to maturity.

Christians grow to spiritual maturity by the process of edification (Acts 9:31). The churches were being strengthened. If a church is a strong church, there you will find peace, true biblical peace. A strong church will find agreement on the interpretation of Scripture. The strong church will do what God instructs the church to do. It should be the goal of every Christian to replicate the church in Acts 9:31; the churches had peace and were being strengthened. The majesty of God in God's word should be a primary means for bringing peace and strength to the church.

The strong peaceful church will express the fear of the Lord and experience the comfort of the Holy Spirit. The fear of God does not mean a Christian feels tyrannized by God and thus fearful of God. It means they respect God because they understand a few things about God. They know that Jesus Christ is the God-man, the full and final prophet, priest, and king. The early church knew who God was and what God was capable of doing, unlike the greatest part of the evangelical church today. Many Christians are unable to describe the nature and character of God and many do not even know the Ten Commandments. The Holy Spirit comforted them because the Holy Spirit encouraged them by sending the Word of God through the preaching of the apostles and disciples.

God performed miracles to prove that He had given Peter the authority to speak for God. God performed the miracles so the myriads of generations to come would believe the Word of God. God performed those miracles so the Word of God and the Spirit of God would enable you to believe the truth.

The picture of the first thirty years of the church ought to be the norm for the church in every successive generation. Churches throughout the world ought to have peace. They ought to be strengthened by the Word of God. They ought to have a proper fear of the Lord. The Holy Spirit ought to bring encouragement to every soul.

The early churches experienced peace (Acts 9:31) and many believed on the Lord (Acts 9:42). Peace and faith are inseparable doctrines of Christianity. Every soul that has faith in God will have peace with God. False faith and pseudo peace is an anomaly that is more or less evident among secular professing evangelical churches. Yes, professing churches may be growing rapidly, but do they have true peace? Are they being strengthened by the Word of God or the words of men? Are they walking in the fear of the Lord? Does the Holy Spirit encourage the prosperous mega-churches or do they find encouragement from celebrities in other professing churches and perhaps unbelieving celebrities?

Do we believe the Lord is present with His church as He was with early church during their first thirty years? If so, do we expect the church to increase and for many to believe in the Lord?

21. Truth for the Young Church

God's voice and the work of the Holy Spirit are necessary for the conversion of unbelieving sinners and the sanctification of sinful believers. God's voice is the subject of much discussion among evangelical churches. Understanding how God speaks requires a careful examination of the whole counsel of God.

There are numerous occasions recorded in the Bible of God speaking in an audible voice. However, God communicates to the human race without using an audible voice. "For since the creation of the world His invisible attributes are clearly seen, being understood by the things that are made, even His eternal power and Godhead, so that they are without excuse" (Romans 1:20). God speaks in nature to all rational human beings. The law of God written on the hearts of all men is further evidence that God speaks in a general sense to all rational people (Romans 2:14-15).

God spoke the truth to Cornelius. He was a Roman soldier with a rank equivalent to a captain. He commanded a cohort of soldiers that could have ranged from 300 to 600 men. Cornelius would understand the concept of authority and the importance of communicating the truth.

God spoke to Cornelius in a natural and general way. The Bible says he was devout and God-fearing. He was God-fearing because the law of God was written on his heart. Cornelius had a desire to worship because the first commandment provokes worship. He was also charitable thus listening to the second table of the law. God also used a supernatural vision to compel Cornelius to send for the apostle Peter. However, Cornelius was not a believer. The guilt of his sin and sins weighed heavy on his soul. God

spoke to Cornelius in a way that is natural to all men. God
also spoke in a special way through the voice of an angel. All
men hear the voice of God in a natural and general way to a
greater or lesser degree. God also speaks in a special way to
particular people. God's special way of speaking to His
people is the Word of God.

While God was speaking to Cornelius at Caesarea in a
natural and general way, God was speaking to Peter at Joppa,
nearly 30 miles away in a special way. God gave Peter a
vision that confirmed God's previous promise to the Gentiles.
The promise is found in the Word of God. "And in that day
there shall be a Root of Jesse, who shall stand as a banner to
the people; For the Gentiles shall seek Him, and His resting
place shall be glorious" (Isaiah 11:10). The voice of God
made it plain that the nationalism of Judaism had fulfilled its
purpose with the coming of the Lord Jesus Christ. The voice
of God must be heard, not only by the Israelites, but also by
many nations.

The book of Acts reveals the embryonic nature of the
Old Testament church and how it was growing to maturity
under the New Covenant. The church grew under the New
Covenant because the voice of God was indiscriminate with
the preaching of the gospel. The Word of God is very clear
that many were added to the church daily. "Then those who
gladly received his word were baptized; and that day about
three thousand souls were added to them" (Acts 2:41). "And
believers were increasingly added to the Lord, multitudes of
both men and women" (Acts 5:14). The names and specific
events associated with their conversions are not mentioned
until we get to the Ethiopian eunuch, a foreign Jewish
proselyte. The next conversion mentioned is that of Saul, a
Christian-hating, born and bred Jew. Then we come to
Cornelius in our text. Although thousands more were
converted to Christianity, these are the only three examples of
personal and specific conversions. Unfortunately, evangelical

Christians have turned a personal individual relationship with Christ into a worldview that robs the church of its public corporate collective identity. The focus on individualism has created havoc in the church and I would even say turned the young progressive church into an old stagnant church.

Individualism seems to prevail not only in society, but also in the church. The emphasis in the Bible is upon the community of God's people as a whole, not on the individual standing alone.

In the Old Testament, Israel referred to God's people. In the New Testament, the church is God's people. Individualism is the energy source for the exploding concept known as individual interpretation. Mix relativism to the recipe and biblical truth becomes a matter of individual preference.

Private worship and family worship is a duty of the individual Christian. However, the church has a collective duty to worship the triune God. Unfortunately, individualism will lead Christians to worship individuals rather than worshipping God. Not having the Word of God to guide him, Cornelius worshipped Peter. "As Peter was coming in, Cornelius met him and fell down at his feet and worshiped him. But, Peter lifted him up, saying, 'Stand up; I myself am also a man'" (Acts 10:25-26).

The great need is to gain a better understanding of the church in its progress. Every generation should view the church as an embryonic church – that is a young church. The Holy Spirit is present with a young church. It was present in the young church in the household of Cornelius. "The Holy Spirit fell upon all those who heard the word" (Acts 10:44) The emphasis on the work of the Holy Spirit is not on the whole number present, but upon those who heard the Word of God. Cornelius and the many who gathered with him remind the church of a young model congregation.

What would a model congregation look like based on the young church in the household of Cornelius? Cornelius was instructed to speak to Peter with these words. "So I sent to you immediately, and you have done well to come. Now therefore, we are all present before God, to hear all the things commanded you by God" (Acts 10:33). The model congregation is present at the times appointed. "We are all present." How many times does the church gather for worship and say, "we are all here." Christians ought to present themselves before God in worship, not for their own edification, but to praise and exalt reverently and solemnly the name of God the Father, God the Son, and God the Holy Spirit. The congregation meeting in the home of Cornelius worshipped with reverence according to Luke's inspired account. Cornelius said, "We are present before God." Our presence in worship is before God not before men; therefore, entertainment is out of the picture. The church is not able to entertain God.

The young church in the home of Cornelius was a congregation that wanted to hear the commandments of God. "We are all present before God, to hear all the things commanded you by God" (Acts 10:33). They did not gather to see or be seen, but to listen to the Word of God. They did not come to be gratified or entertained, but to listen to the Word of God. They came to hear the full counsel of God's Word without prejudice. Those who gathered were seeking God yet that congregation acted with greater respect for true worship than most congregations today.

The preacher preached the whole counsel of God. Preachers do not have the power to change a heart or increase the sanctification of any soul. Those are things the Holy Spirit has to do. It is the Holy Spirit who blesses the Word and it is the Holy Spirit that gives growth to the converted soul. God's sovereign grace saves and sanctifies.

Many years ago, General Electric advertised their products with this slogan: "progress is our most important product." Not all the progress of industry, technology, and communication has improved the moral condition of the human race. If axiomatic proverbs are important, then the words of wisdom for Christians should be "truth is our most important product." Truth properly acquired and vigorously defended will have a dramatic, but wonderful effect in your life and on the society in which you live.

There are two principles in Peter's ministry to the young church in the home of Cornelius that should get the attention of the old church down on Main Street or wherever it is located.

The first principle is the seizure principle. Christians must take hold of the truth. To put it another way, they have to engage in the process of acquiring the truth. Peter took hold of the truth and the Bible says Peter opened his mouth (Acts 10:34). The religious leaders in Jerusalem tried to stop Peter and the other disciples from preaching the truth of the gospel, but Peter's response to them was, " we cannot but speak the things which we have seen and heard" (Acts 4:20). Even unbelievers can see the difference between simply knowing truth and taking hold of truth. Everyone has some understanding of truth in a general sense. For instance, everyone understands the truth that God exists. They may not like the truth and they may try to suppress it, but they cannot avoid the general truth relative to God's existence. Those who belong to Jesus Christ not only understand truth in a general sense; they have a more specific understanding of truth. When God speaks to His people, they listen to Him. They may not fully understand, but God will graciously speak again and again so they will be able to grasp the truth. For example, God spoke to Peter through a vision of a great sheet with ceremonially unclean animals, accompanied with a voice. The Bible says this happened three times (Acts 10:9-15). In the final analysis, Peter listened and took hold of the truth that there is no prejudice in the gospel of Jesus Christ. God will be glorified if Christians take hold of the truth

The second principle is the perseverance principle. After Christians receive the truth, they must continue in the truth. Someone may hear and learn some truth, but that does not mean one can hold to the truth. After Peter discovered the truth of the gospel under the New Covenant, he persevered in the truth. He went to the house of a Gentile, the young church in the home of Cornelius, demonstrated his confidence in preaching the gospel to all nations (Acts 10:34-43). The only way your can persevere in faith and life is to have certain assurance you have God's truth. Peter said, "I certainly perceive" (Acts 10:34). God's revelation of truth to Peter was profound to the point of absolute certainty. Peter had been taught all his life not to associate with Gentiles. When Peter entered into the home of Cornelius, Peter said to them, "You know how unlawful it is for a Jewish man to keep company with or go to one of another nation. But God has shown me that I should not call any man common or unclean" (Acts 10:28). God corrected Peter's understanding of truth by declaring that God does not show favoritism (Acts 10:34).

One of the reasons there is so much spiritual poverty in this country at this time is the absence of taking hold of the truth by professing Christians. The principle of seizing the truth has taken leave from professing Christians as it has throughout the history of God's people. The Old Testament saints had the special privilege of having a church/state. The spiritual and political body was one. The law of God ruled in every sector of life, both private and public. Even though the Old Testament saints had the privilege of having God as their president, legislator, judge, and preacher, they would often fail to seize the truth from the mouth of God.

The people of God during the ministry of Hosea the prophet suffered as the modern church suffers today from the lack of obedience to the seizure principle relative to truth. The prophet Hosea visited the church/state, Israel, just before the fall of the Northern Kingdom in 722 B. C. The economy was great, religion flourished, but a great majority of the religion was false religion. In the midst of prosperity the nation of Israel was about to suffer great calamity because of false religion. However, the prophet Hosea warned the people. "Hear the word of the LORD, you children of Israel, for the LORD brings a charge against the inhabitants of the land: There is no truth or mercy or knowledge of God in the land" (Hosea 4:1). Hosea gave three reasons for the spiritual poverty of his day. There was no truth among the people of God. They did not listen to God thus; God's relationship to the people was severed. When there is no truth, there is false witness. There was no mercy. Truth will always show mercy. There was no knowledge of God. A soul without the truth starves the soul of the right knowledge of God. Ignorance of God leads to hopelessness. If truth, mercy, and the knowledge of God disappears from the life of the church or the culture where the church lives, then you can expect the downfall of society.

Christians must seize the truth of the gospel in the same way Peter seized it. Then they must hold on to the truth of the gospel. Christians must hold on to the gospel of peace. Without peace, they are at war with God. Christians must hold on to the truth of the death of Christ on the cross. It was His death that removed the guilt of sin and established the bond of peace with God. Christians must hold on to the truth of the resurrection of Jesus Christ. The hope of eternal rest is the finished work of the first born from the dead, the Lord Jesus Christ. Christians must hold on to the truth that Jesus is the Judge of the living and the dead.

22. Tradition in a Young Church

Acts 11:1-18

The news of the conversion of Cornelius, a Gentile convert, spread rapidly throughout Judea. Since Jerusalem was the center of apostolic activity, Peter returned to Jerusalem. When Peter arrived in Jerusalem, "those of the circumcision contended with him saying, 'you went in to uncircumcised men and ate with them'" (Acts 11:2). The reference to "those of the circumcision" probably consisted of believing Jews. They were probably Jewish nationalists, but they believed the gospel.

The evangelistic ministry of Philip, Saul, and Peter should have stirred the hearts of the believing Jews to praise and give thanks to God that the gospel was going into the entire world. The saving grace of Jesus Christ should have caused them to praise God, but rather they argued with the men who obeyed the Lord Jesus Christ. The language of the Bible is they "contended" with Peter. Contended means to dispute or argue. Peter had argued with the unbelieving Jews on previous occasions, but Peter had learned that it is never wise to argue against God. God commanded Peter. Peter obeyed God. Then the Jewish believers began to argue with Peter. They were actually arguing against God.

Some Jewish believers in Jerusalem called Peter to the carpet because Peter went in and ate with a Gentile. Peter did not violate biblical law by eating with a Gentile. It was a violation of Jewish tradition. God gave the law to the Israelites during their wilderness trials. There were certain restrictions relative to Gentile participation in worship. Certain feasts were associated with worship. The Gentiles were prohibited from participating in those meals. Jewish tradition had distorted what God originally intended for the law to accomplish.

Tradition is at the center of this contention and argument between Peter and the Jewish believers. Unbiblical tradition continues to visit the church in every generation. The Pharisees contended against Jesus, because they loved unbiblical tradition. The scribes and Pharisees came to Jesus saying, "Why do Your disciples transgress the tradition of the elders? For they do not wash their hands when they eat bread." He answered with a rhetorical question: "Why do you also transgress the commandment of God because of your tradition." (Matthew 15:1-3)

It is important to examine the meaning of tradition to determine the usefulness and abuse of tradition. The word "tradition" literally means "to hand over or pass down some aspect of knowledge or experience." From a biblical perspective the word tradition is generally used in a negative sense. It is used positively, but not often. Tradition may be derived from false doctrine, but it may be true to the Word of God. The salient point of this whole discussion is the pursuit of truth. Is tradition useful? Yes, if it is based on a true objective standard. Should Christians hold on to tradition? Yes, if it is based on the Word of God, because the Word of God is true.

Christians may defend tradition because it affects every aspect of life. Tradition is passed from one generation to the next by way of parents, friends, society, and from the church. However, tradition can interfere with your understanding of how to interact with all the circumstances of this life. Tradition can interfere with your understanding of the gospel as it did the Jewish believers in Jerusalem. They misunderstood the gospel because the false doctrine of their tradition had deceived them.

The good news of Cornelius and his conversion should have caused rejoicing. Instead Peter was chastised, rebuked, and censured. This event ultimately brought division to the church. Why did these religious people, who say they believe in God, want to argue with God?

Peter was not innocent of presumptuous resistance to God's Word. God gave Peter specific instructions to "kill and eat" but Peter said, "not so Lord." Even though Peter received the words directly from God, Peter resisted God's Word. Peter knew very well that God could and did repeal the ceremonial laws. When God speaks it is clear, but sinful minds are not very keen on clearness. God's instruction to Peter was very clear. "What God has cleansed you must not call common" (Acts 11:9). The argument was over. Peter finally understood that God had broken down the wall between Israel and the Gentiles. It was not easy, but Peter finally came to grips with God's truth, the truth that supremely surpassed the tradition of the Jews.

The believing Jews could not accept the truth that God had abrogated the ceremonial laws. When they heard of Peter's obedience to God, they were ready to argue with Peter. Peter came and listened to them, but was ready to present his argument, from the truth and by the witness of six men. Most of the time, fault finding professing Christians protest because of bad and inaccurate information. What were the facts? First, God spoke to Peter and to Cornelius. Second, God repealed the ceremonial laws. Third, the Holy Spirit fell upon them.

God's direct discourse and the supernatural appearance of the Holy Spirit were sufficient to not only convince Peter, but anyone else that the uncircumcised Gentiles were saved by the grace of God. However, Peter did not depend on the immediate work of God and probably for a good reason.

Peter reminded his opponents of God's promise. "Then I remembered the Word of the Lord, how He said, 'John indeed baptized with water, but you shall be baptized

with the Holy Spirit'" (Acts 11:16). Peter remembered what
Jesus said just before His ascension into heaven. "You shall
receive power when the Holy Spirit has come upon you"
(Acts 1:8). Peter thus concluded that God was sovereign in
salvation over Jews and Gentiles alike.

Peter could not argue against God and neither could
those who had originally opposed Peter. "When they heard
these things they became silent; and they glorified God,
saying, 'Then God has also granted to the Gentiles repentance
to life'" (Acts 11:18). Human ignorance will never be able to
stand against divine wisdom. It is most dangerous to say, "I
know better than God."

This text should cause Christians to rethink the
tradition passed on to them. The church must not treat
confessions and traditions as if they were equal to Scripture in
authority. On the other hand if the confession or the tradition
is true to the Word of God, then it is useful. Unfortunately,
tradition is the primary support for existing religious, social
and political institutions and practices in the United States.
However, to replace tradition with ungodly and unbiblical
programs will produce another monster in the church.
Ungodly tradition is a work of the flesh. However, Christians
may overcome ungodly tradition. "For the weapons of our
warfare are not carnal but mighty in God for pulling down
strongholds, casting down arguments and every high thing
that exalts itself against the knowledge of God, bringing
every thought into captivity to the obedience of Christ" (2
Corinthians 10:4-5). Jesus Christ died on the cross for His
disciples and He expects them to bring every thought into
captivity to the obedience to Christ.

The passion of every Christian should be to think like
God thinks and obey what God commands. Unfortunately,
tradition is the primary support for the religious institutions in
America. Many church programs, liturgy and doctrine are
laid on the foundation of church tradition. Almost every

dimension of Christian activity in the church has argued against God and argued for tradition. Why are particular churches skeptical about changing tradition? They are like those of the circumcision. They follow those who have lived before them. Dr. Harold Parker explains the danger of believing interpreted history, without returning to the primary source.

> The second error lies in the tendency for the student to follow the authority ahead of him in Indian file, deeper and deeper into the morass of error. If the first of the secondary authorities is wrong in fact or judgment, then all who follow him will be in error also, for they are on the same path. They will remain in error until the primary sources are checked again, (*Studies in Southern Presbyterian History*, by Harold M. Parker, Jr., p. 56).

I am not arguing that all tradition is bad and that it is not useful, but it must be measured by the Word of God, rightly interpreted.

When Peter heard God tell him to "kill and eat" Peter argued against God, but God told Peter two other times. Peter finally listened to God (Acts 11:7-10). Sometimes redundancy is necessary to make a point. If God has granted you repentance to life and you belong to Jesus Christ, then make Him your object of worship in your personal life, your family life and the when you gather to worship with God's family on the Lord's day.

The young church began by following the Word of God. "When they heard these things they became silent; and they glorified God saying 'Then God has also granted to the Gentiles repentance to life'" (Acts 11:18). Salvation should have been easy to understand and worship was simplified, but what happened? Tradition found its way back in the church.

It was not too long after the coming of Christ that tradition began to replace the Word of God. Now sixteen centuries later salvation is grossly misunderstood and worship is as complicated as it was before the coming of Christ. Liturgy has replaced or at least has become more important than the meaning of God's Word in many churches. The intended meaning of the law of God in God's Word was to show the beauty and marvels of God's saving grace, yet sinners argue for the ugly and mundane. Tradition in the young church is the cause for tradition in the old church. Every generation must be reformed by the Word of God.

23. History of Places and People

Acts 11:19-30

People and places have occupied the attention of historiographers from the beginning of time. History is a record of people, places, and events. It would be difficult to trace the development and advancement of the church without using names of people and places. An understanding of church history will help Christians understand the doctrine of the church. For instance, Christians understand the saving grace of Jesus Christ, because they understand the history of God's redeeming grace. Christians have the Bible, which is the only inspired and true history of God's people. God gave His people an infallible history of the growth and development of the church, so they may have a better understanding of His saving grace. The history of redemption is important to the salvation of the soul.

Antioch holds an important place in church history. Some historians call it the "main base for the whole Euphrates frontier" during the Hellenistic period (*The Zondervan Pictorial Encyclopedia of the Bible*, vol. 1, p. 185). The New Testament speaks of two cities named Antioch. One is known as Antioch of Pisidia, which was located in the province of Galatia (modern day Turkey).

The other Antioch is Antioch of Syria, simply referred to as Antioch. Antioch of Syria mentioned in Acts chapter eleven is primarily a reference to the Greek culture and not the Jewish culture. A Greek city in the Roman Empire would be interested in politics, not religion. Even though a Greek city would engage in some religious activity, it would be considered morally corrupt and undesirable for those who worship the true and living God. Antioch was also a commercial center with little interest in philosophy or cultural purity. Antioch of Syria became an important place in the history and development of the New Testament Church. Antioch was important because it played a major role in the fulfillment of the promise the Lord Jesus Christ made to His church. "You shall be witnesses to Me in Jerusalem, and in all Judea and Samaria, and to the end of the earth" (Acts 1:8).

Antioch was the least likely place to receive the message of God's saving grace through the work of Jesus Christ because of its pagan proclivities. However, the Lord appointed Antioch as the main port of embarkation for the church expanding to the "end of the earth." The fact that God used a place like Antioch as a launching place to carry the gospel to the ends of the earth, should be a source of encouragement to Christians.

If God sends renewal, reformation, and revival, the place God chooses may not receive his Word *immediately*, but rather *mediately*. To put it another way God uses means or instruments to evangelize the world. If you are a Christian then you are the means that God uses to take the gospel to the whole world. God may not change your city immediately, but He will use His people to be witnesses of His grace.

Antioch was the place God used, but places are incapable of making disciples. Somebody took the gospel to Antioch. Although their names were not mentioned, they were men from two different places. One place was Cyrene, a Greek city in North Africa. The other was Cyprus, an island in the Mediterranean Sea.

The historical context of Peter's sermon in Jerusalem at Pentecost is important. The Bible says there were devout men from every nation under heaven for the great feast in Jerusalem. It specifically mentions Cyrene (Acts 2:5-10). Some went back to there native cities because of persecution (Acts 11:19).

God appoints men who are particularly equipped for the purpose of expanding His kingdom. One man particularly gifted was Barnabas. After the elders in Jerusalem heard of the church growth in Antioch, they sent Barnabas to assist the new believers at Antioch. Barnabas was a Jewish Levite from Cyprus. The apostles nicknamed him Barnabas, which they translated as Son of Encouragement. The Greek word translated Barnabas literally means "Son of Nebo." The apostles took the liberty of translation thus calling him Son of Encouragement. Maybe they were encouraged because Barnabas was known as the man in the nascent church to sell his property and give it to the apostles. He was a man of dedication and integrity. Barnabas was the kind of teacher that could encourage the disciples to fulfill the mission of making disciples.

Saul, who will later be known as Paul the apostle was also associated with the church at Antioch. The elders at Jerusalem sent Saul to his hometown at Tarsus. Barnabas was acquainted with Saul from the time of Saul's first contact with the elders in Jerusalem (Acts 9:27). Apparently the Spirit of the Lord motivated Barnabas to find Saul and bring him to Antioch. Barnabas needed someone to help him with the ministry to the Gentiles. Barnabas knew Saul's qualifications. Saul came from a well to do family since Roman citizenship was generally held only by the upper class. His social standing implies that Saul probably received the equivalent of the best university education available in his day. Saul was a Hebrew of Hebrews. It follows then that Saul must have lived by Jewish law. Saul studied at the feet of Gamaliel, one of the most influential of the Jewish Rabbi's. Saul was a determined man which is obvious by his participation of the death of Stephen (Acts 8:1). An educated, motivated, and converted man with ten years of additional study and meditation under his belt would place him on the top of the list of prospective ministers for the mission of making disciples.

The Story of Barnabas and Saul at Antioch is a historical account of God ordaining the right people to be at the right place to begin the extension of the church into the fertile field of the world. The inspired history of places and people instrumental in the mission of making disciples is very useful for every generation of a young particular church. Every disciple of Christ ought to recognize that God has placed him or her at a particular place, at a particular time to be a witness of God's saving grace.

A follower of Christ should follow Christ into places that Christ would visit such as a wedding where the best wine was served (John 2:1-10). Jesus went to places that tax gatherers and sinners were present. Barnabas and Saul did not stay in the comfort of their pious religious domain. They stepped out of their comfort zone and God used them for His glory.

Barnabas and Saul stayed in Antioch "for a whole year [and] they assembled with the church and taught a great many people" (Acts 11:26). The mission that Christ gave them was to make disciples and teach the whole counsel of God (Matthew 28:19-20). The Bible indicates that they taught a large number of new converts, but there is no evidence to suggest that it was a mega-church. The modern church growth experts ought to study the places and people of the young church in the Book of Acts. They will find principles for church growth inspired by God.

"The disciples were first called Christians at Antioch" (Acts 11:26). People identify followers of Jesus Christ by the term "Christian". Yet there is not any evidence in the Bible that followers of Christ ever called themselves Christians. Since Christians are followers of Jesus Christ, they are identified by association to Jesus Christ, the second person of the Trinity. Unfortunately we live during a time when the greater part of the Western civilization treats the word Christian as a byword in a pejorative sense.

The lesson from this text is to find the place where you can serve and glorify God. Identify yourself with Christ and your association with Him will give reason to the unbeliever to call you a Christian.

24. Young Church Meets the State

Herod the king refers to Herod Agrippa I, a vassal king who ruled the territory of his grandfather, Herod the Great. He had James put to death and Peter put in prison to gain favor with the Jews. Herod wanted to mistreat and oppress the church, for reasons unknown except from the promise of the Lord Jesus Christ, that His disciples will be persecuted (John 15:20).

Since the Jews wanted to suppress the Christian religion, it was of mutual benefit to Herod to suppress, if possible, the mission and ministry of the church. It is the essential godly nature of the church that threatens civil government. If individuals were the threat then why didn't Herod go after Simon the Zealot, one of the original twelve disciples? The title attached to Simon's name should have been reason enough to pursue him rather that James the brother of John. The Lord Jesus Christ changed Simon's zealous thinking, but nevertheless he was identified as a zealot.

An explanation of the Zealot movement during the period of the Acts of the Apostles will clarify this historical event. The Zealot movement had its roots in the Maccabees during the second century B.C. By the time of the birth of Christ, the Zealot party was actively fighting the Roman conquest in Palestine. The last stand of the Zealots was at the fortress of Masada in 73 A.D. The Zealots were a combination of religious and political Jews who hated Roman government control. The Romans interfered with Jewish traditions. Herod's job was to maintain the peace of Rome while preserving some Jewish tradition. Zealots would have been a threat to Herod's job and religious life. Herod did not want any particular personality suppressed, he wanted to suppress the church.

The church is the body of Christ, thus it makes perfectly good sense to say that unbelievers, like Herod, hate the body of Christ, which is made up of individual believers. Herod did qualify a few among the church for persecution, but that was merely a political decision.

The principle to understand from this portion of Scripture for the young church is also applicable for every generation. It was the state against the church. The state and the church are ordained to carry out their respective duties according to the Word of God. How can the state carry out its godly purpose if it is not morally bound to the law of God? Dr. Robert L. Dabney is right to say that "God has, indeed, by the law of Nature and revelation, imposed on all the citizens and on magistrates the duty of obedience, and ordained that men shall live in regular civil society, under laws" (*The Practical Philosophy*, by R. L. Dabney, p. 378). The law of God is written on the heart. The apostle Paul leaves no room for escaping the reality that everyone, including the minister of the state, "by nature do the things in the law" (Romans 2:14-15).

Herod suppressed his knowledge of God's law and exercised prerogatives that did not belong to him as the minister of the state. The Bible is not ambiguous on this matter. "For rulers are not a terror to good works, but to evil...For he is God's minister to you for good...he is God's minister, an avenger to execute wrath on him who practices evil" (Romans 13:3). Herod should not have murdered James and he should not have imprisoned Peter, but the church did not react with swords and spears. Does this mean that the church is to be silent on government abuses? One of the leading liberal European theologians of the mid 20th century explained his view. Although, I have no affinity to his theological system, I do agree with some of what he had to say about the relationship of the state to the church. Oscar Cullmann said, "the Church's task with regard to the State is thus clear...it must remain in principle critical toward every State and be ready to warn it against transgression of its legitimate limits" (*State in the New Testament*, by Oscar Cullmann, p. 91).

Earthly kingdoms and political governance are principal tempters used by Satan. Satan tempted the Lord Jesus Christ with earthly kingdoms. Many wicked men have been tempted by earthly kingdoms. The temptation by Satan in the wilderness was secular and political. "Then the devil, taking Him up on a high mountain, showed Him all the kingdoms of the world in a moment of time. And the devil said to Him, 'All this authority I will give You and their glory'..." (Luke 4:6).

The history of the church in relation to the state has proven again and again that the state cannot ignore God. Human governments are not merely an expression of human will, but of a will regulated and measured by eternal principles. It is the rebellion against those eternal principles that set the state against the church. The Bible teaches that all power in heaven and earth is committed to the Lord Jesus Christ. He is the Ruler of the nations, the King of kings and the Lord of lords. The state has not been given the authority, right, or power to abuse its subjects contrary to the law of God.

Since an ungodly state does not have a soul to serve God, it fears the power of the church. During the reign of Herod, the church was growing and expanding. Herod saw the church as a threat to the state. However, "The Word of God grew and multiplied" (Acts 12:24).

The irony of this paradigm is that the Word of God is the measure of morality for the state. The State has an obligation to regulate its own conduct and legislation in conformity with the teaching of the Word of God (Romans

2:14-15). The state has a moral responsibility, just as individuals within the state have a moral responsibility.

Herod's attack against the church 2000 years ago was no different than the state attacking the church in the present time. Unfortunately, the church has given the government carte blanche to run rough shod over ecclesiastical and spiritual matters. Today rather than seeing the increase in the study of the full counsel of God and the acceptance of the Word of God as absolute truth, the individual democratization of the church is the order of the day. The dominion of the secular and the denigration of the sacred have led the church down the unpleasant path called statism.

Statism is a concept that views the civil government as the ultimate authority. Statism taken to its logical end means that the state is the means of salvation. There is a popular pledge that Americans frequently announce that should dispel any idea that the state has ultimate authority. The pledge is that in the United States we are "one nation under God." Actually it should read "one nation against God." However if we really believe that we are "one nation under God" then we really believe that statism does not exist. God is the ultimate authority and God mandates the extent of government authority. The lurking philosophy behind the statism concept is humanistic secularism. Humanism gives man the ultimate authority and secularism teaches that this life is all that counts.

Not many, but a few American theologians anticipated the church's agreement with humanistic secularism by the middle of the 19th century. In a letter to Dr. Breckinridge, James H. Thornwell wrote his friend dated January 17, 1842: "The Church has almost dwindled down into a secular corporation; and the principles of this world, a mere carnal policy, which we have nick-named prudence, presides in our councils..." (*Life and Letters of James Henley Thornwell*, edited by B. M. Palmer, p. 228). If the church bows its knee to humanistic secularism and the state believes it has ultimate authority, then the church bows it knee to the state.

The following examples reflect the attempts of the state to usurp the authority of God.

- Today the education of God's covenant children has been given to the state.

- Today the institution of marriage is a state-controlled institution. (I believe the state regulates marriage and family life beyond God's intended purpose.)

- Today homosexuality has become an acceptable life-style even to the extent that legislators, educators, and alleged adjudicators of justice agree with the public conscience in the sanction of same sex marriage.

- Today the biblical work ethic is almost unknown in the western economic system because the state legislates against God's plan.

It is a sad day when the church has become so "secular" as Thornwell says that people, even professing Christians, cannot distinguish between the state and the church. The present perception of the function and purpose of the church and state is contrary to the teaching of Scripture. It is ungodly role reversal. The state promises salvation and the church promises social justice.

It is time for God's people to return to the kind of faithfulness that the early church turned to in their time of need. The church needs to pray and be diligent in their calling. When God uses means to accomplish his purpose, the church should not say, "you are beside yourself." It is not beyond God's capacity and benevolence to answer prayers, reform the church and restore a godly society. It is not beyond God's sovereign hand to deliver His people from the hands of a tyrannical state. God delivered Peter from the hands of a tyrannical state.

When Herod, representing the state, attacked the church James died, Peter was in prison and Herod appeared to triumph. However, in the end, Herod was dead, Peter was free and the Word of God triumphed. The death of Herod is a remarkable example of how God will ultimately judge wicked government leaders unless they believe the gospel and submit to God. The description of Herod's death is horrible. "So on a set day Herod, arrayed in royal apparel, sat on his throne and gave an oration to them. And the people kept shouting, "The voice of a god and not of a man!" Then immediately an angel of the Lord struck him, because he did not give glory to God. And he was eaten by worms and died" (Acts 12:21-23). "The voice of god and not of man," the people cried out. Herod allowed himself to be put in the place of God.

An angel of the Lord stood by Peter. An angel of the Lord struck Herod down. The church will stand. The state will fall.

There are two dynamics in this text. The first teaches the church that God is sovereign even when the state invades the church. The second teaches that the church will prosper even in the face of individual losses (Stephen, James, and Peter). The church will prosper because the Word of God assures Christians that God is the ultimate authority, both in the secular world and the spiritual world.

25. The Missionary Enterprise

Acts 13:1-12

The Christian missionary enterprise belongs to the Church. I make a distinction between the missionary movement and the missionary enterprise. The missionary movement is the organized effort by the modern church and some parachurch organizations to take the gospel to foreign countries. The missionary enterprise is the biblical model of making disciples. The missionary enterprise was a major factor in the first thirty years of the church.

My purpose in this chapter is to give a doctrinal explanation of the missionary enterprise. Every Christian has a mission, so it may be said that every Christian is a missionary. However, not every Christian has been called to a special labor in a specific field for the purpose of taking the gospel to a particular people group.

Since the time of Abraham, God's people have moved from place to place carrying the truth of God's saving grace with them. However, during the first thirty years of the young church in the New Testament, the mission of the church enlarged under the ministry of the apostle Paul. The mission efforts of the apostle Paul ought to be studied to better understand the missionary enterprise of the church.

The word missionary comes from the word mission. The word mission literally means "to be sent" or more specifically mission means "to be sent to do something." In His high priestly prayer the Lord Jesus made it clear to the disciples that he had been sent on a mission from God the father. "As You sent Me into the world, I also have sent them into the world" (John 17:18). The Lord Jesus Christ sends His church on a general mission to glorify God. There are specific missions that will glorify God.

The mission of the church is not the same thing as the ministry of the church, yet the mission and the ministry cannot be separated. A good biblical definition of the ministry of the church is found in Paul's letter to the Ephesians.

> And He Himself gave some to be apostles, some prophets, some evangelists, and some pastors and teachers, for the equipping of the saints for the work of ministry, for the edifying of the body of Christ, till we all come to the unity of the faith and of the knowledge of the Son of God, to a perfect man, to the measure of the stature of the fullness of Christ; that we should no longer be children, tossed to and fro and carried about with every wind of doctrine, by the trickery of men, in the cunning craftiness of deceitful plotting, but, speaking the truth in love, may grow up in all things into Him who is the head—Christ— from whom the whole body, joined and knit together by what every joint supplies, according to the effective working by which every part does its share, causes growth of the body for the edifying of itself in love. (Ephesians 4:11-16)

The ministry of the church primarily consists of equipping the people of God for works of service. It is the established or particular church that devotes itself to the ministry of the church. If the ministry follows the Word of God, then the mission will be thoroughly established.

The missionary enterprise is not merely an evangelistic endeavor. The missionary enterprise has a much wider responsibility than that which is normally taught in seminaries. The established church or particular church at Antioch was the center of attention for sending out missionaries to extend the landmarks of the Christian religion. The ministry of the church at Antioch was in order. The church at Antioch had a foundation of sound biblical doctrine. If the Christian missionary enterprise prospers, it must have unity of doctrine. From the evidence available, the preachers and teachers at Antioch were in doctrinal agreement.

The church at Antioch fasted, prayed, and laid hands on two men who were selected for missionary service. "Then, having fasted and prayed, and laid hands on them, they sent them away" (Acts 13:3). This verse is brief, but full of doctrine for missions. The missionary enterprise begins with fasting and prayer. The church at Antioch realized the spiritual nature of the mission by fasting and praying. They also choose spiritually gifted men for the mission of taking the gospel to the ends of the earth. God sends men on a mission who are equipped to do the work of ministry. The church at Antioch, with the prophets and teachers having oversight, was the sending unit.

Laying of hands is probably not ordination. Barnabas had already been sent to Antioch by the elders. Saul was set apart by the Lord Jesus Christ. The laying of hands was the solemn commission given to Barnabas and Saul for the missionary enterprise.

The Christian missionary enterprise, like any other Christian endeavor, uses ordinary means to accomplish God's purpose. Missionaries are not more spiritual than other Christians. The work of a missionary is not a specialized field. Missionaries are men called, prepared, equipped, and ready to take the full counsel of God to people anywhere in the world. The Holy Spirit enables men to carry out the mission. Godly elders will recognize the necessary gifts of men to serve the missionary enterprise.

The missionary enterprise has two primary objectives, summarized in Matthew's gospel. Jesus says to His disciples, "Go therefore and make disciples of all the nations, baptizing them in the name of the Father and of the Son and of the Holy Spirit, teaching them to observe all things that I have commanded you; and lo, I am with you always, even to the end of the age" (Matthew 28:19-20).

The two objectives of the missionary enterprise are to make disciples and teach the whole counsel of God. The commandment from the Lord Jesus Christ was to "make disciples." The commandment is often confused with making converts. It is not the mission of the church to make converts, because the church is not able to make converts. Only the Holy Spirit can convert the soul.

The Lord gave the church exclusive authority to obey His command and complete the mission of making disciples and teaching the full counsel of God. Church membership is not the mission of the church. It is the result of the mission of the church. The authority given to admit and dismiss members of the visible church belongs to the elders of local particular churches. The plain reading of Scripture and common sense testifies that no other organization can effectively carry out the mission of the church, because only the church has authority to carry out the missionary enterprise.

The missionary enterprise is the collective work of the church because making disciples begins with apologetics and evangelism.

> The aim of apologetics is to defend the possibility of theology as a science, where 'science' is understood in the broad sense of being an objective inquiry into some existing objects by means that allow for the disclosure of their nature to the mind, in short a disciplined inquiry into the truth. (*Truth in the Flesh*, by John Hartung, p. 125)

Paul the apostle often employed apologetics as he engaged in the noble work of making disciples (Acts 22:1; 24:10ff). The first step in making disciples is presenting the gospel of the kingdom of Jesus Christ so the person will have an opportunity to believe the gospel. If he or she believes the gospel he or she is a disciple.

The second objective of the missionary enterprise is to teach the full counsel of God. The disciple must inquire into the holiness of God and the sinfulness of man. Although the holiness of God cannot be fully understood and the sinfulness of man fully explored, there is the demand for holiness of life. Jesus said, "If you love Me, you will keep My commandments" (John 14:15). Teaching holiness has always been a mission of the church even in the Old Testament congregation. The Prophet Hosea explains this dimension of the mission. "For I desire mercy and not sacrifice, and the knowledge of God more than burnt offerings" (Hosea 6:6). According to the inspired prophet Hosea, the holiness of God begins with understanding, not with outward religious practices.

The biblical missionary enterprise is to make disciples and teach the full counsel of God. The ministry of the church is to equip disciples for the mission. Therefore, every believer participates in the missionary enterprise.

In the course of their missionary work, Barnabas and Paul found a false prophet.

> Now when they had gone through the island to Paphos, they found a certain sorcerer, a false prophet, a Jew whose name was Bar-Jesus, who was with the proconsul, Sergius Paulus, an intelligent man. This man called for Barnabas and Saul and sought to hear the word of God. But Elymas the sorcerer (for so his name is translated) withstood them, seeking to turn the proconsul away from the faith. Then Saul who also is called Paul, filled with the Holy Spirit looked intently at him and said, "O full of all deceit and all fraud, you son of the devil, you enemy of all

righteousness, will you not cease perverting the straight ways of the Lord?" (Acts 13:6-10)

Elymas is called a sorcerer who was alleged to do supernatural things with the aid of evil spirits. The Greek word translated sorcerer is *magos*. He was also a Jewish magician named Bar Jesus which literally means Son of Salvation. His specialty was using words falsely to further his own personal agenda. The sorcerer or magician was allegedly a student of metaphysics and the supernatural world. The magician was a leach on society, but a successful leach. The evil art of sophistry was his tool. He knew how to use words and work on people's emotions. He was expected to heal the sick, spark a romance or perhaps the mundane chore of invoking gods for the sake of business and travel safety. The magician promised his clients that he could expel demons or bring disaster to an opponent in a political campaign. The magician was a religious con artist. The magician named Bar Jesus and many like him were the chief enemies of the missionary enterprise in the life of the young church.

However, the lies of a magician are no match for the Word of God. Whether it is the sorcerer in the 1st century pre-modern world or the sophist in the 21st century postmodern world, Christians have a responsibility to stand against these evil men with the Word of God.

Sergius Paulus wanted to hear the Word of God. He was willing to challenge his own paid consultant. The Bible describes Sergius Paulus as an intelligent man. He was prudent and wanted to understand the Word of God. He lived in the same kind of world that Christians live in today. He lived in a world where the law never satisfied the demands of justice. Sergius Paulus was intelligent in the sense that he at least speculated that somewhere, somehow he might find an answer to the demands of the law of God. The magician hated the truth of the gospel and tried to convince the proconsul to turn away from the faith. Since the fall of man in the Garden of Eden, the world has been filled with sophisticated deceiving liars like Elymas.

It is necessary for Christians to engage in the culture but they will likely encounter men like the deceiver Elymas and the inquirer Sergius Paulus. The postmodern world is full of people who allegedly tell the truth and therefore shape a postmodern culture. The following is a summary list of people who shape the thinking and lives in a postmodern culture.

Entertainment industry: The majority of their work produces filth, immorality and exchanges the truth for a lie.

Consumer industry: Advertisers in the business and sales industry mislead the public with every gimmick known to man.

Politicians: They make promises they cannot and do not expect to keep in order to manipulate the culture they serve.

Legal profession: Lawyers twist the facts and judges adjudicate on the basis of twisted facts.

Educator: Educators teach according to the directions of the bureaucrats who control the purse string of the institution.

Christians live in this mixed up world and it is there that they engage in the mission God gives them. The mission is to make disciples by teaching the truth based on the whole counsel of God. Tell the truth to the entertainment industry. Tell the truth to the business world. Tell the truth to politicians. Tell the truth to lawyers. Tell the truth to educators. Christians have the responsibility to participate in the missionary enterprise of the church by telling the whole truth and nothing but the truth.

26. Model for Establishing Churches

Acts 13:13-52

  Christians participate in the mission and ministry of the church by making disciples and teaching the whole counsel of God. The result is the establishment of local particular churches. Paul's experience at Antioch Pisidia represents a New Testament model for establishing churches. It begins by seeking out those who are seeking God. Paul found them at the Jewish synagogue. It was there that Paul preached a sermon to those allegedly seeking God.

  Although preaching is offered to God in worship, it has wonderful effects on the people of God. One of the great benefits of preaching is the confirmation of the faith. The establishment of the faith includes the process and content of the Christian life. Establishment of the faith has two dimensions, the establishment of personal faith and establishment of collective faith. Personal faith includes the Christian's personal relationship with God. The collective faith of God's people in a particular location is necessary for the establishment of the church.

  Individualism is an enemy of the collective faith of God's people. If those who profess to be God's people adopt Individualism as a worldview, the model for establishing a particular church will not follow the biblical pattern. God's people are individuals and must have a personal individual relationship with God. However, when the noun forming suffix, "ism", is added to the word individual, it describes an ideology or becomes the worldview of the person. The following definition will keep Individualism in perspective.

  This worldview places priority on the power of the individual creature instead of the sovereign God.

Christians are the only people who are really and eternally given individual rights and at the same time Christians are under the rule of a sovereign monarch, the Lord Jesus Christ. Jesus said, "You shall know the truth, and the truth shall make you free" (John 8:32). A Christian is one who is adopted into the family of God and is an individual sibling among many siblings. It is the duty of all Christians to reject the philosophy of individualism and accept the sovereignty of God as the ruling principle in life. (*Theological Terms in Layman Language*, by Martin Murphy, p. 56)

Individualism is particularly destructive to the biblical model for establishing particular churches. It is the establishment of individual Christians into one body that establishes a particular church.

Barnabas and Paul went on the mission to make disciples and teach the full counsel of God at Antioch in Pisidia. The mission is necessary to establish a particular church. Luke wrote the acts of the Apostles to give an account "of all that Jesus began both to do and teach" (Acts 1:1).

Jesus said, "I will build My church" (Matthew 16:18). Jesus taught the reality of the establishment of the church, and Luke explains the biblical model for establishing particular churches. The Lord is very careful to give his people all they need to accomplish the task he gives them. Christians should be thankful that they have this portion of God's word to instruct them in the establishment of churches.

The modern terminology for establishing churches is "planting churches." The expected result is "church growth". Almost without exception, the term "church growth" carries with it unbiblical concepts for establishing churches. Many evangelical denominations have strict rules for starting a local particular church. Many denominations believe their rules must be followed for church growth. One rule is to hire a professional to check the demographics. It is important to classify the socio-economic classes to determine if there is enough money to support the massive investment in land, buildings, and facilities to insure church growth. Then the husband and wife (the church planting team) must be screened to see if they possess the functional gifts necessary to carry out this elaborate plan. Finally, the couple must take psychological tests to determine if they are mentally in tune with the culture they intend to mobilize. The modern church plant accentuates features that will attract unbelievers to the alleged worship service. The emphasis today is on contemporary music in worship, even if the lyrics are contrary to the teaching in the full counsel of God. The emphasis today is on fellowship and friendly services. Deemphasize doctrine; it will stunt church growth. The preaching is a short homily with a stress on the perceived felt needs of the audience. There is more emphasis on psychological analysis than it is on soul searching. Many churches have entrusted the hope of church growth in sound bites and video images.

Paul and Barnabas moved into an area and went to the local Synagogue, read the Word of the Lord and preached a sermon. That is how they established churches. They preached a sermon, but it was not short. His sermon introduction was, "Men of Israel, and you who fear God, listen."

Paul addressed two categories of people that needed to hear the gospel. The Jews believed God and hoped for the arrival of a Messiah. The Jews needed to hear the gospel. The Gentiles worshipped God, but they needed to hear the good news of God's saving grace through the Lord Jesus Christ.

Paul's sermon consists of two parts. The first part is a lengthy explication of the history of redemption beginning with Moses. The second part is the gospel message of forgiveness and justification. "Therefore let it be known to you, brethren, that through this Man is preached to you the forgiveness of sins; and by Him everyone who believes is justified from all things from which you could not be justified by the law of Moses" (Acts 13:38-39). The forgiveness of sins is an essential doctrine because all men are sinners (Romans 3:23). Martin Luther is credited for saying, "forgiveness of sins through Christ is the highest article of our faith." The forgiven sinner will find peace, joy, and hope in the eternal and favorable presence of God. Paul also preached the doctrine of justification. Paul's summary of the doctrine of justification is "everyone who believes is justified" (Acts 13:39). A brief explanation of this doctrine will be helpful.

> The word justification used in relation to the doctrine of salvation in Scripture is always used in a forensic (legal) sense. It is a divine act whereby God declares the elect of God, who are sinners and deserve condemnation, to be acceptable in His sight. The forensic (legal) language in the Bible explains our standing before God. For instance, "Who shall bring a charge against God's elect? It is God who justifies" (Romans 8:33). (*The Essence of Christian Doctrine*, by Martin Murphy, p. 126).

Paul's sermon to the unbelieving Jews and Gentiles explains the good news that sinners may be saved by the grace of God and have assurance of salvation. The collective number of those who believe, constitute the church.

Paul's sermon does not end with an altar call. It does not end with an appeal to live a morally upright life. It does not end on a positive upbeat note. Paul ends the sermon with a warning (Acts 13:40-41). Paul quotes from Habbakuk where God warns the prophet and the people of God that His judgment is upon them (Habbakuk 1:5). Likewise, if anyone hears the Word of God and ignores it, they are asking for God's judgment.

The New Testament Model for establishing the church includes preaching. The text indicates that the preaching had an effect upon the town. After the sermon the Gentiles begged Paul and Barnabas to come back and preach the next Sabbath. The Word of God had captivated the people. It was not the craftiness of a program or the personality of Paul, it was the Word of God, by the power of the Holy Spirit that brought them back. The contemporary model for establishing churches depends almost entirely upon personality and programs.

The Jews constituted the religious establishment in Antioch and they opposed the gospel message (Acts 13:45). Why did the present religious establishment despise the Word of God? This curious question is applicable to the establishment of the church. Some of the Jews understood the established church but they obviously did not preach forgiveness and justification. They preached the Law of Moses (Acts 13:39). They were outraged because Paul preached the gospel message of forgiveness and justification.

The Jews allowed Gentiles to come to the Synagogue. The Gentiles were allowed to listen to the reading of the Word of the Lord. Maybe the Gentiles would be invited to join the Synagogue and become good members by following the tradition of the established religion. The unbelieving Gentiles would join with unbelieving Jews. Paul realized that he could not establish a church with unbelievers, even though the existing church claimed to be believers.

When the Gentiles heard the Word of God they believed the gospel. Why did some people believe the truth of the God's word and other's reject it? The answer is found in the Word of God. "Now when the Gentiles heard this, they were glad and glorified the word of the Lord. And as many as had been appointed to eternal life believed" (Acts 13:48). It was by divine appointment that many believed and the church at Antioch of Pisidia was established. It is a model for establishing the church.

27. Principles for Making Disciples

Acts 14:1-28

God sent Paul and Barnabas on a mission to make disciples, which is necessary to establish churches. They set out on their journey from Antioch of Syria. They went to the island of Paphos, on to Antioch in Pisidia and then to the region that is now commonly known as the republic of Turkey. The ancient city of Iconium was their next stop. There is no such place today known as Iconium, but modern archeological studies indicate that the city of Iconium did exist for about 400 years.

Paul and other missionaries in the early church seemed to have developed a pattern at every place they visited. In every new town they visited the existing Synagogue. They read the Word of God and then preached a sermon.

There is no evidence in the Bible that making disciples included miraculous healings or giving life to a dead body. The purpose of miracles was to attest that God gave them extraordinary powers to prove the mission was by God's authority. The miracles also validated the inspiration of their words and to prove the words were from God.

The whole counsel of God commands Christians to make disciples. Therefore, making disciples is a matter of doctrine. Paul and Barnabas followed the doctrine from the Lord. Paul and Barnabas preached the doctrine of Christ and a large number of Jews and Greeks believed the gospel (Acts 14:1). However, one might be deceived to think that preaching and teaching the doctrine of Christ would unify the church. The evidence from Scripture reveals that controversy follows the preaching or teaching the doctrine of Christ and controversy leads to persecution (Acts 14:2).

At Antioch of Pisidia the Jews were filled with envy at the preaching of the Word of God. The Jews contradicted and cursed the missionaries of Christ (Acts 13:45). The Jews even stirred up the devout and prominent women and chief men of the city (Acts 13:50).

The pattern continues at Iconium. After preaching the Word of God the unbelieving Jews stirred up the Gentiles and poisoned their minds against the missionaries. "Poison the minds" is translated from the Greek word *kakoo* that literally means to "embitter" or in its most literal sense it means to "mistreat".

Although there were many believers, there was a multitude of unbelievers. The Bible does not give any reason to believe that people who embitter the minds of other people against the doctrine of Christ are in a favorable relationship with God. Unfortunately, some professing believers are infected with embitterment. The Lord Jesus said, "false Christs and false prophets will rise and show great signs and wonders to deceive, if possible, even the elect" (Matthew 24:24).

It all starts with controversy over doctrine. The dissension leads to division, which is exactly what happened at Iconium. "The multitude of the city was divided: part sided with the Jews and part with the apostles" (Acts 14:4). Controversy, dissension and division has been a repeated pattern for two thousand years of church history. When controversy dissension and division meet sinners face to face, they seek the line of least resistance, which is outward peace. The disastrous effect of maintaining outward peace over false doctrine is the destruction of the church.

One reason for the fall of Jerusalem in 586 B.C. may be traced to outward peace over false doctrine.

> Because from the least of them even to the greatest of them, everyone is given to covetousness; And from

the prophet even to the priest, everyone deals falsely. They have also healed the hurt of My people slightly, saying, 'Peace, peace!' When there is no peace" (Jeremiah 6:13-14).

It is the destructive deceit of Satan that says, "peace, peace when there is no peace." Another trick of Satan is to "agree to disagree." John Calvin said, "Shall we make open war against God in order to be at peace with men?" (*Concerning Scandals*, by John Calvin, p. 56). The following questions are relevant for every individual Christian.

Question: Am I willing to sacrifice a favorable relationship with God to obtain a favorable relationship with man?

Question: If the full counsel of God is being taught and preached, why is there so much division and dissention in the church?

Question: Are churches throughout this land preaching the doctrine of Christ, the true doctrine of Christ?

The true and full teaching of Scripture will separate the sheep from the goats. The process is painful, but the result is good, because the doctrine of Scripture unites those who belong to Him now and forever.

The persecution at Iconium moved Paul to Lystra and Derbe. Paul began teaching and observed a man crippled from birth. Paul commanded the man to walk and God healed the man. The people shouted, "The gods have come down to us in the likeness of men!" (Acts 14:11). The people were ready to worship Paul and Barnabas. The Book of Acts exposes false worship on numerous occasions. The Law of God relative to worship is, "You shall have no other gods before Me. You shall not make for yourself a carved image—

any likeness of anything that is in heaven above, or that is in the earth beneath, or that is in the water under the earth; you shall not bow down to them nor serve them..." (Exodus 20:3-5). These commandments apply to believers and unbelievers (Romans 2:14-15). Human beings were created to worship God, but because of the fall (sin) they worship the creature rather than the Creator. The history of the human race is a history of worshiping people. Every person has an inclination to worship particular, private, and public gods, shaped according to their own imaginations. However, rational people are experts in inventing idols. An idol is a false god. All men do not worship the same false gods, but all men are guilty of idolatry. The two objects of worship by the people in Lystra were Paul and Barnabas. It is a very common form of idolatry. It is the idolatry of human popularity. Gods in human form are ordinary to every culture and every generation. They have existed since the Garden of Eden.

The people at Lystra have one thing in common with unbelievers, they invent strange gods. The people of Lystra rightly observed that healing the crippled man was a work of God, but they wrongly tried to make false gods of Paul and Barnabas. Religious celebrities have become the object of worship for many professing Christians. It is a sin to idolize sinners by means of human popularity. The unbelievers at Lystra were guilty of gross idolatry. Christians are vulnerable to popularity cult worship.

What is the source of false gods? It is self esteem, the spark of divinity, the center of creation, or any other psychological, sociological or theological name. The source of false gods is self worship. Nebuchadnezzar had a bad case of self-worship. Nebuchadnezzar did not claim to have a little spark of divinity. He had a big raging flame of self-worship. "I am and there is not one else besides me" (Isaiah 47:8).

Although the Holy Spirit of God healed the man, it appeared that Paul was the ultimate cause of the healing. The people became mad with ecstasy of wonder. They attributed the work of God to a man. The people at Lystra did try to legitimize the appearance of their gods through the lives of Paul and Barnabas.

It was when the unbelievers at Lystra attempted to sacrifice to Paul and Barnabas, Paul said, "why are you doing these things?" The honor, glory, and dignity of God had been attributed to Paul, the chief of sinners. It was nothing more than gross idolatry. Do you know how easy it is for vain minds to be carried away by the misunderstanding of reality? We live at a time in western civilization when reality has almost become meaningless. The multiplied sinfulness is having its effect on an entire cultural milieu. God allows nations to walk in their own ways. "Nevertheless He did not leave Himself without witness, in that He did good, gave us rain from heaven and fruitful seasons, filling our hearts with food and gladness" (Acts 14:16-17). All of God's creation wonderfully reveals His creative power. It is fatally dangerous to become so secularized that eternity has no place in the secular world. Paul's response was, "we…preach to you that you should turn from these useless things to the living God" (Acts 14:15). The miracle impressed the unbelievers at Lystra, but the Word of God and the good news of Jesus Christ had no good effect on their souls.

With the influence of unbelievers from Antioch and Iconium, persecution was inevitable.

> Then Jews from Antioch and Iconium came there; and having persuaded the multitudes, they stoned Paul and dragged him out of the city, supposing him to be dead. However, when the disciples gathered around him, he rose up and went into the city. And the next

day he departed with Barnabas to Derbe. (Acts 14:19-20)

Paul went to Derbe and made many disciples and then returned to the cities he had previously visited (Acts 14:21). It may sound as if Paul went into the town of Derbe, held a crusade and returned to Lystra, Iconium, and Antioch in a short period of time. It is difficult to determine the length of time Paul stayed in Derbe, but it is playing loose with the text to believe that Paul was there for just a few days. He may have stayed there for weeks and maybe even months. His first missionary journey lasted nearly two years. We read the text with our modern minds without considering the length of time Paul spent at each place.

Making disciples did not occur overnight. It took time and it still takes time today. The biblical principles of making disciples are progressive and ascend from the beginning student to the mature student. Paul was aware of how easy it was (and still is) for Christians to lose sight of the kingdom of God.

Some of the churches Paul visited on his first missionary journey did lose sight of the purity of the gospel, which means they lost sight of the kingdom of God. Paul's letter to the Galatians was a letter to the churches he visited on His first missionary journey. Some of these churches were overtaken with another gospel (Galatians 1:6-10). Instead of remaining in the faith, they sought to be justified by the works of the law (Galatians 3:1-4).

Paul returned to each city to continue the process of making disciples and spending time to strengthen the souls of the disciples (Acts 14:21-22). Although Luke uses a word that often translates into English as "soul" and it is a word that has a wide range of metaphysical implications. Although Scripture is silent, Paul may have the reasoning mind, which is a component of the metaphysical soul, as his object of strengthening. The Christian mind must be repaired or to use Paul's word "strengthened" to withstand the persecution and tribulation ahead.

Disciples not only need to be strengthened; they must be encouraged in what they have already believed. The kind of encouragement Paul gave is the kind that Christians need for assurance of faith. Many professing Christians believe that assurance of faith is a charismatic gift. Assurance is a gift for sure, but it is a result of sound doctrine and sound doctrine will always accompany encouragement.

Making disciples has the benefit of preparing the student of Christ for the narrow way that leads to life. The narrow way is the way of tribulation. This is not the same as persecution. Persecution comes from unbelievers. Tribulation refers to the difficult and perilous times that Christians will encounter from professing believers and unbelievers. Paul strengthened, encouraged, and urged the disciples to remain in the faith, he reminded them of a truth almost ignored by modern professing Christians. "We must through many tribulations enter the kingdom of God" (Acts 14:22). Tribulation encompasses all the pain and misery of this life, but Christians are always strengthened and encouraged with the promise of God's future blessing. The promise is not tribulation; it is much tribulation. Life's problems are not resolved when God changes the heart of a sinner. It is the process of discipleship that brings the believing sinner to an understanding of how to deal with pain, misery, and problems of this life.

With all the pressures and problems that Christian disciples face, how will they continue in the faith? God's answer is simple, but almost universally ignored among Christians. "So when they had appointed elders in every church, and prayed with fasting, they commended them to the Lord in whom they had believed" (Acts 14:23). The word "appoint" is used only two times in the Bible. It originally

carried the meaning of "stretching forth the hand to vote."
Paul used the word again in 2 Corinthians 8:19 advising the
Corinthian Church that Titus had been appointed by the
churches to travel with Paul.   Since the reference is to a
plurality of churches they must have voted to send Titus. The
full corpus of Scripture would indicate that it would be
incongruous for the apostle Paul to assign someone to a role
of spiritual leadership, if the people would not agree to
become disciples under that particular person. Therefore, the
local church was in agreement with the appointment of elders.
The elders are responsible for the spiritual care and growth of
the entire congregation.

I will take up the subject of church government in the
next chapter (Acts 15) and how elders are to rule over the
church. Suffice it to say at this point that the gospel is subject
to corruption without sound church government.

Biblical principles for making disciples will bring joy
to the church. Three principles that are non-negotiable:

> 1. Christians must sacrifice to stabilize the church
> according to the whole counsel of God. Paul said,
> "we must through many tribulations enter the
> kingdom of God" (Acts 14:22).   Christians must
> strengthen and encourage the souls of believers in the
> truth of the gospel.
>
> 2. Christians must organize the church under godly
> leadership.
>
> 3. Christians must pray that they will be faithful
> disciples and they will disciple others.

28. Biblical Church Government

Acts 15:1-35

The Lord has given His church two guiding principles so that Christians may effectively carry out the mission of the church. The two principles are inspired truth and inspired order.

These principles presuppose the presence and powerful work of the Holy Spirit. The first and most important principle is the word of truth. The Lord Jesus said, "I am the way, the truth and the life" (John 14:6). Christ the living Word is the ultimate source of all truth. He has given Christians His written Word so they might know the truth and obey Him in all things. The second principle is a definitive church government to insure purity of doctrine and maintain order in the church.

Paul's first letter to the Corinthian Church indicates disorder and confusion in the local church. Paul's inspired instruction was "Let all things be done decently and in order" (1 Corinthians 14:40). The language Paul used was that of a military metaphor. A good military organization will have an orderly disposition in all its parts. How much more would you expect God to order His kingdom. Every aspect of God's economy is arranged according to order. Principally it is perfect order, but because of this sinful world the church is never perfectly ordered. Even so, the church has been given an example of church order in Acts chapter fifteen. The church should consider it carefully since it is the Word of God. The success of the mission of the church depends on how well the church governs itself.

Acts chapter fifteen begins with a dispute over the gospel. The question arose over whether or not there could be two gospels. The elders and apostles assembled as a council to hear the doctrine. Then Peter rose to speak to the question. Peter argued that to make circumcision necessary to salvation would be the equivalence of tempting God. Anyhow, the Jews were not even able to bear the yoke of the law. Peter closes his argument with the truth that Jews and Gentiles alike obtain salvation by grace through faith in Christ. Barnabas and Paul continued the debate with an explanation of God's marvelous works among the Gentiles. Then James takes the floor and basically agrees with Peter and acknowledges that Paul is right. James quotes Old Testament Scripture to defend the gospel of truth (Acts 15:6-21).

The decision of the court was in agreement with the Word of God. Since the representatives of the court are under constraint to judge justly, they must not disagree with God's constitution. There were no known dissenting votes among the members of the church court. The evidence weighs heavily that the opponents to God's constitution did not even labor their case. Luke's inspired account of that church meeting is that "it pleased the apostle and elders, with the whole church..." (Acts 15:22).

The elders and apostles answered the theological question by applying the two principles of truth and order to bring the controversy to a resolution. If the doctrinal and theological controversies are not settled, there will certainly be disorder and confusion in the church. The church must remember the words of the prophet Amos: "Can two walk together, unless they are agreed?" (Amos 3:3)

When I hear people say, "let's just agree to disagree" it makes me cringe. It is not possible to agree to disagree. It is possible to agree that there is a contradiction and division on some matter or the other. But it is not possible to let the contradiction stand as a valid proposition. Contradiction is contrary to the character of God. To live with contradiction is to live with a lie. Godly thinking people cannot agree with contradiction.

God has given the means to resolve doctrinal and theological disputes or any contradiction that raises its ugly head in the church. The principle that God has given the church to resolve doctrinal and theological disputes is church government. It is the source of peace and harmony for the church. The word "government" comes from the word "govern" which essentially means to rule by right of authority. Church government derives its right to rule from God's authority. Church government is like any biblical doctrine, it is not possible to have two different doctrines of church government. God does not give two gospels or two laws or two Holy Spirits, and He does not give two church governments.

The form of government in Scripture is elders representing the local congregation. It is a concept found in the Old and New Testament. Israel in the Old Testament functioned in a church/state relationship. The people of God were in a covenant relationship with God. The ultimate rule of the nation was by the hand of God, through His appointed representatives. Moses appointed "able men, such as fear God, men of truth, hating covetousness; and place such over them to be rulers of thousands, rulers of hundreds, rulers of fifties, and rulers of tens. And let them judge the people at all times…" (Exodus 18:21-22). God established the nation of Israel and gave them various moral, ceremonial, and judicial laws to regulate the state and establish worship principles. The representatives of the people were referred to as the "elders of the people" (Exodus 19:7). The government of God's people in the Old Testament is representative and constitutional.

The fundamental principle is that God rules by order. In the New Testament the civil government is distinct from the church. The civil government ought to order its affairs according to God's natural law (Romans 2:14-15) and apply the general equity of Old Testament judicial case laws to maintain order in society. Elders are responsible for spiritual oversight of the church (Acts 14:23; Titus 1:5-6; 1 Timothy 5:17; Acts 20:28). Elders in a particular local church also have the responsibility to meet with elders of other particular congregations as a church council to resolve disputes common to all the churches. This duty of the elders is particularly applicable to doctrinal disputes.

The council at Jerusalem exemplifies rule by order. Paul took the gospel controversy to a church court of godly men to get a ruling. The court consisted of men from various churches. The men were called elders. The Bible says they came together to consider a doctrinal dispute.

Paul did not try to tyrannize the church with his apostolic authority. Tyrannical behavior is evidence of an autonomous disposition. Autonomy is self-rule which is against God's rule. Paul did not call for a general election to get a democratic opinion. The Bible does not hint of any tyrannical despotism, or congregational democracy. The church court at Jerusalem consisted of elected representatives from the churches affected by the controversy. Those representatives were sent to rule by order. From the evidence in Scripture, elders were essential to the government of the church. The elders at the Jerusalem council apparently worked hard to come to an understanding of the controversy over whether or not there could be two gospels. The Bible says, "when there had been much dispute..." (Acts 15:7).

The word "dispute" comes from a Greek word which literally means, "to inquire into" and therefore "to deliberate about the inquiry." One of the distinctive failures of the modern church is the lack of deliberation and inquiry into doctrinal disputes. The church of the Lord Jesus Christ is divided because of the well-established and growing trend toward ecumenical denominationalism. However, there is little interest in resolving doctrinal differences. The root of the problem is an unbiblical form of church government.

Luke points out that the "brethren" were the subjects placed under the duplicity of doctrine (Acts 15:1). If they are brethren, they should have every desire to settle the controversy. Brethren implies kinship, a covenant relationship and therefore, a unity of doctrine should be the norm. The Pharisees, the brethren back in those days, had turned the covenant of circumcision into a covenant of works. The way of salvation according to the denomination of the Pharisees was, "follow the tradition."

The Acts 15 church meeting was the first denomination in the New Testament church. One was the denomination of the justification by works and grace and the other denomination was justification by grace through faith. The modern church consists of hundreds of denominations subsumed under the banner of the Christian religion.

Some of the differences are serious and others are so trivial they may be classified as adiaphorous. The church is divided so many different ways. Let me point out a few of the major divisions, not to mention hundreds of less known and less disputed controversial divisions. The church is divided between naturalism and supernaturalism. The supernatural branch of Christianity is divided between the Evangelical and Sacerdotal. The Evangelical is divided between the particularist and the universalist. Then the universalist is divided between the Wesleyan and the Lutheran. The Particularistic is divided between the particularistic Calvinist and the inconsistent Amyraldian. The Evangelical church is divided between covenant theology and dispensational theology. The Reformed church is divided between the supralapsarian and the infralapsarian.

And the list goes on and on and on. Why do these controversies exist? The church is unable to decide which gospel is the right gospel. Here is the dilemma! The church has adopted an unbiblical form of church government which prevents the church from deciding doctrinal disputes. There have been a few church councils in the history of the church that developed a creed to maintain orthodoxy. For instance, the end of the 5th century A.D., the church of the western world basically agreed on the doctrine of God determined by the councils of Nicea and Chalcedon. There have been other church councils throughout the history of the church, but more often than not, the decision and creeds that followed, further denominated the church. By the end of the 17th century, the church of the western world was greatly divided on the doctrine of God's sovereignty in the salvation of sinners. The division has exponentially increased in the past couple of hundred years.

If God is the governor of the Universe then there must be a government that He finds pleasing to Him. If the church remains true to its mission, then the church must order its affairs after God's plan outlined in the Word of God.

When false teachers come on the scene, they must be confronted with sound doctrine. If they fail to repent and the dispute cannot be settled in the local church, it must come before an ecclesiastical assembly consisting of representatives from the whole church.

When the elders deliberate on a theological controversy, a judicial decision must follow. The full counsel of the Word of God must be the basis for every judicial decision. If the decision is contradictory to the Word of God, then the constitutional principle was abused or ignored. Obviously if the decision is contradictory to the Word of God, rule by order was not applied. Godly elders do not ignore the Word of God.

Most church courts today simply advise the church on doctrinal issues and even moral indiscretions. Advice is not enough. The Word of God is not an advisory manual. Members of the church are under obligation to uphold the Word of God.

The model church in Acts 15 describes a faithful church. The justification for the decision was not popular opinion or tyrannical lordship. The justification was not arrogance or pride. The model church described in Acts 15 made its decision to embrace one gospel based on rule by order and constitutional government. Faithless times and faithless people, whether in 50 A.D. or 2000 A. D. will always find a reason to excuse a false gospel and spurious salvation on the basis of the manifold church governments that allow and in some cases promote hypocrisy and schism.

Every Christian will one day come face to face with the decision: "Which church is the faithful church"? Every Christian ought to ask the question: "Are the apostolic principles for church government actually practiced in the local particular church"? The principles are simple, authentic, and biblical.

29. Continue Making Disciples

Acts 15:36-16:5

The apostle Paul left the council in Jerusalem with one intent and purpose. His purpose was to continue the mission God had given him to make disciples by teaching and preaching the whole counsel of God. The question of which gospel was the right gospel had been settled. There was no need to come back to Jerusalem in six months to listen to the opinion of a committee. The church court at Jerusalem spoke with full and final authority. The decision of the elders at Jerusalem preserved both the doctrine of the church and the unity of the church. I cannot stress enough the purpose of church government, because evangelical churches have been so deficient in explaining the relationship of the gospel to church government. The purpose of church government is to preserve the doctrine of our holy Constitution, the Bible. In so doing we preserve the unity of the church and in so doing we preserve the future of the visible church on earth.

With the doctrine of the gospel preserved, Paul and Barnabas went back to Anitoch of Syria and resumed teaching and preaching the gospel that was so dear to them. Making disciples was the mission so the brethren may be strengthened by many words (Acts 15:32). After a short period of time Paul urged Barnabas to continue the mission of making disciples. Paul's plan was for the both of them to return to the churches that they had visited prior to the Jerusalem council.

Then after some days Paul said to Barnabas, "Let us now go back and visit our brethren in every city where we have preached the Word of the Lord, and see how they are doing." Now Barnabas was determined to take with them John called Mark. But Paul insisted that they should not take with them the one who had departed from them in Pamphylia, and had not gone with them to the work. Then the contention became so sharp that they parted from one another. "And so Barnabas took Mark and sailed to Cyprus; but Paul chose Silas and departed, being commended by the brethren to the grace of God. And he went through Syria and Cilicia, strengthening the churches" (Acts 15:36-41).

Barnabas wanted to bring Mark with them on the mission, but Paul disagreed with Barnabas. This is a minor disagreement compared to the disagreement that Paul had with the Judizers who wanted to change the true gospel of Christ. Furthermore the disagreement with Barnabas was between two godly men who had suffered greatly together for the cause of the mission to make disciples. They were together almost to the point of death, yet they found themselves in sharp disagreement. There is no indication that they became angry towards each other. However, they could not reach a consensus relative to this conflict.

This is a perplexing aspect of Paul's life. Why did two godly men divide over what appears to be an insignificant issue? The only reason for Paul's insistence that Mark not return on the mission was Mark "departed from them in Pamphylia, and had not gone with them to the work" (Acts 15: 38).

The context begins with the church at Antioch sending Paul and Barnabas on a missionary journey. Mark accompanied them on the trip, however Mark abruptly returned to Jerusalem while Paul and Barnabas were in Asia Minor. There is no other mention of Mark until Paul and Barnabas had this sharp disagreement about whether to take Mark on the next missionary journey. The young man Mark comes from a family of committed disciples of Christ. For example, after Peter had been freed from prison he went to Mark's mother's home where they had gathered to pray (Acts 12:12). From the information available, Mark did not abandon the

Christian faith. He simply failed to continue with Paul and Barnabas on their first missionary journey.

Now on the second missionary journey, Paul did not trust Mark for the rigorous trip ahead. Barnabas did have confidence that Mark was ready to make the trip. Although Paul and Barnabas were godly men, they were sinners. Satan uses every opportunity to divide the people of God. Satan is a deceiver and deceit is the father of division.

Barnabas was Mark's cousin (Colossians 4:10) which may have influenced Barnabas. It would have been wrong if Barnabas made his decision strictly on the basis of his affections for Mark. If Mark came to them and admitted his fault and wanted to prove that they could depend on him then Barnabas had good reason to want Mark to go and Paul should have considered Mark's request.

However, there may have been good reason that Paul refused to allow Mark to join him on the second missionary journey. The Bible does not explain why Mark did not fulfill his commitment on the first missionary journey. Mark may have failed to remain faithful to his call to the ministry. When Christians make promises and commitments, there is a certain expectation. Paul could have yielded to the request of Barnabas, but experience had proven that Mark could not be trusted. From Paul's perspective, Mark had been an unfaithful servant in the first missionary. The Bible reveals that the church supported Paul's decision. The church had more information to make a godly decision. The brethren commended Paul. The brethren did not commend Barnabas. So for this reason we would naturally expect there was more to Mark's abrupt return from the first missionary journey. The elders at Antioch agreed with Paul's decision not to take Mark on the second missionary journey. Barnabas went to his hometown and took Mark with him.

Later Mark did prove to be reliable. It takes time to prove one's trustworthiness. A private in the Army proves the ability to be a sergeant. A lieutenant proves his ability to be a general. A student proves his ability to become a teacher. A Christian must show evidence that his or her words are truthful and actions are faithful. Paul was considerate and loving enough to let Mark prove his faithfulness. Mark was given the opportunity to prove his faithfulness and he did prove to be faithful. In Paul's letter to Timothy, Paul wanted Timothy to bring Mark with him to Rome. Faithful men called to the ministry need time to mature. The honor of Jesus Christ rests in the balance. Paul had good reasons for his distrust and Barnabas had good reasons for his trust in the young disciple named Mark.

Paul returned to Derbe and Lystra. Someone had been faithful in making a disciple of a young man named Timothy. The Bible indicates that Paul wanted Timothy to go with him so he took Timothy and circumcised him because the Jews in that region knew he was the son of a Greek father, therefore Timothy was an uncircumcised young man.

It may seem strange that Paul stopped his missionary journey to debate the necessity of circumcision for the salvation of God's elect and then almost immediately have Timothy circumcised for the sake of the gospel. Although the elders in Jerusalem had determined that circumcision was not necessary for salvation, he knew that the Jews would show no respect for young Timothy. As a young man, he would need every advantage.

Paul took young Timothy, a new convert to Christianity, under his care after he had refused to bring young Mark with him on the second missionary journey. Paul's purpose was to be a spiritual father to the young Timothy, something that Mark retreated from in his youth thus making Mark ill equipped for the ministry.

Timothy was faithful and Paul gave him the opportunity to prove himself a faithful servant of Christ. Paul's wisdom and discernment proved to be an advantage for the whole church. Later in Paul's ministry he wrote a letter to the Philippian church explaining Timothy's ministry to the church.

> But I trust in the Lord Jesus to send Timothy to you shortly, that I also may be encouraged when I know your state. For I have no one like-minded, who will sincerely care for your state. For all seek their own, not the things which are of Christ Jesus. But you know his proven character, that as a son with his father he served with me in the gospel. (Philippians 2:19-22)

Timothy was faithful and determined to make disciples. He was concerned for other people. He worked well with other people. The interest of Jesus Christ was central to his life and ministry. Timothy was a man that could be trusted. He was not the kind of person that would retreat during the heat of the battle.

Although the Bible warns against dissensions, God in His providence concurrently used the dissension between Paul and Barnabas for the advancement of the kingdom of God on earth and the glory of God. The church must continue making disciples. Therefore, she must make every effort to restore and practice sound church government for the preservation of the gospel. At the same time Christians must remember that they will not agree on every practical matter. Barnabas put the disagreement behind him and continued to make disciples. Paul put the disagreement behind him and continued to make disciples. The mission of the church: Continue making disciples!

30. The Church in the Culture

Acts 16:6-40

The first thirty years of the New Testament church laid the foundation for the purpose, mission, and ministry of the church. The purpose of the church for every generation is worship. The mission of the church is to make disciples and teach the whole counsel of God. The ministry of the church is to equip the saints to serve in the kingdom of God. This brief exposition has already covered the first twenty years of the young church. Paul's second missionary journey began around A.D. 50. The next ten years established the application of the mission and ministry for the future church. The New Testament church will identify itself in the kingdom of God and express itself to the culture.

The church is part of the kingdom of God. The kingdom of God as it relates to the created order also includes the culture in which we live. The kingdom concept is not exclusive; it is inclusive. The kingdom of God includes the church and the culture. The cultural concept designates a way of life. Christians tend to go in one of two directions with the cultural concept. They tend to blame the culture for all evil or glorify the culture. Culture is an expression of the worth of a society. The culture represents the customs and the institutions of a social group expressed by art, science, and religion or any other valuable discipline associated with a particular social group.

The culture and the church will be in conflict until the mission of the church is complete. Making disciples is the responsibility of the church after the Holy Spirit changes the heart. To put it another way, the Holy Spirit reforms the soul of sinner, so he or she is enabled to believe the gospel. With a new mind and a new determination to follow the Lord, a child of the kingdom will desire reformation of the culture.

Christian reformation means improve or change what is wrong, corrupt and unsatisfactory in the church. Reformation means Christians will seek to understand the Word of God. Reformation means Christian conduct themselves according to the Word of God. The basis and essence for reformation is found in God's commandment to subdue the earth (Genesis 1:28). The fall destroyed the essence of human dignity and the authority and power to rule over creation. Therefore, personal and cultural reformation is necessary.

Jesus explains the cultural mandate in terms we can understand: "Father as you have sent me into the world I also have sent them into the world" (John 17:18). The cultural mandate in this sinful world encompasses evangelism, making disciples and stewardship or any number of disciplines that are considered necessary to accomplish the mission.

Paul's mission to make disciples and teach the full counsel of God is in principle the mission of every Christian. Paul's second missionary journey took him into places that were culturally diverse. Paul traveled over a large area in Asia Minor and Southern Europe. It is impossible to determine every contact and what effect his ministry had on that region of the world. The Bible reveals glimpses of his travel and in some cases sufficient detail to determine his activity as it concerns the spread of the gospel. He started his second missionary journey by traveling through Galatia which is modern day Turkey and then on to Macedonia which is modern day Greece (Acts 16:6-10).

He arrived at Philippi. The cultural milieu at Philippi was a mixture of Asians, Greeks, and Romans. The culture had a philosophy of life about the arts, science, and religion, but they did not acknowledge the true and living God. This was the setting which the apostle Paul began to make disciples at Philippi. Paul started with the available resources. There were no auditoriums or buildings available. Paul's method for making disciples was God-centered. Paul depended on God's providence to lead him to the right place and the right people. He did not spend money on extensive demographic studies to determine the need for making disciples. Philippi did not have a Jewish synagogue. Jewish law required ten males with their families to form a synagogue. Therefore, on the day for worship, Paul looked for a place of prayer and found it down by the river "where prayer was customarily made" (Acts 16;13). There were only a few women and Paul spoke to them.

> Now a certain woman named Lydia heard us. She was a seller of purple from the city of Thyatira, who worshiped God. The Lord opened her heart to heed the things spoken by Paul. And when she and her household were baptized, she begged us, saying, "If you have judged me to be faithful to the Lord, come to my house and stay." So she persuaded us. (Acts 16:14-15)

The mighty work of God is necessary to make disciples. It was not the gospel message that changed the heart of Lydia. The Bible reveals the supernatural work of the Holy Spirit which is, "the Lord opened her heart" (Acts 16:14). Before the Lord opened her heart, she had a closed heart. The action, represented by the word "opened", is something that happened to her. The change of heart was necessary for the message of the gospel to break through to Lydia's soul. Lydia's new mind, will, and affections made the gospel message a delight to every part of her being. She became a disciple of Christ because the Holy Spirit enabled her.

A positive response to the Gospel is contingent upon the mighty work of God. Sometimes there are negative responses to the gospel (Acts 7:59; 13:50;14:2). Then other times there are positive responses like we find with Lydia. She had been praying which indicates she was seeking God. Although she was not a Jew, she worshipped God. She listened to the truth from God's messenger. She not only listened, she was not argumentative and received the sign of the covenant between her and God, the sacrament of baptism (Acts 16:15). The mighty work of God comes from God not man. Making disciples and teaching the full counsel of God is the responsibility of the church. Satan will try to stop Christians from making disciples. While Paul was in Philippi, Satan used an unbelieving Gentile to obstruct Paul from making disciples.

> Now it happened, as we went to prayer, that a certain slave girl possessed with a spirit of divination met us, who brought her masters much profit by fortune-telling. This girl followed Paul and us, and cried out, saying, "These men are the servants of the Most High God, who proclaim to us the way of salvation." And this she did for many days. But Paul, greatly annoyed, turned and said to the spirit, "I command you in the name of Jesus Christ to come out of her." And he came out that very hour. But when her masters saw that their hope of profit was gone, they seized Paul and Silas and dragged them into the marketplace to the authorities. (Acts 16:16-19)

Those who are hostile to Christ will oppose the mission of the church. Even those who profess a covenant relationship with God may work against the mission of the church (Acts 4:1-3). Jewish religious leaders were greatly disturbed because the apostles were teaching the people and proclaiming the resurrection of the dead. The leadership in the Old Testament church at that time was evil and corrupt.

Sinful cultures hate the kingdom of God. A culture without Christ thrives on greed; Material wealth and possessions becomes their god. A culture without Christ lives for self-interest and immediate gratification. The voice of a culture without Christ is "I want what I want, and I want it now."

The culture at Philippi needed a change of heart so they could understand the message of the gospel. Unfortunately, the Philippians saw Paul as a religious fanatic. They thought Paul wanted to restrict business and commerce. The changing culture in the United States believes Christians want to restrict commerce if Christians oppose abortion.

Paul saw three converts as a result of his faithfulness to make disciples. First was Lydia, an Asian woman. The Greek slave girl delivered of a demon by the power of God, it is presumed she became a believer. The third convert was the Philippian jailer.

The Bible does not say how many became disciples of Christ, but Luke used the word "brethren" to describe the church at Philippi (Acts 16:40). God adds to His church daily. Then the church instructs them in His word. When God blesses His church with new converts, Christians must be ready to make disciples. Reformation in the church will have an influence on reformation in the culture.

31. Study the Bible

Thessalonica was the next stop on Paul's second missionary journey. Thessalonica was a major seaport city in Greece. There was a synagogue at Thessalonica so Paul first went to the Jews, and then to the Gentiles. Although the Jews persecuted him, Paul knew they had the Word of God. Paul knew that the Jews were looking for the Messiah. They read the law and the prophets, but misunderstood them. They were willing to listen to the apostle because they had the Word of God.

Paul reasoned with them (Acts 17:2). Paul presented an argument that required evidence. Paul's technique is not uncommon. In order to prove something, arguments are necessary. Paul's argument was that Christ had to suffer and rise again from the dead. Ultimately that would mean Christ was the Messiah. The Jews had anticipated the coming of the Messiah for many centuries. The Jews did not need to be convinced God was the redeemer of His people. They needed to hear the Redeemer had already appeared in the flesh. Paul explained the Scriptures (Acts 17:3). The word "explained" literally means to "open up". Paul opened the Word of God so it might be evident that Jesus Christ was the Savior of His people. Paul's explanation was "that the Christ had to suffer and rise again from the dead, and saying, 'This Jesus whom I preach to you is the Christ'" (Acts 17:3). The technique Paul used is not complicated and the content is not difficult to apprehend and believe.

Christ had to suffer
Christ had to rise again from the dead;

Therefore, the Christ I preach is the promised Messiah.

Paul gave them reasons to explain why Christ had to suffer. God pours His wrath and judgment on sinful men and the only hope is the forgiveness for the guilt of the sin of Adam; and all the particular sins that result from the sinful nature. Christ had to suffer because of the sin of Adam, commonly known as "the inherited guilt" and the sins of all men as a result of sin nature. Christ suffered the miserable death of a criminal for the sake of those whom God has called to himself.

Obviously a dead man is not a savior. After suffering for the sins of men and women and offering a perfect sacrifice to God, Christ was resurrected from the dead because sinful men must have a living Mediator. The one factor that sets Christianity apart from any other world religion is the bodily resurrection of Jesus Christ. Most Christians have heard the gospel story so many times that the resurrection becomes nothing more than a tidbit of information. If Christians expect to make disciples, they must put the resurrection of Christ as the single most important feature of our argument and explanation. Furthermore, their argument and explanation of the resurrection must rest upon the Word of God.

Only some of the Jews were persuaded. Others were not persuaded. God seeking Greeks were persuaded in a much larger number. The English Bible also says that some leading women joined Paul. Another possible translation is "wives of prominent men" (Acts 17:4).

The new disciples needed instruction from the full counsel of God. Teaching the Bible is necessary to make disciples. When the Bible says they "joined Paul and Silas" the word joined connotes an assignment by voluntary association. It would be like a man joining the Army and looking to a superior for guidance and direction (Acts 17:4).

The new disciples wanted someone to teach them the Word of God to confirm their faith. Those who were persuaded to follow Christ recognized the need to elevate to the place that they too could make disciples. However, Paul did not have the power to persuade them to believe without the work of the Holy Spirit first giving them the ability to believe Paul's explanation of Scripture.

Although many were persuaded, there were those who were not persuaded. Unbelievers do not like the threat of condemnation, which is the preface to any teaching of God's grace. The unbelieving Jews at Thessalonica were confronted with their sin and ultimately God's wrath and condemnation. The thought of God's displeasure is not a pleasant thought.

The unbelieving Jews were envious. They wanted Paul discharged from his missionary enterprise. When they realized they could not stand against the evidence that Paul had so masterfully articulated, they sought to destroy him. The unbelieving Jews instigated and conspired to start a riot because their argument against the gospel failed.

Why did the unbelieving Jews go to the civil magistrate? Did they not bring their own religious laws into disrepute? When wicked men set their minds on devilish plans, they take no pains to meet their goal. It is strange that Paul preached the gospel of peace, but it provoked people to fight one another.

Those unbelieving Jews were angry, because their religious belief system was falling apart. So much so that when they could not find Paul and Silas, they went after Jason. Apparently, Jason had hosted Paul and Silas, so the unbelieving Jews declared Jason guilty by association.

The lies of those unbelieving Jews is the norm for unbelievers. Their only tool is the one given to them by their master, Satan himself. Deceit is Satan's tool and all his followers must apply for the same tool, because they are left without any argument against the gospel. Christians must not be discouraged when they are slandered and mistreated for the sake of the gospel.

Christians should take comfort when they treat their profession of faith with integrity. Christians may earn the same name that Paul earned. He was charged with turning the world upside down. Paul did not turn the world upside down. Making disciples and teaching the full counsel of God does not turn the world upside down, but rather it turns the world right side up. It is the lies of Satan that turn the world upside down.

The unbelieving Jews troubled the crowd and the rulers of the city by means of deceit. The unbelieving Jews incited a state of confusion. If there is any such thing as turning the world upside down, it is a state of confusion. An upside down world describes the present condition of the United States at the beginning of the 21st century. Furthermore, the church is in a state of confusion, thus the church may be said to be upside down. If Christians have courage to make disciples and the same Christians are charged with turning the world upside down, the truth is that upside down is right side up.

Paul's preaching caused an uproar at Thessalonica, but the Lord had plans for Paul to continue making disciples.

> Then the brethren immediately sent Paul and Silas away by night to Berea. When they arrived, they went into the synagogue of the Jews. These were more fair-minded than those in Thessalonica, in that they received the word with all readiness, and searched the Scriptures daily to find out whether these things were so. Therefore many of them believed, and also not a few of the Greeks, prominent women as well as men. (Acts 17:10-12)

The Bible says the people at Berea were more fair-minded. Literally the words "fair-minded" are derived from two Greek words translated "well born." Translated without any context it refers to people of more noble character by virtue of birth. Noble men are mentioned in Scripture several places (Luke 19:12; 1 Corinthians 1:26). It is not likely that Luke intended to say that men are more virtuous because they were born of rich or aristocratic parents. There are recorded occasions in the late Greek and early Roman Empire when the legal adoption of a son was being executed by law and stipulations were made that prohibited the adopted son from being sold into slavery. For instance in one secular Greek manuscript it was said that a son was "well born and of free parents." Apparently being of noble birth gave the person certain advantages. Being of noble birth probably afforded a better education, a better sense of tolerance and sense of confidence in intelligent communication. Does the noble-minded man have an advantage over others in a less privileged place in society? Yes, because generational continuity is the mark of a society. A generation of God seekers will very likely produce another generation of God seekers. Perhaps that is the case of the Bereans. Although all the details are not known, the Bereans were more willing to learn and investigate Paul's gospel message.

The Bible says they received the Word with all readiness. The Bereans were willing to listen. They were not looking for a way to criticize and condemn; they wanted to know the truth. They did not have preconceived notions about Paul's message. They were not afraid of what they might hear. They were not puffed up with pride. Proud men are disinclined to listen to the Word of God, because it speaks to the heart. The Bible does not use unpretentious language therefore its effect is profoundly convicting. If the Bereans received the Word of God with a diligent eagerness to learn from the Word of God, how much more should Christians be confirmed in the faith by searching the Scriptures.

The Bereans searched to see if Paul's message is true. The Bereans searched the Bible, the only Bible they had which was the Old Testament. They searched to determine if the testimony of Scripture proved Paul's doctrine. Many of the Bereans found it to be true, because many of them believed, both Jews and Greeks. The Holy Spirit enabled them to believe and they were persuaded by Scripture. They examined the Scriptures daily to discover the full counsel of God. They searched the Scriptures to understand the nature and character of God. They would want to know if God was a spiritual being or if He possessed material substance. They would want to know if God was independent of creation or did he cause himself to come into being. They would want to know if God had any limits, thus did God have a beginning and would He have an end. They would want to know if God was changeable. They wanted to know who God is and what God does.

They would want to know about man. How did man come into existence and what is man's final destiny? If it was possible for man to be in a favorable relationship with God, then certainly they would want to know how to live in the world that God had placed them. The full counsel of God answers all those questions and many other questions concerning faith and life.

Christians should search the Scriptures daily even though they may find something in the Bible that may seem to be unpalatable. It may even seem mysterious at some points to some degree.

In 1976 Dr. Harold Lindsell wrote a book titled, The *Battle for the Bible* that rocked the evangelical world. Dr. Lindsell said the "battle rages, not among those in the liberal tradition where the issue is already settled, but among those who profess to be evangelicals." The issue was the infallibility and the inerrancy of Scripture. The assault has been and remains vigorous against the Bible, not so much as a body of literature, but as the final authority to speak to every aspect of faith and life. Through the centuries, the Bible has been the objective standard for evangelical churches. The Bible was the foundation upon which the famous orthodox creeds, confessions and catechisms came to be the summary of the only infallible rule of faith and practice.

32. Defender of the Faith

Acts 17:16-34

Paul continued his ministry of making disciples in the city of Athens. Paul entered a new cultural milieu. Athens was a place of notable recognition as early as the 5th century B. C. The Greeks defeated the Persian army thus making Athens a great city. Athens became a center for literature, art, science and philosophy. Socrates and Plato were at home in Athens. It was the home of Grecian drama and the place that historians spoke about the future of Greece. Athens was known for its acute and probing interest in the human mind, laws of thought and demonstrations of rhetoric unparalleled in that world. Even though hundreds of years had passed from the golden era at Athens, it was still the intellectual center for that part of the world.

Paul went to the synagogue and reasoned with Jews and Gentile worshipers (Acts 17:17). It was in Athens that Paul went to the market place. The market place was the center of public activity. It was at the market place that Socrates spoke about immortal questions. People went to the market place to discuss subjects of interest or to hear the latest news. Paul went to the market place to discuss the Christian religion with the philosophers.

The Athenian culture had different views on how to make sense out of life. The two prominent schools of philosophy that remained at Athens were the Epicureans and Stoics.

The Epicureans taught that the goal of life was to attain the greatest pleasure with the least amount of pain. Without mentioning any of the technicalities of that worldview, we live among Epicureans today. The North American culture has a worldview that makes pleasure the great good in life. Avoid pain at all costs. The focus is "let me do what pleases me with the least discomfort." Materialism is the present day Epicurean worldview, along with its cousin, consumerism.

The other prominent school at Athens during Paul's visit was the stoic school of philosophy. Basically it taught that life consisted of good and evil. This worldview relies on chance. They may say, "make the best of whatever happens." Chance is the present day Stoic worldview. The Roman Emperor, Marcus Aurelius was influenced by the Stoics. He believed the Romans must be willing to endure the hardships of life for the sake of the Roman Empire.

Luke indicates that Paul addressed the Areopagus (Acts 17:19-22). The reference to the Areopagus was probably the rulers of the city who were responsible to oversee religious discussions. In Paul's opening remarks he said, "Men of Athens, I perceive that in all things you are very religious" (Acts 17:22). Paul quickly shifted the discussion from religion to theology. Paul was a defender of the faith. He began his speech with apologetics.

Paul was successful in bringing the full counsel of God into his sermon (Acts 17:22-32). Paul began with the nature and essence of God's character, then he explained the nature of the human condition before God, and finally the resurrection.

Paul probed deeply for the benefit of those who were looking for something more than a sensation. Paul could not say much about the Epicurean philosophy because it requires endless diversions to survive the constant changes of life.

It is more likely that Paul's sermon was primarily directed toward the Stoic philosophers. The Stoics were students of Zeno of Cyprus. The stoic name was derived from the Greek word *stoa* which referred to the place that Zeno gathered his students. They would sit with him on a porch to study. They believed that god was reason itself.

Therefore, man was expected to exercise his rational faculties to live in harmony with creation. However, the Stoics realized that the best exercise of reason was merely survival, therefore they taught a form of fatalism that taught a person had to take the bad with the good. Stoic philosophy attempted to find something to unify the diversity in the world.

Paul's answer was "that they should seek the Lord in the hope that they might grope for Him and find Him, though He is not far from each one of us" (Acts 17:26). The word "grope" has an interesting history in the Greek language. The English word "grope" is derived from the Greek word *pselaphao*. The same Greek word is translated "touch" in Luke's gospel. Jesus told those who doubted, "See My hands and My feet, that it is I Myself; touch Me and see, for a spirit does not have flesh and bones as you see that I have" (Luke 24:39). The Greek word *pselaphao* was derived from the Greek word *psallo* translated "making melody." When music is in harmony is has a unique effect. It brings unity from diversity. The unique experience of finding God and touching Him, figuratively speaking, brings unity to a confused soul. A touch or a glimpse of God is only possible if the church teaches the whole counsel of God. The Bereans endeavored to touch God by searching the Scriptures daily (Acts 17:11). I wonder how many people today believe that they have risen above Stoic philosophy?

If the first agenda of the church begins with social programs, political activities and behavioral modifications, the sinfulness of diversity will overcome the desire to seek the Lord. If the church begins with a proper understanding of God and teaches the whole counsel of God, then making disciples will glorify God.

Even though people are scattered over the face of the earth, and even though there are great differences among the cultures of the world, in due time, they should seek God. It is not our duty to play God. As Paul explains, it is God that appoints times and boundaries. The apostle John said, "The wind blows where it wishes and you hear the sound of it, but do not know where it came from and where it is going; so everyone who is born of the Spirit" (John 3:8). The presence of God is essential to his nature and character.

Most people have some sense of God's presence. The Psalmist explains God's presence in the simplest of terms.

> Where can I go from Your Spirit? Or where can I flee from Your presence? If I ascend into heaven, You are there; If I make my bed in hell, behold You are there; If I take the wings of the morning, And dwell in the uttermost parts of the sea, Even there Your hand shall lead me. (Psalm 139:7-10)

The presence of God is real, now and in the future. It is not possible to escape God's presence on earth, in heaven, or in hell. However, understanding God's presence is difficult when people rely on their limited human sense experience. The connection between God's presence is contingent upon our understanding of our existence. Specifically, the Word of God declares, "for in Him we live and move and have our being" (Acts 17:28). Humans are not miniature models of God. God is independent. All creation is dependent on Him for everything. God gives life and existence by His Spirit. The basis for understanding the presence of God is our understanding that we are totally dependent upon God for our mere existence.

The Stoics were well aware of Paul's triad expression of existence. Life, movement, and existence are the normal patterns of humanity. Sometimes Christians take those patterns for granted, as if they had the power of life, movement and existence apart from God. God created the world, God sustains the world, and governs the world and everything in it. Absolute and ultimate dependence on God is enough to bring Christians to their knees in humility.

Humans are not able to save themselves in any sense of the word. They cannot save their bodies and they cannot save their souls. Since man cannot save himself, God commands all men to repent (Acts 17:30). Tear down the altars of all known and unknown gods and turn to the true and living God for salvation.

Unfortunately, the disdain for serious inquiry into the nature of God is common among professing evangelical Christians. Evangelicals have turned to "let's just have faith." The propensity among Christians in the postmodern world is to believe something without evidence. The biblical model for defending the faith is the way to overcome the faithism of the modern church.

The Athenians pursued philosophy to understand life. Some people pursue the study and practice of religion to understand life. Paul addressed the Stoics and Epicureans with the truth of life, judgment, and resurrection of the body. The concept of life may be understood from three biblical perspectives. The first perspective is the secular life of the unbeliever. It is a life of darkness, an estranged life without fellowship with God. The secular life of the unbeliever is a life under the tyranny of Satan. The secular life of the unbeliever leaves one with a sense of hopelessness and the threat of judgment. The next perspective is the secular life of the believer. It is a life of light with an intimate fellowship with God. The secular life of the believer is not free of sin, but sin does not rule over the believer. The secular life of the believer places all confidence for the power of life, movement and existence in the hands of almighty God. The final perspective of life described in the Bible is eternal life or life everlasting. To put it another way, life is not mere existence.

The Satanic view of life is self preservation. In Job 2:4 Satan said, "Skin for skin! Yes, all that a man has he will give for his life." If Christians do not understand the meaning of life, they too will fall into the trap of self preservation. The person who has a right standing with God will live forever in a favorable relationship with God. The person who does not have a right standing with God will exist forever, but under the hand of God's divine justice. Daniel explains the good and the bad. "And many of those who sleep in the dust of the earth shall awake, some to everlasting life, some to shame and everlasting contempt" (Daniel 12:2). There is an everlasting life for the believer and everlasting life for the unbeliever.

To exist under the mighty wrath of God and endure the eternal punishment is that portion the Word of God describes as everlasting contempt. Daniel's prophecy is an awesome truth found throughout Scripture. If we put eternal life in a right perspective it will help us put secular life in a proper perspective.

The postmodern scholar may try to explain life through scientific inquiry, but he cannot explain judgment. Christians can explain the final judgment, because they understand life. Paul warned of the coming judgment in the sermon to the Athenians. God has "appointed a day on which He will judge the world in righteousness by the Man whom He has ordained" (Acts 17:31).

Paul crafted his words carefully. He knew the Athenian Stoic philosophers would dismiss the final judgment as mythological. However, they would not and did not dismiss the idea of the resurrection, because then the judgment becomes an eternal matter. The final judgment has eternal consequences and Christians have every reason to warn unbelievers about the final judgment.

Rational creatures will not escape the final judgment in this life or in the life to come. (See Psalm 50:4; Romans 2;16, Hebrew 9:27; Hebrews 10:30). Since the Bible speaks so abundantly about the final judgment, Christians ought to work hard to understand this doctrine. John describes the final judgment in the book of Revelation.

> And I saw the dead, small and great, standing before God, and books were opened. And another book was opened, which is the Book of Life. And the dead were judged according to their works, by the things which were written in the books. The sea gave up the dead who were in it, and Death and Hades delivered up the dead who were in them. And they were judged, each one according to his works. (Revelation 20:12-13)

During the final judgment, the book of life will be opened. It is difficult to understand the extent of this symbolism, but one thing is certain; the book of life is an absolute standard. The pure truth will be revealed from the book of life. The judgment will determine the legal standing of the professing Christian with God. It will measure the moral constitution of every person. The evidence in Scripture is powerfully persuasive that Christians will stand before the all-powerful divine Judge of heaven and earth.

The question is not who stands before the judgment seat, but what happens at the judgment seat. First, the unbeliever stands condemned in the judgment. Then those who were justified by faith in Jesus Christ are forgiven. Although Christians will stand before the judgment seat, they will not find condemnation or eternal punishment. To put it another way the unbeliever will receive the negative element of the final judgment, but the Christian will receive the positive element. The works of the Christian will be tested. If those good works are found to be in Christ, they are approved and accepted by the Judge who is Christ Himself. Another positive effect of the judgment seat of Christ is that it is the place God's children are given rewards for doing good. The Bible does not give the specific details about the rewards, because if we are indeed Christians, we seek not the high place, but rather we seek the faithful place.

Paul connects the final judgment to the resurrection. It is the resurrection, which leads to eternal existence and the life to come. One of the promises associated with our salvation is the resurrection of the dead. Like the judgment, resurrection is for all people, but the resurrection will have a different meaning for believers than it will for unbelievers.

> Do not marvel at this; for the hour is coming in which all who are in the graves will hear His voice and shall come forth; those who did the good deeds to a resurrection of life, those who committed the evil deeds to a resurrection of judgment. (John 5:28-29)

For Christians the resurrection and final judgment opens the door to our eternal home with God the Father, God the Son, and God the Holy Spirit. Greek philosophy and religion did not believe that the dead would ever stand up again. They did not believe in the resurrection.

At the end of Paul's sermon some of the Greeks mocked him, but others believed in the final judgment and the resurrection. Why did some of the Athenians believe? They believed because God is sovereign and those whom He called repented, trusted Christ, and became disciples of Christ. The consequences for not repenting and trusting Christ is the final judgment and eternal condemnation. Instead the inspired example is that Paul asserted the truth about Jesus and the resurrection. The doctrine of the resurrection will always provoke questions. For that reason Christians must be ready to defend the faith.

33. Courage in a Corrupt Culture

Acts 18:1-17

Paul's passion was to make disciples regardless of what he had to do or where he had to go. Paul moved from one city and culture to another. He was deliberately determined to fill his life with the mission that Jesus Christ had given him. Courage was a mark of his determination. The biblical principles for making disciples are the same for every generation. However, it takes courage to make disciples in a corrupt culture.

The Corinthian culture has similarities to the modern western culture. To better understand Paul's mission, Christians should try to get a glimpse of what it was like to live in Corinth. Paul left Athens, the literary and cultural center and went to Corinth, the commercial capital of that part of the world. Corinth was depopulated several times before the coming of Christ because of earthquakes and war. Julius Caesar rebuilt the city in 46 B. C. and it was repopulated with freed men from Italy, Jews, and other Orientals thus making it a cosmopolitan city. Corinth was a city of wealth and prosperity during the time of the Roman Empire. It was one of the favorite cities of the Roman Emperors. It had a population of about 200 thousand free men and about 500 thousand slaves. (See *The Zondervan Pictorial Encyclopedia of the Bible*, vol. 1, p. 960-964 for more on the city of Corinth).

The wealth and the prominence of the city made it notoriously wicked. Luxury and immorality probably best describes the city. It was a multi-cultural city with a variety of worldviews. Corinth was a commercial city bringing with it all the advantages and disadvantages of wealth. Corinth was a religious city since it was the center for the cult of love known as the goddess Aphrodite. The temple of Aphrodite was the home of a large number of temple prostitutes. The result was that corruption became synonymous with the city of Corinth. It would be similar to any major city in the United States.

Even though there was a dim picture of the ethical atmosphere in Corinth, there was a witness of absolute ethics by the existence of a Jewish Synagogue. The Jewish Synagogue gave the apostle Paul a platform to take the gospel to these wicked cities in the Roman Empire. Unfortunately many of the Jews did not find any relevance for the gospel of Christ. To them Christ was simply not the Messiah they expected.

Modern man, unable to make any tangible contact with the Corinthian culture, is able to conceive slightly of the social, economic, political, and religious landscape. Furthermore, that conception should help Christians understand their roles and responsibilities to take the gospel into every city and culture.

Christians today face the same struggles, the same handicaps, and the same adversities, in principle, as those of the apostle Paul. Unfortunately, some who believed and called upon the Lord God omnipotent rejected the full counsel of God. The religious Jews despised the gospel of God's grace. The atheists rejected Paul's teaching. The religious Jews and the atheists joined hands to persecute a godly and faithful servant of God.

Yet in all the persecution, in all the emotional and physical taxation of his soul, Paul continued to be faithful. The political powers of Rome were no match for God's servant. The raging materialism did not stop Paul. The dysfunctional culture of the Mediterranean basin did not stop Paul. The courageous Paul put his mission above the desire to be happy.

For those reasons, Paul could write the Corinthian Church and say, "Blessed be the God and Father of our Lord Jesus Christ, the Father of mercies and God of all comfort" (2 Corinthians 1:3). Corinth was a wicked place, but Paul found great confidence in his relationship with God. Paul's certainty was that "having been justified by faith, we have peace with God through our Lord Jesus Christ" (Romans 5:1). With absolute certainty Paul said, "There is therefore now no condemnation to those who are in Christ Jesus" (Romans 8:1). The wickedness in this world will not prevail over the church. God's commandments and promises do not change because a culture finds them unpalatable. The Word of God belongs to those who are in Jesus Christ throughout human history and every culture in the world.

The evil one uses persecution and intimidation to curtail the mission of the church. However, God's promise of divine protection accompanied God's commandment to make disciples. "Now the Lord spoke to Paul in the night by a vision, 'Do not be afraid, but speak, and do not keep silent; for I am with you, and no one will attack you to hurt you; for I have many people in this city'" (Acts 18:9-10). The Lord gave Paul three commandments with three corresponding promises.

The first commandment was "Do not be afraid." It is necessary to clarify the language found in the English Bible. The translation is a good translation, but in Greek grammar there are grammatical forms to express negatives. One negative expression is "do not begin to do something" and the other is "stop doing what you've been doing." The Lord knew Paul's heart so the Lord removed Paul's fear with the injunction, "stop being afraid." Fear implies doubt, diminishes faith, and robs the mind of its rational ability. Fear immobilizes courage.

Sin is the father of fear. Paul was a sinner as all Christians are sinners, so the Lord gave sinful believers a promise. The Lord said, "I am with you." The Lord said to Issac, "I will be with you" (Genesis 26:3). The Lord said to Joshua, "as I was with Moses, so I will be with you" (Joshua 1:5). Some of the last words spoken by the Lord Jesus Christ are "lo, I am with you always, even to the end of the age" (Matthew 28:20).

The Lord also commanded Paul to keep on speaking (Acts 18:9). Fear will often keep people from speaking. Speech is necessary to make disciples and to teach the full counsel of God. The power to speak the truth is non-negotiable for the mission of the church. As the church enters the twenty-first century, western civilization has an all-encompassing truth crisis. The relativity of truth never entered the scene in the western world until the 18th century. Two centuries later the question is no longer "Is it true?" but "whose truth is it?" Truth now belongs to that power that stands to gain the most in the game of truth. Christians will continue to speak the truth. Paul was faithful to speak the truth in spite of the consequences. While Paul was in prison he wrote the church at Ephesus, "I am an ambassador in chains; that in it I may speak boldly, as I ought to speak" (Ephesians 6:20).

The corresponding promise to keep on speaking is "no one will attack you to hurt you" (Acts 18:10). Paul needed encouragement after the physical abuse he experienced on previous occasions. Paul continued making disciples and teaching the whole counsel of God for a year and a half in Corinth without any restraint or abuse (Acts 18:11).

God's protection for Paul is particularly interesting in light of current trends in this country when there is so much discussion over the relationship of church to state. The Jews did try to attack Paul at Corinth. The Jewish representative of the Old Testament church turned against Paul and brought him into the secular court. Lucius Gallio, the civil governor, heard the ambiguous charge brought against the apostle Paul.

He heard the case and concluded it was a religious matter. It is clear that Gallio interpreted Roman law so that the government respected the religious customs of the people. Paul had not broken any Roman laws and the state had no right to interfere with spiritual matters, except to maintain peace. Although Gallio did not protect Paul against the false charges of the Jews, he did not find it in his jurisdiction to interfere in controversial religious questions (Acts 18:15).

John Calvin and the Scottish seceders saw Galileo's decision as a disaster, while others see him as the wise magistrate establishing the doctrine the separation of church and state. This text is the seed for which future church fathers would establish a biblical understanding of the church/state relationship.

Paul was released unharmed. However, one of the Jews, Sosthenes, was beaten at the hands of the religious leaders. The Lord used the state to protect Paul from any harm. The Lord Jesus kept his promise, as He always has and will continue throughout eternity.

The third commandment is "do not become silent" (Acts 18:9). The Lord's corresponding promise was "I have many people in this city" (Acts 18:10). God had chosen many people to be His own, but someone had to tell them about God's amazing grace. Paul took his message from the Old Testament and applied it to the New Testament church.

> How then shall they call on Him in whom they have not believed? And how shall they believe in Him of whom they have not heard? And how shall they hear without a preacher? And how shall they preach unless they are sent? As it is written: "How beautiful are the feet of those who preach the gospel of peace, Who bring glad tidings of good things!" But they have not all obeyed the gospel. For Isaiah says, 'LORD, who has believed our report?' So then faith comes by

hearing, and hearing by the word of God." (Romans 10:14-17)

God's people must not be silent, because they are the instruments to tell the good news of God's saving grace. Courage in a corrupt culture is a sign of a faithful disciple of Christ.

34. Unity of Doctrine and Practice

Acts 18:18 – 19:7

Paul was an itinerate missionary. His mission was to make disciples and organize particular churches. Although he stayed longer at some places, he moved from place to place making disciples.

Paul left Corinth and returned to cities and regions "Strengthening all the disciples" (Acts 18:23). This begins Paul's third visit to the churches and commonly referred to as the third missionary journey. Paul wanted to make sure the disciples were confirmed or fixed in the faith. The Word of God was the basis of their doctrine and their practice was empowered by the Holy Spirit.

There is a brief, but very important interlude recorded in the book of Acts that introduces Apollos, a fellow worker in the kingdom of God.

> Now a certain Jew named Apollos, born at Alexandria, an eloquent man and mighty in the Scriptures, came to Ephesus. This man had been instructed in the way of the Lord; and being fervent in spirit, he spoke and taught accurately the things of the Lord, though he knew only the baptism of John. So he began to speak boldly in the synagogue. When Aquila and Priscilla heard him, they took him aside and explained to him the way of God more accurately. And when he desired to cross to Achaia, the brethren wrote, exhorting the disciples to receive him; and when he arrived, he greatly helped those who had believed through grace; for he vigorously refuted the Jews publicly, showing from the Scriptures that Jesus is the Christ. (Acts 18:24-28)

Apollos was a gifted scholar and preacher who appears on the scene in Ephesus and later moved to Corinth. The Apostle Paul mentions him as a prominent minister to the Corinthians in his first letter to the Corinthians. Apollos was an Alexandrian Jew, a fact not to be taken lightly. Alexandria was known for its library and scholarly accomplishments. It was the city in which the Old Testament was translated into the Greek language from its native Hebrew and Aramaic. The great Jewish philosopher Philo called Alexandria his home. Without going into the details of Philo's contribution to the Judeo-Christian world of the first century, it is sufficient to say that he was well known by Jewish Rabbi's and the Christian fathers of the first three centuries.

The Word of God reveals gifts and abilities of Apollos. He was an "eloquent man." He was eloquent because of his command of words. An eloquent speaker is one who has a large treasure of words and their meanings and can use them properly. The word "eloquence" reinterpreted in the postmodern world means one is able to make words sound charming and sophisticated. Apollos had a thorough knowledge of Scriptures. Literally, the Greek text indicates he was exceedingly knowledgeable in the Scriptures, thus some translations have "mighty in Scripture." With his home in Alexandria, his great learning and understanding of Scripture, it is most likely that he would have studied with the best Old Testament Bible scholars of that day. Therefore, it is likely that Apollos studied the Old Testament with Philo.

Apollos was, "instructed in the way of the Lord." The way of the Lord is mentioned often in the Old Testament, but in the New Testament I find no mention except by John the Baptist. I take it that the way of the Lord was God's special revelation of Himself at any given point in redemptive history always looking ahead to the coming of the Messiah.

Apollos was fervent in spirit. He had conviction and whatever Apollos knew he was not afraid to express himself, because he was a man of principle. Assuming he had mastered the skills of logic and rhetoric, as any Alexandrian scholar would have, Apollos was the not the man to argue with about religion.

Apollos "taught accurately the things of the Lord, though he knew only the baptism of John" (Acts 18:25). Apollos understood the Holy Spirit in the Old Testament, but not the work of the Holy Spirit in the New Testament. For instance, Apollos may not have known about the teaching of Jesus on the Holy Spirit in John chapter three. When Apollos first arrived at Ephesus he "knew only the baptism of John."

When Paul returned to Ephesus he found some men who were baptized according to the Old Testament purification rituals. Apparently, Apollos was still thinking in terms of the Old Covenant. The baptism of John was under the Old Covenant. The baptism performed by John the Baptist was associated with the Old Testament act of ceremonial purification. There were various baptisms in the Old Testament associated with the Levitical laws.

The book of Hebrews mentions various baptisms or as some English translations refer to washings in the context of the Old Testament sanctuary and services (Hebrews 9:10). A careful study of the book of Hebrews and the book of Leviticus will reveal the various baptisms that were part of the Old Testament worship rituals and consecration of priests and kings. John the Baptist anticipated the new covenant and possibly realized that his ministry was part of the transition from the old to the new. To treat the Old Testament baptism of John the same as the New Testament covenant baptism is completely without merit. Apollos was intimately acquainted with John's baptisms, because he understood and knew all of the liturgies and implications of the Old Testament washings for purification and consecration. He taught accurately everything that he knew based on his understanding of the Old Testament. It is possible that when he first arrived at

Ephesus he may have been a disciple of John the Baptist or John's followers. The evidence from Scripture is not sufficient to say that Apollos was preaching the resurrected Christ when he first arrived to Ephesus.

Aquila and Priscilla meet Paul in Corinth and became close friends. They moved to Ephesus and heard Apollos preach. After they heard Apollos preach in the Synagogue they took him aside, very likely into their home and explained the gospel more accurately. Two laymen, probably not well educated, just average working people, were able to explain the finishing touches that Apollos needed to declare the death, burial, resurrection, and ascension of the Lord Jesus Christ. Apollos, Aquila and Priscilla became fellow workers in the early church. Aquila and Priscilla did not go to the preacher immediately after the sermon in the presence of the congregation and confront his doctrine. They explained the Word of God privately, so as not to cause a stir in the congregation. Aquila and Priscilla saw the lack of understanding in the ministry of Apollos and they explained the full counsel of God. Apollos was humble and received the instruction. Everyone, including the preacher, is subject to learn from other members in the body of Christ.

The church stood tall as the fellow workers in God's kingdom worked together rather than against each other. The doctrine of the church gathered people together so that the composite unity of the church was a witness of God's grace.

If individual Christians will humbly and diligently study the full counsel of God with grace and thankfulness, it will reveal the doctrine of composite unity. Christians must work together with the gifts and skills that God has given them so the church may experience composite unity.

The composition of the Protestant church has lost its once significant and distinctive place in western civilization. The Protestant church has squandered its inheritance. However, it is not beyond the scope of God's grace to revive her again. When the church is reformed by the full counsel of God's Word, revival will be the expression of that reformation. The individual parts of the collective church must cohere to the Word of God. Any coherence among sinful people must come from a single objective source. The only objective source for Christians is the Word of God. Truth is not by discovery of human perfection, for there is no such thing as human perfection among sinful human beings. Truth axioms in the Word of God are infallible. However, truth axioms are so despised that the prominent English Christian scholar and sociologist, Dr. Os Guinness said, "what remains in the West is a world of lies, hype, and spin." Dr. Guinness summarizes the state of western culture with the incisive observation that "truth is dead and knowledge is only power...To believe otherwise is seen to be naïve, obscurantist, or reactionary. Worse, it is to be morally blind to the dark impulses that poison the traditional distinctions between truth and falsehood, right and wrong, and character and image" (*Time for Truth*, by Os Guinness, p. 13). Unfortunately, professing Christians have abandoned the truth axioms. The abandonment of truth means there is no composite unity in the church.

It is common for the people of God assembled under the name of Jesus Christ to find fragmentation comfortable and composite unity repulsive. The mission of modern church is to make disciples that are committed to unity of doctrine and practice.

35. Universal Nature of Christ

Acts 19:8 – 20

Although Paul found disciples in Ephesus, they had not heard the full counsel of God. The true disciples of Christ belonged to the church, but they were still influenced by the professing disciples of Christ.

> And he went into the synagogue and spoke boldly for three months, reasoning and persuading concerning the things of the kingdom of God. But when some were hardened and did not believe, but spoke evil of the Way before the multitude, he departed from them and withdrew the disciples, reasoning daily in the school of Tyrannus. And this continued for two years, so that all who dwelt in Asia heard the word of the Lord Jesus, both Jews and Greeks. (Acts 19:8-10)

The gospel of Christ was not limited to Jerusalem, Antioch, Perga, Galatia, or any other region that Paul had previously visited. Jews everywhere knew about the Messiah and thus the Christ. They may have misunderstood him, but they knew about Christ. Some of the Jews were looking for the Christ and they found him as Paul, "spoke out boldly for three months, reasoning and persuading them." Some of the Jews were not looking for Christ although they went to the synagogue each week. The knowledge of Messiah was universal among the Jews, but the application of the gospel was a sweet smell to some and a despicable smell to others.

The evangelical church in North America has compromised the full counsel of God to soothe the pain that unbelievers feel when they are confronted with the Word of God. Paul went to the existing synagogue to make disciples and teach the full counsel of God. Paul discussed the full counsel of God and tried to persuade the unbelievers to receive the Word of God. More specifically Paul tried to persuade them "concerning the things of the kingdom of God" (Acts 19:8). Like many religious professing Christians today, the unconverted Jews had little interest in the kingdom of God. Their interest was for the kingdom of this world. When Paul left the synagogue he took the disciples with him.

The evangelical church in North America at the beginning of the twenty first century has similar distinguishing marks as the Old Testament synagogue. The evangelical church is soaked with unbiblical tradition. Making disciples according to the doctrine of Scripture has been forgotten. Church growth is the passion of many churches. Making disciples ought to be the passion. The mission of making disciples begins the process of ministry to the disciples.

Paul's plan found in the inspired Word of God is normative and desired above the plans of sinful men devised by the standards of the world. Paul's plan for establishing a church consisted of three vital principles.

1) Leave the existing religious institution when it is obvious it cannot be reformed.
2) Rent a building or secure a place to meet without any unnecessary burden.
3) Teach the Word of God everyday.

Some of the ancient manuscripts adds that Paul taught from the fifth hour to the tenth, meaning from 11 a.m. to 4 p.m. This was the typical time for the midday rest period. It was probably the only time the hall was available and the rent was probably cheaper during that time. Also, it was the time of day when people had free time. Paul made disciples and over a two year period all that lived in Asia heard the Word of the Lord, both Jews and Greeks (Acts 19:10).

Paul's church growth manual was the Word of God. Church growth experts may try to imitate the true gospel with a false gospel. It will not work. Even the demons know the difference in the real and the spurious. The Jewish exorcists tried to imitate Paul, but the demons did not recognize the Jewish exorcists. The Bible explains how the possessed man was provoked by the demon so that the man physically assaulted the Jewish exorcists. Notice that the evil spirit did not say anything against Jesus or His disciple, the apostle Paul.

Even the demonic world recognizes the person and nature of Jesus Christ. Christians are too quick to dismiss the universal nature of the Lord Jesus Christ. People everywhere in all walks of life recognize a fake. Many could say, as the demon possessed man said, "I recognize Jesus and I know about Paul, but who are you?" (Acts 19:15).

The church has a purpose, which is to worship the triune God. The church has a mission, which is to make disciples and teach the whole counsel of God. The church also has a ministry.

> And He Himself gave some to be apostles, some prophets, some evangelists, and some pastors and teachers, for the equipping of the saints for the work of ministry, for the edifying of the body of Christ, till we all come to the unity of the faith and of the knowledge of the Son of God, to a perfect man, to the measure of the stature of the fullness of Christ. (Ephesians 4:11-13)

Paul's summary of the ministry of the church is in harmony with the mission of the church.

> The mission of the church and the ministry of the church complement each other. The ministry of the

church begins by "serving the Lord with all humility" (Acts 20:19). The servants of the Lord, (apostles, prophets, evangelists, pastors and teachers), are responsible for "equipping the saints for the work of ministry." The word "ministry" is derived from the word "minister" which literally means "to serve". The ministry of the church consists of serving in the body of Christ. (*The Present Truth*, by Martin Murphy, p. 34).

Christians must be fully trained to engage in the mission of making disciples and teaching them the full counsel of God. Paul used three metaphors to describe an immature church. It will act like a child. The immature church will be tossed to and fro and carried about with every wind of doctrine. If she is not completely prepared, she will be influenced by the trickery of men into doctrinal error. The mature church on the other hand speaks the truth in love.

The apostle Paul had seen the reality of the universal nature of Jesus Christ in his travels throughout the Middle East and Southern Europe. The Christian church expanded during Paul's ten year mission. The universal nature of Jesus Christ was the forefront of Paul's ministry. If Christians look at the full and final purpose of the gospel ministry, then the glory of God will shine forth in a dark world.

It is the universal nature of Jesus Christ that makes the church universal. The universal church simply refers to the whole number of the elect from the beginning of time, including those at the present time and those that shall be gathered together under Jesus Christ who is the head and the king of the church.

If Christians really believe the church is universal in its character, they need to escape from the tunnel vision mentality. God's people see the bigger picture and engage faithfully in God's plan for His church.

36. Cultural Revolution

Acts 19:21- 41

Ephesus was a city in Asia Minor of significance and importance to the spread of the gospel. Ephesus was a large city of about 300,000 at the time of Paul's ministry. Ephesus was a port city bringing people through Ephesus from all parts of the world. It was the home of a theater that would seat an estimated 25,000 people. Ephesus was the home of the temple Diana which was known as one the wonders of the ancient world. Think of Ephesus in terms of a mega-city, which would be comparable to any large city in the United States. It was in this context that Paul began making disciples. There was church growth throughout Asia Minor.

Paul's ministry at Ephesus was lengthy in comparison to some of his missionary endeavors. Paul ministered to the Ephesian Church for two years. The book of Acts and the letter Paul wrote to the Ephesians reveals the success of his ministry in and around Ephesus. Study both accounts to grasp the principles in the Word of God and contend with them until the principles are obvious, or dismiss them as meaningless to the present time and culture.

Every Christian has the responsibility to make disciples and teach the disciples the full counsel of God. The Word of God delineates a structure for the mission. Some people have a direct role in making and teaching disciples, where others have an indirect role. For instance, the elders of the church are accountable for the spiritual welfare of the congregation so the individual members will be equipped for the mission. The Bible has a clear order for the roles of each individual member. The elders are supposed to submit to the Word of God as the regulative principle for all of faith and practice. Local congregations ought to submit to the elders, the family should submit to the spiritual leadership of the father, and so on. The apostle Paul followed the structure and order from God's Word so that the mission of making disciples would not fall short of the expected results.

Paul entered many cities and suffered persecution. Other times the people would simply reject him. However, many of the Ephesians accepted the gospel of Jesus Christ. In fact, the gospel ministry caused a cultural revolution at Ephesus.

The words culture and revolution need a brief definition to put Paul's ministry in context. A culture is a way of life. Dr. David Wells has given as good a meaning to the word culture as I can find. He says a culture consists of "sets of meanings and morals, beliefs and habits that arose in specific contexts of history and religion" (*God in the Wasteland*, by David Wells, p. 9). Some people speak of a culture as being on equal terms with a society. There is a slight distinction. A culture is the intrinsic value of a society of people. A society represents the collective agreement to the culture. Political philosophers speak of a social contract, but they speak of a culture in terms of "the means, tools, customs, and institutions of a society" (*Dictionary of Philosophy*, edited by Dagobert Runes, p. 88).

Revolution describes the radical significant change that took place in Ephesus as a result of Paul's gospel ministry. Paul did not start an ungodly revolution. He did obey the Lord by making disciples and teaching them the whole counsel of God. Luke's analysis of Paul's ministry in Ephesus was, "these things were accomplished." The Holy Spirit changed the hearts of many people in Ephesus to believe the gospel of Jesus Christ. Paul was busy making disciples which changed the way they lived. The Christians traded in the old ungodly culture for a new godly culture.

The effect that Christianity had on the ungodly culture at Ephesus caused some of the Ephesians to instigate a riot to overthrow the peaceful cultural revolution brought on by the gospel. It should be observed that Luke does not use the word church to describe the Christian converts. He describes the Christian converts at Ephesus in terms of "the Way" (Acts 19:23). Christianity was a new way of life. It was the way of the true and living God. The Lord Jesus Christ was at the center of their religious lives. The change was revolutionary bringing a new set of morals and a new way of life called the church.

It was "the Way" (the church) that disturbed the men who made and sold the silver shrines of Diana. The manufacturer of those silver shrines was big business in the city of Ephesus. The ungodly culture at Ephesus depended on the idolatry and worship of the goddess Diana. Christians today may not have the monstrous temple in Ephesus and accompanying financial and economic benefits from it, but they have plenty of other monumental idols that create billions of dollars in the current economy.

The announcement of the gospel and the power of the Holy Spirit, along with the means of grace in preaching the Word of God transformed some of the people of Ephesus. The transformation was significant enough so that it penetrated the entire culture. The people quit buying the silver shrines. The business people were outraged because their pocket books and bank accounts dwindled.

Demetrius, a silversmith in Ephesus, saw the threat of the Christian cultural reform. He gathered the other silversmiths together and collectively they incited some of the citizens of Ephesus to wrath. Demetrius appealed not only to the economic effect, but also to religious motives. "So not only is this trade of ours in danger of falling into disrepute, but also the temple of the great goddess Diana may be despised and her magnificence destroyed, whom all Asia and the world worship" (Acts 19:27). Demetrius wanted to gain the support of the citizens, so that the civil authorities would then have a reason to crush the Christian revolution. The Ephesian Christians demonstrated their faith and commitment to the Word of God. The cultural relevance of the Christian religion depends on faith and ideals. Unfortunately, that is where many professing Christians stop. They believe, but they privatize their faith. They keep it at home and leave the public square to the ungodly vultures of cultural tyranny. The cultural relevance of the Christian religion depends on faith and ideals, but it also depends on the practice of Christian principles in the public sector.

When the way of life for the Christian conflicts with another way of life, the battle over cultural authority begins. Cultural authority is the contest between unbelievers and believers. The disrespect for the Christian religion has devolved from one generation to another generation for so long that the decline has robbed Christians of their freedom.

The truth of God's Word will cast its light over the culture. Truth will inspire discipline and constraint upon the culture. The absence of truth from the Word of God will cause cultural collapse and the culture will decline to the point of chaos and confusion.

It is time for the professing Christians in this country to invade the culture. If the millions who profess Christianity are merely professing Christians, you may think that the mission is impossible. It is not. Christians are called to be faithful. Noah was faithful with only a few. Abraham was faithful with only one heir. Elijah stood against 100's, Jeremiah against the entire nation. Evidence from Scripture and through 2000 years of church history reveals the myriads of Christians who stood against the odds of the secular predominate culture. A promise accompanied the mission Christ gave the church. The Lord's promise was, "I am with you always, even to the end of the age" (Matthew 28:20).

The religious lies of any culture will not survive against the truth of the Word of God. The truth of the Word of God will expose the emptiness of idolatry and the man-made gods of culture. The truth of the Word of God clearly and calmly proclaimed will transform culture.

The proponents of the modern religious culture will rise up against the gospel, if the gospel interferes with their cultural milieu. They will do it in the name of religious zeal and patriotic pride in an effort to exterminate the gospel of Jesus Christ and consequently the full counsel of God.

God may send someone like the town clerk at Ephesus to give Christians temporary relief (Acts 19:35-41). Many theologians have turned the town clerk at Ephesus into a hero for Christianity.

However, the town clerk showed no love for Christianity. All he did was to save the Ephesians from self-destruction. He simply acted according to his nature. He wanted to save himself and his city. He knew very well that an unchecked riot could have caused the city of Ephesus to lose its free status in the Roman Empire. The town clerk was merely jealous to save his wicked and perverted culture.

The cultural revolution in Ephesus was the result of Paul and his companion's faithfulness to the mission of the church. They made disciples and taught them the full counsel of God. A peaceful revolution reformed the culture. The change in the Ephesians way of life was the result of their change of heart and mind. If you are reformed by the Word of God and the power of the Holy Spirit, you may cause a cultural revolution.

37. The Discipleship Plan

Acts 20:1-12

The first thirty years of the church demonstrated God's plan for making disciples and teaching the full counsel of God. Paul the apostle was instrumental by laying a foundation for the future church. Paul traveled throughout Southeastern Europe and Asia Minor with the mission and ministry of the church before him. There are plenty of men throughout the history of the church, who like the apostle Paul, were simply faithful to the Word of God.

Paul was faithful to evangelize. The good news of God's saving grace was the announcement to people wherever Paul went. The announcement was, "believe on the Lord Jesus Christ." The next step in Paul's faithfulness was to bring the Christian converts an understanding of the full counsel of God. The Word of God introduced the disciples to a new world and life view, a Christian world and life view. Paul understood that sound preaching and teaching of God's Word must accompany conversion. Christian discipleship is a term that describes the value of instructing a student with the Word of God.

Sound words are necessary in preaching and teaching for discipleship purposes. Paul's explanation is to, "Hold fast the pattern of sound words which you have heard from me, in faith and love which are in Christ Jesus" (2 Timothy 1:13). A brief quote will help summarize the application of this text.

A summary of sound words is not equal to quoting Bible verses. It has often been said that biblical texts may be found to prove almost anything. Unbelievers, liberals, the ignorant and scholarly alike use Bible verses taken out of context to prove their opinions. One Bible verse does not equal the entire Word of God. The goal of every Christian should be to gather a summary of the Word of God so that God is exalted and man is put down. For instance, the doctrine of God must be relative to God's nature and the doctrine of man must be relative to man's nature. When we hold fast to the healthy words of Scripture we will save ourselves and our progeny from theological error. Error in doctrine will almost inevitably lead to error in practice. When a man believes wrongly he will act wrongly. The very cause of division, schism, quarrels, and bickering in the church is a result of wrong teaching. Why? Because we have ignored the outline of healthy words from Scripture. (*A Westminster Catechism*, by Martin Murphy, p. 210-211).

Although sound preaching and teaching is the essential ingredient for discipleship, it also requires a godly relationship between the teacher and the student.

> After the uproar had ceased, Paul called the disciples to himself, embraced them, and departed to go to Macedonia. Now when he had gone over that region and encouraged them with many words, he came to Greece and stayed three months. And when the Jews plotted against him as he was about to sail to Syria, he decided to return through Macedonia. And Sopater of Berea accompanied him to Asia—also Aristarchus and Secundus of the Thessalonians, and Gaius of Derbe, and Timothy, and Tychicus and Trophimus of Asia. These men, going ahead, waited for us at Troas. But we sailed away from Philippi after the Days of Unleavened Bread, and in five days joined them at Troas, where we stayed seven days. (Acts 20:1-2)

The first healthy sign of good discipleship is the evidence of a good relationship between the teacher and the disciples. Paul literally sent for the disciples at Ephesus. The word "called" is a strong word, which infers that Paul insisted on their presence. His purpose for assembling the disciples was not merely to hug their neck. Paul exhorted them, which I believe is a more accurate rendering of the Greek word. He encouraged them with words consistent with his teaching. After spending two years with them, he was ready to visit the disciples of Christ in other places.

The second healthy sign of good discipleship is the faithfulness and instruction of the teacher to the disciples. Paul went back to Macedonia and Greece and encouraged them. The encouragement was with many words. Although Paul may have visited several of the churches in Greece such as Philippi and Thessalonica, he probably spent the winter, in Corinth. There was more trouble at the Corinthian Church than the other churches on his circuit. However, Paul invested in the lives of God's people everywhere.

The best investment a Christian will ever make in this world is by pouring his or her life into someone else. Paul was not only willing to pour his life into other people, he was willing to sacrifice to do it. However, Paul's sacrifice was not careless. For instance, when Paul got word that the Jews intended to kill him, he changed his travel plans, so he could continue sacrificing himself to make disciples (Acts 20:3).

When Paul was ready to make the trip to Jerusalem, he strategically sent the right men to the right places. Although it is not necessary to rehearse each name associated with his ministry, suffice it to say that Paul placed them in the places they could best serve in continuing the work of making disciples (Acts 20:4-5).

The pattern was the same for each visit. Christians should not overlook what may seem insignificant to the development of the church. Please take note of Paul's trip as he came to Troas and stayed seven days. There is an interesting inspired account of what happened on Sunday. "Now on the first day of the week, when the disciples came together to break bread, Paul, ready to depart the next day, spoke to them and continued his message until midnight" (Acts 20:7).

The disciples were assembled, apparently by the elders of the church at Troas. The English words "came together" are passive in the Greek text. That means someone brought them together and that authority belongs to the elders of the church. The purpose of assembling the disciples was for worship. The two elements of worship mentioned in this text were the Lord's Supper and preaching.

The people were anxious to hear the preaching of the Word of God. There is no mention of the time the worship service began, but the preaching continued until midnight. Sunday was a regular workday; so most people would not be able to get to the assembly until seven or perhaps eight p.m. Even so, that is four hours of preaching with the exception of the time spent in other elements of worship such as the sacrament of the Lord's Supper. There may have been other elements involved in worship such as prayer, singing of Psalms or giving an offering. However, none are mentioned at this meeting for worship.

The point Luke intends to emphasize is the preaching and teaching ministry. Today people could not stand, sit or lie down for four hours or even three hours of preaching and teaching. However, this text does not teach that a worship service must go for four hours and most of that preaching and teaching the Word of God. The purpose of a lengthy sermon was to strengthen the disciples. The reason those people could sit and listen to the Word of God for four hours is simple. They lived at a time when words were meaningful and often the only source of communication. Today we live in a world that demands pictures and entertainment. Christians go to a movie theater and sit quietly to watch a movie for two or three hours. The entertainment industry conditions the mind with fast track switching of the scenes so that the mind never has to concentrate. The result is that many people go to church, a misnomer, looking for passive entertainment. They want the worship experience to be an emotional response based on jokes, stories, skits, anecdotes, music or some other form of entertainment.

Paul's visit was such that it was the only time he could spend with the disciples. However, this text does teach that the exposition of the Word of God is central to the worship service and obviously the Lord's Supper accompanied the preaching of the Word. It has often been said that this text proves that preaching too long will cause people to fall asleep. It is true that Eutychus fell asleep and fell out the window to his death. Some liberal theologians claim that Eutychus was not dead that he just lost his breath. Luke was a physician and if he said the boy was dead, he above all people should know. I think the tragedy of his death was really a blessing. The Holy Spirit using the apostle Paul gave the young man life. In some sense it depicted the power of the resurrection. Paul's preaching surely included the fact that we all die, but we shall all be raised again on the last day. Can you imagine attending a church service, someone dying during the service and then raised from the dead? The events of that night were so significant the people stayed for a time of informal discussion and fellowship that lasted until day break. The assembly of the disciples must exalt God and encourage the believers (Acts 20:11).

Every church ought to ask these probing questions.

- Is the church engaging in the mission to make disciples?
- Is the ministry consistent with the mission that Christ has given the church?

- Has man-made worship replaced sacred godly worship?

Worship was in a state of disarray during the time when the Israelites were under the rule of God. Long before the destruction of the Temple in Jerusalem (586 B.C.) God condemned their false worship. "Their land is also full of idols; They worship the work of their own hands, that which their own fingers have made" (Isaiah 2:8). Over one hundred fifty years later God said, "I will utter My judgments against them concerning all their wickedness, because they have forsaken Me, burned incense to other gods, and worshiped the works of their own hands" (Jeremiah 1:16). Sinful professing people of God in every dispensation tend to turn God's prescription for worship into man-made pomp and formal pageantry. The way to prevent false teaching and false worship is to follow the discipleship plan found in the Word of God.

38. Godly Counsel for the Church

Paul was a faithful preacher and teacher, but he was also a godly pastor to the people of God. His pastoral counsel is godly counsel for the church in every generation. Paul gave godly counsel to the Church at Rome when he said, "do not be conformed to this world, but be transformed by the renewing of your mind, that you may prove what the will of God is, that which is good and acceptable and perfect" (Rom. 12:2).

The Holy Spirit enables a child of God to receive godly counsel. Making disciples and teaching the disciples the full counsel of God ought to result in a change of behavior. The Christian disciple ought to formulate a Christian world and life view. Unfortunately, repentance may not be obvious in the professing Christian life.

Christians may not act like Christians for several reasons. The professing Christian may not be a Christian. Since Christians are not free from sin, they may be overcome by sin. Christians may not know how to act, because they have not received the benefit of God's counsel. More specifically, they may not have received the benefit of the teaching from the full counsel of God.

The Lord Jesus gave the children of God a promise just before he ascended into heaven. "But you shall receive power when the Holy Spirit has come upon you..." (Acts 1:8). The Word of God gives Christians every reason to believe they have been empowered by the Holy Spirit. "Now may the God of hope fill you with all joy and peace in believing, that you may abound in hope by the power of the Holy Spirit" (Romans 15:13). It is the Holy Spirit that enables the Christian to receive godly counsel.

This sinful world will cause suffering, misery, pain, and confusion. Therefore, Christians must seek godly counsel from the Word of God. The Psalmist with the power of the Holy Spirit and the love of God in his heart said, "Trouble and anguish have overtaken me; Yet, Your commandments are my delights" (Psalm 119:143). The Word of God was his delight.

Paul's farewell visit with the Ephesians is an inspired account of a pastor giving godly counsel to the church. It is inspired and normative. Christians ought to read this portion of God's Word often and accompanied by prayer.

> Therefore I testify to you this day that I am innocent of the blood of all men. For I have not shunned to declare to you the whole counsel of God. Therefore take heed to yourselves and to all the flock, among which the Holy Spirit has made you overseers, to shepherd the church of God which He purchased with His own blood. For I know this, that after my departure savage wolves will come in among you, not sparing the flock. Also from among yourselves men will rise up, speaking perverse things, to draw away the disciples after themselves. (Acts 20:26-30)

The most obvious counsel from this portion of God's Word is the necessity for elders in the church to teach the full counsel of God and lead the congregation.

The church simply cannot carry out the mission and ministry of the church without elders. The Word of God requires the appointment of elders for every church. Elders are recognized by their "example to the believers in word, in conduct, in love, in spirit, in faith, in purity" (1 Timothy 4:12). They have the very heavy responsibility of leading the church in worship and ministry for the spiritual welfare of the members of the church.

If the elders do not receive the benefit of God's counsel from the Word of God, then the congregation will suffer as a result of spiritual deprivation. If elders have the Holy Spirit and receive counsel from God's Word, then they must give godly counsel to the congregation. Paul's godly counsel also reminds the elders, who are to remind the church that the foundation of salvation, peace, joy, hope, and the love of God begins with faith and repentance. Paul's godly counsel to the elders was for the benefit of the whole church. Paul told them that he had solemnly testified to both Jews and Greeks of repentance toward God and faith in our Lord Jesus Christ. It is the mark of a Christian to repent of sins and trust the Lord Jesus Christ.

Paul's godly counsel considers the trouble, travail, hardship, and suffering that may visit the Christian to a greater or lesser degree. The evil one will assault Christians every possible way. Demons exist to bring misery to God's people. It is not a question of whether or not the evil one will assault Christians; it is a question of how often and to what degree. Paul served the Lord with many tears and trials, but he expected chains and tribulation (Acts 21:13).

The counsel of a godly pastor begins with his own willingness to sacrifice. Physical life is important, because we are created in the image of God, but eternal life with a favorable relationship with God is ultimately important. However, the mission and ministry of the church is for this life and has eternal consequences. As Paul said, "But none of these things move me; nor do I count my life dear to myself, so that I may finish my race with joy, and the ministry which I received from the Lord Jesus, to testify to the gospel of the grace of God" (Acts 20:24).

The duty Christians owe Christ is far more important than the duty they owe to this world. However, they must never seek to escape the duty Christ has given them in this world until they finish the race.

Paul's greatest concern was the danger of heresy and false teachers. Paul called them savage wolves and warned the Ephesian elders that they would "draw away the disciples after themselves" (Acts 20:30). Savage wolves will infiltrate the ranks of the church. The savage wolves will introduce false doctrine. Like their father the Devil, the savage wolves will try to mislead the disciples of Christ with false preaching and teaching. Jesus warned the disciples to "Beware of false prophets, who come to you in sheep's clothing, but inwardly they are ravenous wolves" (Matthew 7:15). Savage ravenous wolves may come in the form of celebrated religious leaders. Jesus made a declaratory statement to the Jewish religious leaders during His earthly life.

> Jesus said to them, "If God were your Father, you would love Me, for I proceeded forth and came from God; nor have I come of Myself, but He sent Me. Why do you not understand My speech? Because you are not able to listen to My word. You are of your father the devil, and the desires of your father you want to do. He was a murderer from the beginning, and does not stand in the truth, because there is no truth in him. When he speaks a lie, he speaks from his own resources, for he is a liar and the father of it. But because I tell the truth, you do not believe Me. Which of you convicts Me of sin? And if I tell the truth, why do you not believe Me? He who is of God hears God's words; therefore you do not hear, because you are not of God. (John 8:42-47)

It is the purpose of false preaching and false teaching to draw away the disciples or to put it more literally drag away the disciples of Jesus Christ. The pride and selfish ambition of false preachers and teachers will corrupt the

Word of God and pervert the doctrine of salvation. There is a logical progression to Satan's plan.

> Misleading leads to heresy.
> Dragging away represents apostasy.
> Apostasy is the abandonment of the faith.

Factionalism and teaching ambiguous doctrine are the primary reasons for the exodus of large numbers of professing Christians from the alleged evangelical church in North America. The elders of the church are the backbone of the spiritual health of the church. Could it be that God is sending a message to churches throughout this land to get their attention?

If unconverted people are admitted to the membership and communion of the church, those unconverted members may become unconverted elders and unconverted elders will destroy the growth of the body for the building up of itself in love. Since God gave His church elders to shepherd the church of God, the whole church should take note of what God expects from the elders of the church. Paul explains the duty of the church, specifically the elders of the church, in a brief defense of his ministry. "For I have not shunned to declare to you the whole counsel of God" (Acts 20:27). If preachers would preach the full counsel of God, then God's people would not be turned away by the false preaching. If elders would teach the full counsel of God, the wolves would have no effect on the disciples of Jesus Christ. Preaching the full counsel of God may be uncomfortable at times. It will cut to the bone and convict Christians of their sins and their duty to serve God in this life. Preaching and teaching the full counsel of God will make the church sound, because the voice of Jesus Christ becomes the master of the soul.

The counsel of godly pastors is for the protection of God's people from perverted doctrine which leads to uncertainty, confusion about the word of His grace, and finally unbelief. The only way to have joy and peace in Jesus Christ is to know that entry into the kingdom of God is sealed with the inheritance purchased for God's adopted children by the sacrifice, death, resurrection and ascension of Jesus Christ.

39. Dilemma of Religious Tradition

Acts 21:1-26

There are times when the truth is inescapably obvious and there are times Christians must be satisfied with God's revelation, however limited it may appear. For instance, the Word of God commands the church to make disciples, but the Word of God does not reveal the methods and programs to complete the mission. The Bible does give the church principles that should be applied to the mission of making disciples. Paul's life is an example for individual believers and the church collectively. Over a period of nearly twenty years, his resolve to make disciples was never shaken. His commitment never faltered. His sacrifice is unquestionable.

Paul's ministry at Ephesus lasted about two years and he returned to Jerusalem to deliver the collection made by the Gentile churches for the poor saints in Jerusalem (Romans 15:25). He stopped at various cities and found Christians greeting him and praying with him. Then as today, "The man who is in the family of God has friends all over the world."

Some of his Christian friends urged Paul not to go to Jerusalem for fear of his safety and maybe his life (Acts 21:10-11). They wanted Paul to remain with them and continue the mission of the church. Paul's response was the same unwavering resolve he demonstrated throughout his ministry. Paul said, " For I am ready not only to be bound, but also to die at Jerusalem for the name of the Lord Jesus" (Acts 21:13).

Suffering for the right reason always pleases God. Suffering requires sacrifice and sacrifice is an expression of love. If you have the love of God in your heart, then suffering for God's glory is an act of genuine worship to God.

When Paul arrived in Jerusalem the church greeted him apparently with a warm welcome. The next day the elders called a Presbytery meeting with James moderating. Paul gave a detailed report of those things, which God had done, through his ministry. God had worked in Paul's life. The Holy Spirit changed his heart and the full counsel of God had reformed him. In the modern church, Christian leaders are busy planning strategies for church growth, but they should be busy making disciples.

After Paul reported the work of God among the Gentiles, the elders point out that massive numbers of Jews have converted to Christianity. Unlike the Jews, the Gentile converts were not weighed down with religious tradition. The Jews were thoroughly acquainted with the Old Testament; unfortunately, a long train of religious tradition came with their conversion to Christianity. The Jews were looking for the Messiah, but they were jealous for the ceremonial law. The Jews were ardent Nationalists. Temple worship still functioned in Jerusalem. They loved their heritage and certainly did not want to turn it loose.

Paul's opponents caricatured him as a teacher who turned the hearts of the Jews away from the Law of Moses. It was a false report, but religious people get worked up over changes in tradition and religious worship. Some particular churches do not follow the biblical model of elder leadership. The pastor is the leader and his religious followers follow his suggestions step by step.

The advice from the elders was to seek the respect of the Christians at Jerusalem by helping four indigents with the expense of completing their Nazarite vow, which required Paul to join with them. This is not the time or place to give a history of the Nazarites and the vows associated with the Nazarite, but I will use the brief comments of one more qualified than me to explain the meaning and practice of the

Nazarite. The Jewish historian Josephus in his famous Antiquities said this of the Nazarite vow.

> When any have made a sacred vow, I mean those that are called Nazarites, that suffer their hair to grow long, and use no wine, when they consecrate their hair and offer it for a sacrifice, they are to allot that hair for the priests [to be thrown into the fire]. Such also dedicate themselves to God, as a corban, which denotes what the Greeks call a gift, when they are desirous of being freed from that ministration, are to lay down money for the priests; thirty shekels if it be a woman, and fifty if it be a man; but if any be too poor to pay the appointed sum, it shall be lawful for the priests to determine the sum as they think fit. (*Antiquities*, 119, Josephus)

The Jerusalem elders reaffirmed their previous decision not to require anything of the Gentile converts except that they "keep themselves from thing offered to idols, from blood, from things strangled, and from sexual immorality" (Acts 21:25). The elders appear to have the unity of the church in mind. Two very different religious backgrounds came into conflict. The old Jewish heritage and the new wine of the Gentiles threaten disunity to the church. The Jewish Christians had clearly abandoned any sacrifice for the atonement, but they continued other ceremonies of the law.

However, the elders in Jerusalem tolerated the traditions and customs the Jews. Paul participated in a Nazarite vow and the liturgy associated with it. Although Christians are free from the yoke of the ceremonial laws, it may have been premature to call the Jews to cease and desist from all of the ceremonial laws. Some would be more detestable than others, but the Nazarite vow would be the last one eliminated in the early church. Paul even admitted in his letter to the

Corinthian church that, "to the Jews I became as a Jew, that I might win Jews; to those who are under law, as under the law that I might win those who are under the law" (1 Corinthians 9:20).

Paul worked for years to collect money for the poor in Jerusalem.   Maybe Paul thought the Gentile financial contribution might ease the tension and bring unity to the culturally and ethnically divided church. Paul had suffered beyond human comprehension and now he must prove again his integrity and consistency for the sake of the gospel. Paul rose to the occasion. Without any argument, without any scene at all, Paul humbled himself to conquer because the mission Christ had given him was in the balance. Paul was not a slave to human ordinances, but he had liberty of conscience to bear the infirmities of the weak. "Give me liberty or give me death" was the cry of Patrick Henry. Those words were and still are the crowning mark of determined men. Paul was determined not to abandon the mission that Christ had given him.

Unbiblical tradition is easy to accumulate, but difficult to abolish. The dilemma of religious tradition will often replace the purpose, mission and ministry of the church.

40. Habit and Continuity of Persistence

Acts 21:26 – 22:21

The compromise of fundamental truths is the result of the sinful nature and generational continuity. When turmoil, confusion, and strife enter the scene of intelligent human discourse, the resulting hysteria overshadows the truth. It is the nature of a sinner to deny absolute, eternal truth and embrace personal relative ideas.

The cultural crisis in the Western world at the beginning of the 21st century has devolved from previous generations under different labels. Technology and information transmission has exponentially multiplied the energy of false and misleading theories of truth. An emotionally driven media and legal maneuvers have perpetrated the crisis in this country by distorting or avoiding truth.

Nearly 2000 years ago the apostle Paul faced the same dilemma under a different set of circumstances. The nascent church in Jerusalem failed to maintain the habit and continuity of persistence. Paul had followed the advice of the Jerusalem elders by participating in a Nazarite vow.

> Therefore do what we tell you: We have four men who have taken a vow. Take them and be purified with them, and pay their expenses so that they may shave their heads, and that all may know that those things of which they were informed concerning you are nothing, but that you yourself also walk orderly and keep the law. (Acts 21:23-24)

However, some Jews from Asia saw Paul in the Temple who had probably been in Ephesus during the uprising of the Ephesians against Paul. They hated Paul and his mission, so this was an opportunity for them to stir up the Jews in Jerusalem against Paul, since it is obvious that they considered Paul their enemy.

The reason the unconverted Jews falsely accused Paul is because they were enemies of Christ and enemies of Christianity. Like political zealots, religious zealots are dangerous. They incite the masses. The angry Jews shouted to the mob in the temple, (sort of like being in a building falsely referred to as the church), "Men of Israel, help us" (Acts 21:28). They acted as if Paul was the most dangerous criminal in Jerusalem. Their passions were unbridled for their intense hatred against the truth. They hated to hear the truth that Jesus Christ had fulfilled the law thus making salvation a gift from God. These unconverted Jews could no longer find diversions to satisfy their guilty condition before God.

Satan took advantage of the opportunity to deceive the people and set the people in a rage against Paul. This vicious attack against the gospel of Jesus Christ is ultimately an attack against truth. It is an attack against Christians today as much as it was against Paul.

There are two distinguishing factors that come into play. They are factors Christians face every day. First, the devil's tactics are true to his name, deceiver. The unconverted Jews deceived the people. They said Paul was against the law of God and the Temple in Jerusalem. Not true. Paul did teach that the ceremonial laws found their fulfillment in the Messiah, the Lord Jesus Christ. The blood of bulls and goats in the ceremonial law merely typified the coming Messiah. They also said Paul was against the Temple. Another absurd lie, because Paul was in the Temple to fulfill his Nazarite vow. Then they said he brought Greeks into the Temple. That is not true. Luke's inspired account was that they had seen Paul with a Greek man named Trophimus in the city, but not in the Temple. The devilish lies worked and the whole city rose up against Paul. They literally drug Paul out of the Temple and began to beat him to death. This applies to Christians when they resolve to stand for the truth. Their enemy will use the most effective weapon in the arsenal, that is to tell a lie.

The next factor is God's providential care. God rules over turmoil and confusion. In Paul's case the civil magistrate entered to maintain order in society. Let me be quick to add that is the only responsibility of the civil magistrate. He is to maintain order, but not interfere into affairs that concern spiritual truth. God provided the state to protect Christians against the anarchy of false religions.

False religion will always be against true religion. However, God is in control no matter how bad things seem. If your mission is to make disciples for Christ, then false religious people will rise up against you. The more consistent you are with your mission, the more consistent you will be confronted by the enemy called false religion.

Drawing from these fundamental principles, Christians must persevere in the mission of making disciples and teaching the full counsel of God. Christian commitment, if it is truly a commitment, must be accompanied by habit and continuity unbroken in a sequence following God's eternal truth.

Paul's persistence was habitual. It was second nature for Paul to defend the full counsel of God. He did not pick and choose the times to defend the whole counsel of God. Paul's persistence was not only habitual, it was continuous. When it appeared that the odds were against the truth of the gospel, Paul did not back down. He stayed the course.

The habit of persistence does not come easy, especially for a fluff and puff society. The prolonged and intense abuse of the fourth commandment has produced a nation given to pleasure and laziness. The Bible commands human beings to work and follow the principle of persistence. "Six days you shall labor and do all your work" (Exodus 20:9). It is rare for anybody in this country to work as unto the Lord for six days each week. Pleasure has replaced perseverance in the things of the Lord, but the Bible never indicates that Christians are to persevere in the pleasures of life. Although pleasure is not sinful, it must not replace the mission of the church. Persistence and perseverance in truth produces a productive and prosperous spiritual estate. Paul was a faithful mission-minded man who habitually and continually persisted in the noblest call of life.

Paul's defense before the people in Jerusalem serves as a reminder of his persistent passion to make disciples and glorify God. (Read Acts 22:1-21 to put this exposition in its proper context). His address always begins with grace and dignity. Then he set forth the facts to show that the charges were groundless. The charges were false. The opposition was blood thirsty, but Paul did not give up or give in. Paul was faithful to persist in doing what was right in the eyes of God. Paul was not trying to make friends or enemies; he was trying to make disciples.

Paul's testimony reveals his habit and continuity of persistence in the work of the gospel. He went to Jerusalem to unify the culturally and ethnically diverse church. He wanted everyone to see the abundant grace of God in Jesus Christ. Paul was always ready to tell of the humbling experience he had on the road to Damascus which changed his life forever. A few stumbling blocks and a little persecution did not stop the apostle and never should stop any disciple of Christ.

Christians need to develop the habit of continuity and persistence, not in eating, travel, sports, and other pleasures, but in their faithfulness to the mission Christ has given them.

41. Democracy Without a Conscience

Acts 22:22 – 23:35

During his campaign for President, Mr. Ralph Nader called for a "Vote of Conscience". One of his supporters is reported to have said, "either we vote our conscience or we keep getting candidates like Gore, who doesn't really believe in anything" (*The Washington Post*, Nov. 6, 2000). What did his supporter mean when she said, "we vote our conscience." The "we" in that statement implies a democratic state, one in which the people of that state rule collectively.

The democratization of the church and state in modern western societies created what is often referred to as the tyranny of the people. The Marxist theory caricatures religion and particularly Christianity as merely a scheme to rob the individual of his or her civil and social rights. Karl Marx believed that Christianity was the means by which people are drugged to believe in God. Marx believed, "religion is the opiate of the people." The word *opiate* comes from the word "opium" that is a mind altering drug. Marx did not believe in God and thought workers were controlled by religion like a drug addict is controlled by opium. His solution to the social and civil disorder was to give people a pure democracy.

The mixture of a Marxist democracy with the expression "voting your conscience" invokes a moral dilemma. This country is in a moral dilemma because the mission of the church has taken on an unbiblical masquerade in recent history. For instance, the church growth movement and its offspring organizations subtly dismissed the biblical mandate of making disciples and introduced flagship church growth. In its most crass form the doctrine is, "do what successful churches do to create church growth."

This text in the book of Acts is a brief, but inspired historical account of the Jews in Jerusalem attempting to murder Paul and the defense of his mission. They were ungodly religious men preserving their tradition and acting contrary to the full counsel of God.

The mob of ungodly Jews in Jerusalem charged Paul according to their conscience rather than consulting the full counsel of God. They were ready to kill Paul on trumped up charges. Since the charges were false, Paul was ready to give a defense for what he taught according to the full counsel of God and how his teaching resulted in his actions. Paul believed and taught Jesus Christ was the Messiah, the only way to salvation and eternal life. Paul's witness and testimony reflected his belief that Jesus Christ was the Son of God and the Savior of sinners.

Paul took his message to the whole world, but the world hates the Lord Jesus Christ. The Lord himself explained this very sober doctrine.

> If the world hates you, you know that it hated Me before it hated you. If you were of the world, the world would love its own. Yet because you are not of the world, but I chose you out of the world, therefore the world hates you. Remember the word that I said to you, a servant is not greater than his master. If they persecuted Me, they will also persecute you. (John 15:18-20)

The Lord makes a distinction between a democracy, where people rule themselves and a theocracy, in which God rules. The unconverted Jews acting as a democracy in Jerusalem tried to kill the apostle Paul, because they hated Jesus Christ. The attempted murder of Paul indicates a vote of conscience.

Contrary to the wicked plot of the Jews, the apostle Paul acted honorably and with integrity. The opening words of Paul's defense was, "Men and brethren, I have lived in all good conscience before God until this day" (Acts 23:1). This reveals the conflict between the ungodly Jews and the godly apostle. It raises a moral dilemma. The conscience of the unconverted Jews motivated them to murder a man without a just cause. Their conscience dictated an evil action therefore, their conscience was bad. However, the apostle Paul said he had a good conscience. In this brief exposition I want to expand on Paul's use of the word "conscience."

The moral distinction of the conscience is either a good conscience or a bad conscience. With the present trends in American Christianity, Christians should endeavor to understand the intention behind the oft-quoted little statement "let your conscience be your guide." The conscience is spoken of several times in the New Testament. Paul refers to "every man's conscience" (2 Corinthians 4:2). His doctrine indicates the conscience is universal to all people.

Paul refers to the conscience bearing witness either accusing or excusing (Romans 2:15). In that context Paul infers that their actions show that they are aware of an inward moral law.

The Bible seems to indicate that the conscience is a component of the "mind" and "will" therefore, making the conscience a *soul* function. God has given all human beings a mind, which gives them the ability to make judgments and make decisions according to a standard, either objective or subjective. Based on my study of the Bible and over sixty years of experience with the human race, I observe that God provided a soul to all human beings, consisting of the mind, will, and emotions.

The conscience may distinguish between that which is morally right or morally wrong. The text in Romans (2:14-15) indicates the conscience functions as a witness and a judge. As a witness the conscience tells the person whether his or her belief is right or wrong based on the moral standards he or she has accepted for himself or herself. As a judge the conscience tells the person whether his or her action is consistent with the person's standard of conduct. If the action is not according to the standard held by the conscience, then the conscience gives a guilty verdict. If the action is according to the standard of what the person has accepted then the conscience gives a not guilty verdict.

The conscience is like a little voice that says what you are doing is bad. That is the accusation that Paul refers to in Romans 2:15. On the other hand a little voice may say what you are doing is good. Can you trust your conscience or to put it another way, can you trust that little inner voice? Like every other part of creation the *noetic* effect of sin made the conscience fallible and unreliable.

> The Greek word *nous* essentially refers to the mind, reason, or understanding. The word *noetic* comes from the Greek word *nous*. The *noetic* effect of sin refers to the mind, so the question must be asked: to what extent did the fall of man affect the mind? The *noetic* structure (the function of the mind) refers to the sum total of everything a person knows and consequently believes. For instance, Adam's ability to reason before the Fall was like the rest of creation; it was perfect. The *noetic* effect of sin did not destroy reason, but rather defaced it. (*Theological Terms in Layman Language*, by Martin Murphy, p. 72)

God gave man a standard, which is commonly known as the law of God. It was written on the heart (soul) of man at creation, but the sin of man caused every human being to rebel against the law of God. Before Adam sinned, his conscience was perfectly aligned with God's law. After

Adam sinned, his conscience and the conscience of every human being, was misaligned with God's law. The standard which is God's law never changed. The attitude of the heart changed thus causing the conscience to act according to the sin nature. The question is often asked, what about an unbelieving sinner who doesn't murder or steal? The answer is that human nature is totally corrupt and perverse, but man was not utterly without the desire for self-existence and self-preservation. Therefore, they obey the voice of natural law for self-preservation. People without the saving grace of Jesus Christ do good things for their own satisfaction and their own egotistical purposes.

A brief summary of what the Bible teaches about the unbeliever's conscience and the believer's conscience is necessary to put this text into its proper context.

The unbeliever's conscience is like a warning device that only works part of the time. Sometimes they hear it and sometimes they do not hear it. The unbeliever's conscience is condemning. The Bible refers to it as weak, defiled or seared (1 Corinthians 8:7). The conscience of the unbeliever is deficient of spiritual truth, because the unbeliever's mind hates the Word of God in its fullness, and therefore refuses to accept the Word of God. Paul's reference to the seared conscience is one that continually refuses to heed the warning and finally becomes dull and insensitive to the truth of the Word of God.

The believer's conscience is commending because it is under the influence of the Holy Spirit. The believer's conscience bears witness with the Word of God and is said to be good (Acts 23:1), sincere (2 Corinthians 1:12), pure (1 Timothy 3:9), and without offense (Acts 24:16). The believer's conscience will increase in the knowledge of God and His standards of truth. The result is that he will make a deliberate effort to avoid sin. When the believer does sin he or she is ready to confess his or her sin, so the conscience will commend rather than condemn. Paul is an example for all Christians. His conscience was bearing witness of God's Word by the power of the Holy Spirit. His conscience was judging according to the Word of God. The rule in his soul's mind came from God.

The mob of religious Jews in Jerusalem was nothing more than a democracy without a conscience. Their witness was from unbelief and their judgment was according to the standards of evil. The rule in their soul's mind came from a sinful, unregenerate heart.

How is your conscience? Is it under the influence of the Holy Spirit or is it under the influence of the spirit of man? It is a good conscience when it is under the influence of the Holy Spirit.

The Holy Spirit always and forever bears witness and judges according to the Word of God. When your conscience is controlled by the Holy Spirit and agrees with the Word of God, you can say like the apostle Paul, "I have lived in all good conscience before God until this day."

42. Truth Debates Sophistry

Acts 24:1 - 25:12

The term that best defines the art and skill of defending the truth of Scripture is apologetics. It is an essential function of making disciples. Some words change in meaning over the course of time, so Christians must study the words used in Scripture carefully against the modern use of those words. The word apology had an entirely different meaning 2000 years ago when the Bible was originally written. When Luke wrote the Book of Acts the word apology referred to a written or spoken defense of some particular doctrine. Today the word apology has replaced the biblical doctrine of forgiveness. The apostle Paul was a master apologist. Christians are commanded to be ready, "to give a defense to everyone who asks you a reason for the hope that is in you with meekness and fear" (1 Peter 3:15). Christians today do not feel compelled to defend the religion of Christ. They tell unbelievers to believe.

This text in the book of Acts explains Paul's apology to the Roman Governor Felix. The Jewish leadership in Jerusalem charged Paul with Temple defilement. Luke begins the proceedings by establishing a historical context. "Now after five days Ananias the high priest came down with the elders and a certain orator named Tertullus. These gave evidence to the governor against Paul" (Acts 24:1). Evidence should be based on the truth of what one has seen or knows. For example, when a witness is called to testify at a trial it is to tell what that person has seen or heard. The testimony ought to be accurate and nothing but the truth.

Paul the apostle was trained to defend the truth and had plenty of occasions to practice his skills. Polls are conducted frequently in this country to discover the public attitude relative to truth. Poll after poll indicates that if there is any truth, it doesn't matter. Maybe that is the reason so many of our leaders get away with not telling the truth.

Paul realized he had an enemy and it was not merely those charging him, but the enemy was the evil art of sophistry. The first Christian scholar was probably Clement of Alexandria. Although little is known of his life he was one of the early defenders of the Christian religion. In one of his writings he said:

> The art of sophistry, which the Greeks cultivated, is a fantastic power, which makes false opinions like true by means of words. For it produces rhetoric in order to persuasion, and disputation for wrangling. These arts, therefore, if not conjoined with philosophy, will be injurious to every one. For Plato openly called sophistry "an evil art." And Aristotle, following him, demonstrates it to be a dishonest art, which abstracts in a specious manner the whole business of wisdom, and professes a wisdom which it has not studied. (*Clement of Alexandria, Stromata*, chap. 8)

Sophistry is a subtle false argument. To sophisticate means to mislead by deception and false arguments. To be sophisticated is actually bad, although a new meaning is that a sophisticated person is worldly wise, they are in the know, and on top of things.

Another early church father, Gregory of Nyssa, said, "the argument against Christianity unfolds itself and discloses the tangled web of their sophistries, men of discernment see at once that what they have apprehended is nothing at all" (*Gregory of Nyssa, Dogmatic Treatises*). John Calvin's commentary on Nahum 1:3 is, "I see that the world every-where trifle with God, and that the ungodly delude them-selves with Sophistries" (*John Calvin Commentaries, On*

Nahum, 1:3). The nineteenth century theologian, apologist, and pastor James. H. Thornwell said, "The sophist of speculation is the hypocrite" (*The Collected Writings of James Henley Thornwell, Theological and Ethical*, vol. 2, p. 488).

In the text of Acts chapters 24 and 25, Paul makes his third defense. First he had addressed the mob in Jerusalem, then he appeared before the Sanhedrin and now he is before Felix the governor of Judea. The Jews from Jerusalem came to charge Paul with the hope that Felix would turn Paul over to them or better yet that Felix would have Paul put to death.

The Jewish leaders from Jerusalem brought a spokesman with them. His name was Tertullus. Was he a Jew or Roman Lawyer? He appears to have been knowledgeable with Roman law and has a Roman name so this is probably a Greek translation of a Latin speech. Felix the governor called on Tertullus to state his case.

In the typical style of that day, Tertullus should acknowledge the governor's office and authority. Notice how Tertullus addressed the governor. Tertullus accredited Felix with bringing peace and prosperity to Judea. That was a lie and a big lie on top of being a lie. Felix brought trouble, dissension, suspension, and terror to that part of the Middle East. Then Tertullus alleged that Felix was a man of foresight. That was a lie. Family connections and intrigue got him the position. His corruption caused so much trouble that Nero finally recalled Felix. It is hard to imagine that anyone could be worse than Nero. Tertullus skillfully lied, as any sophist does, to gain favor with the governor.

Tertullus eventually said there were three charges against Paul. First, Paul was charged with being a troublemaker. The *New King James Version* translates it, "creator of dissension" The Greek word is related to the English word "plague." Like an infectious disease it would spread throughout the empire. According to Tertullus, Paul was a real danger for the Roman Empire. Second, Paul was charged with being a ringleader of the sect of the Nazarenes. A ringleader is always considered a threat by the state. Third, Tertullus said Paul tried to desecrate the Temple. Of the three charges this is the only one of significance. Rome had given the Jews permission to impose the death penalty to anyone who defiled the temple. All three charges were merely accusations. However, they were very effectively presented by way of sophistry.

Tertullus stated them as if they were true and ultimately deserved condemnation. Tertullus concluded his arguments with an agreement from the Jews present. He told Felix, "by examining him yourself you may ascertain all these things of which we accuse him." Tertullus assumed that his deception and cunning was so persuasive that Felix would believe him. Tertullus thought Felix should believe the charges because Tertullus made them, the Jews present for the trial agreed, and the democracy, that is the mob at Jerusalem, had voted against Paul.

There was no place for truth, but the sophist seems to forget a fundamental axiom. Truth is always true even if nobody believes it. Falsehood is false even if everybody believes it. Os Guinness has rightly said, "without truth we are all vulnerable to manipulation."

Paul's defense before Felix is radically and truthfully different than the rhetoric of Tertullus. Paul clearly stated that he was not a troublemaker. He was only in Jerusalem for six days. He did not even preach while he was there. Paul disputed no one while he was there. He did not even gather a crowd of people except the democracy without a conscience. Paul admitted he was a follower of the way, but certainly not a ringleader. Anyhow, Roman law allowed Paul to practice his religion just like they allowed the Jews to practice their religion.

Paul's final defense was "I did not desecrate the temple." In fact Paul was submitting to the Jewish law and was ceremonially clean. There was no sophistry in Paul's defense. There was no deception. There was no wrangling with words. Truth was Paul's only defense. A nation, a church, or an individual that gives in to the deception of sophistry, will lose the freedom to tell the truth. For the Christian to use empty words is to make mockery of the head and the king of the church, the Lord Jesus Christ.

Jesus Christ is not like truth, he is truth. His incarnation is real. His sinless life is real. His death on the cross to pay for the sins of God's people is real. His saving grace is real. Everything about Jesus Christ is real and therefore true.

The Word of God is normative as Paul explains, "We demolish arguments and every pretension that sets itself up against the knowledge of God, and we take captive every thought to make it obedient to Christ" (2 Corinthians 10:5). Making disciples will require the use of apologetics against false arguments and sophisticated allegations.

Felix detained Paul for two years (Acts 24:27) and was replaced by Festus. The Jews and Festus tried to manipulate Paul into a situation that may cost Paul his life. The biblical text shows Paul's resolve to continue making disciples. Paul's defense was:

> I stand at Caesar's judgment seat, where I ought to be judged. To the Jews I have done no wrong, as you very well know. For if I am an offender, or have committed anything deserving of death, I do not object to dying; but if there is nothing in these things of which these men accuse me, no one can deliver me to them. I appeal to Caesar." Then Festus, when he had conferred with the council, answered, "You have appealed to Caesar? To Caesar you shall go! (Acts 25:10-12)

43. The Apostles' Doctrine

Acts 25:13 - 26:32

The Book of Acts reflects the doctrine of the apostles. The church summarized the apostle's doctrine and captioned it, *The Apostles' Creed.* Paul said to the Athenians, "I proclaim to you God who made the world and everything it." Christians affirm The Apostles' Creed by saying, "I believe in God the father almighty" (Acts 17:24). Paul said to the Thessalonians, "This Jesus whom I am proclaiming to you is the Christ." Christians say, "I believe in Jesus Christ the Lord" (Acts 17:3). "The Holy Spirit fell upon them (the Gentiles)" and Christians repeat the creed saying, "I believe in the Holy Spirit" (Acts 11:15). When Paul addressed the elders at Ephesus the last time he said, "Be on guard for yourselves and for all the flock, among which the Holy Spirit has made you overseers, to shepherd the church of God which He purchased with His own blood." Christians say, "I believe in the Holy Catholic Church" (Acts 20:28). Paul's testimony to Felix the Roman Governor was, "For the resurrection of the dead I am on trial before you today." Christians affirm the creed by saying, "I believe in the resurrection" (Acts 24:21).

The apostles and other disciples demonstrated utmost faithfulness in making disciples and teaching the whole counsel of God. The apostle Paul was particularly prominent in his role of faithfulness. For nearly fifteen years the apostle Paul traveled throughout Asia Minor and Europe faithfully making disciples and teaching the doctrine found in the Word of God. His appearance before King Agrippa, a Jewish King, and Festus, a Roman governor, is the third and final defense of the apostle Paul before secular authorities. Under the most adverse circumstances, Paul was faithful in his endeavor to make disciples. One verse will set the context for Paul's attempt to make disciples. "So the next day, when Agrippa and Bernice had come with great pomp, and had entered the auditorium with the commanders and the prominent men of the city, at Festus' command Paul was brought in" (Acts 25:23).

The Bible explains that Agrippa entered with, "great pomp." The Greek word translated into English as "pomp" is *phantasis*. The word refers to the imagination and specifically something that is not really real. It was all show or at least of momentary interest. Luke probably chose this word because the importance of the appearance of these great men was only a passing fantasy. All the pomp in this world is passing fantasy. The pomp of that day passed away. They died and eventually the Roman Empire became a historical byword. All the flags, pageantry, and great public display ceased to exist.

After everyone was seated "Paul stretched out his hand" and began his defense and witness (Acts 26:1). The stretching of the hand was the opening gesture for one poised to make a speech before some formal assembly. Paul then sets forth his history as a religious person, especially his acquaintance of the Jewish religion.

Paul was very careful to direct his narrative to the doctrine of messianic salvation. Agrippa understood the hope of the messiah. Festus did not understand, because he did not believe in the resurrection of the dead. Then Paul introduced the Messiah, Jesus of Nazareth, but initially Paul described himself as an enemy of Jesus the Messiah.

Paul's apologetic shifts to prove that God changes the hearts of men, because Paul was living proof. He gave an account of his Damascus road experience bringing it to a conclusion with these choice words coming from the mouth of the Lord Jesus Christ. Referring to the Gentiles Jesus said, "that they may receive forgiveness of sins and an inheritance among those who are sanctified by faith in Me" (Acts 26:18). The doctrine of forgiveness and an eternal inheritance would hold the attention of Agrippa and Festus. Paul asserts that his doctrine is the same as the doctrine of the prophets and Moses: "that the Christ would suffer, that He would be the first to rise from the dead and would proclaim light to the Jewish people and to the Gentiles" (Acts 26:23). Paul essentially challenges King Agrippa to believe the doctrine of the apostles.

Before King Agrippa could say anything, Festus said to Paul, "you are beside yourself! Much learning is driving you mad!" (Acts 26:24). To put it another way Festus thought the apostles' doctrine was for lunatics and crazy people. Paul responds by telling Agrippa and Festus that he is not crazy, but speaks words of "truth and reason" (Acts 26:25). Paul carefully and selectively used words and concepts like truth and reason, words that both King Agrippa and Festus would understand. Paul used the word "truth" because ultimately, it is objective and absolute. Truth is not humanly autonomous. Truth is that which is really real in the mind of God. Just because you *feel* like something is really real, does not make it true. It is real only if it is true in the mind of God. Agrippa and Festus knew very well that the gospel of Jesus Christ and the related promises of the gospel were not just Paul's ideas, if the doctrine is true. Paul said he, "speaks with reason." The word "reason" in this text does not refer to formal logic, but rather sound thinking or probably better yet common sense.

Paul's response to Festus fell on deaf ears, so Paul quickly turns his attention to King Agrippa.

> For the king, before whom I also speak freely, knows these things; for I am convinced that none of these things escapes his attention, since this thing was not done in a corner. King Agrippa, do you believe the

prophets? I know that you do believe." Then Agrippa said to Paul, "You almost persuade me to become a Christian." And Paul said, "I would to God that not only you, but also all who hear me today, might become both almost and altogether such as I am, except for these chains." (Acts 26:26-29)

There you have the inspired record of Paul's last defense and witness to men of authority on this earth. Paul was faithful. Paul had no fear of men. Paul spoke the truth and reason.

The doctrine of the apostles' was a fulfillment of the doctrine of the prophets in the Old Testament. The fulfillment of the messianic promise was "not done in a corner." Making disciples and teaching the full counsel of God was open for the world to hear and believe. Christianity is the most public religion in the history of the world.

Before the advent of Christ the religion of the Old Testament was public. All the Old Testament writings and prophets were public. The appearance of Christ was public. Other religious cultures from the east saw the star that directed them to the place of His birth. The progress of Christianity is publicly displayed in the annals of history. Think of the public nature of Christian influences. The Bible is the most public book in the world. The church is the most collective expression of Christianity in the world. The foundation for many charitable works, hospitals, schools and almost every civic institution has roots in Christianity. The Christian forefathers threw down the gauntlet to the world, the flesh and the devil, attesting to that great truth that Christianity was not done in a corner. The Middle ages attempted to build community and civilization around the unity of apostles' doctrine. They tried to make Christianity the universal religion of Europe. Christianity and the apostles' doctrine were not in a corner. It is time for the church to get out of the corner.

However, in the modern era in this country and Europe as well, the church has been absorbed into the state. Christianity is now in a corner. The religious liberty of the past and the human dignity that accompanied it is now in a corner. The result is a watered down gospel. The result is a civilization without the unity of faith. The American creeds of socialism, individualism, relativism, pragmatism, and utilitarianism have trampled underfoot the apostles' doctrine, because Christianity is in a corner.

When everything is said and done, Christians must remember that the pomp of this world is like a passing vapor that disappears before their eyes. Man-made civic creeds will pass away, but the Word of God will remain forever. Christians must take the doctrine of the apostles' into every part of life so they can say with integrity, this thing was not done in a corner.

King Agrippa was a man in the covenant community. King Agrippa was like the baptized church member who still does not believe. Religious people or to put it another way, baptized religious unbelievers may almost be persuaded, but they remain in darkness.

Baptized religious unbelievers remain in a corner. Paul told Agrippa that he wished for Agrippa to be like Paul "except for these chains." Paul may have intended to use "these chains" as a metaphor for King Agrippa's bondage to Satan. The church is in a corner because of the disregard and disbelief of the Word of God.

Those like King Agrippa **almost** believe that God is sovereign.

They **almost** believe that Christ died for His flock.

They **almost** believe that the Holy Spirit applies the work of Christ to the sinful heart.

They **almost** believe that man is naturally dead in sin.

They **almost** believe in the biblical doctrine of forgiveness.

They **almost** believe that ungodly worship is acceptable to God.

The Protestant church in the Western world is inundated with professing Christians that almost, but not quite, believe the full doctrine of Scripture. They most eagerly believe that doctrine of Scripture that pleases their unbelieving estate.

They almost believe, but not quite. Maybe this provokes a question. What should I do? "Therefore, brethren, be even more diligent to make your call and election sure, for if you do these things you will never stumble" (2 Peter 1:10). Stir up the grace of God that is in you.

When you move beyond "almost believing" imitate the Apostle Paul. Engage in the noble work of making disciples. Trust God to remove the chains and call His people out of darkness into the light by His sovereign power.

44. Godly Confidence

Acts 27:1-44

This text describes an eye witness account of Paul's trip to Rome. Paul had appealed to Caesar and to Caesar he must travel. There are some interesting questions that arise from Luke's personal account of Paul's trip.

Why is this trip the only one described in vivid detail? Apparently Luke kept a daily diary of the weather, the ports, and details of sea travel that would generally only be known by sailors. The answer is, God inspired it because historical details and historical accuracy are important.

Why did Luke go on this trip and not some of the others? Were not some of Paul's other missionary travels just as important as this one? Answer: The providence of God provided for Luke to travel with Paul on his final stretch to Rome.

Although the majority of this chapter concentrates on historical narrative, the disciple should remember that it contains very important doctrine.

Providence
Patience
Stewardship
Evangelism
Generosity

Trust and godly confidence are important doctrines found in this chapter. There is a vast chasm between ungodly confidence and godly confidence. Ungodly confidence is trust in some human invention or convention that relies upon the power of man. At the very least ungodly confidence depends on the sinful human understanding.

Godly confidence is trust in God. Godly confidence is based on an understanding of God because of God's Word, The natural world is under the direct care of God. For instance, it would be godly confidence to understand that the natural elements are consistent with their nature. It represents ungodly confidence to believe contrary to what God has revealed in nature. For example, when there was a low pressure over Libya it caused a strong cold wind over the Mediterranean. For that reason sea travel over the Mediterranean ceased from November to March in ancient times

Paul's warning is consistent with the danger of the natural elements. Paul knew of the danger and warned them saying, "Men I perceive that this voyage will end with disaster and much loss, not only of the cargo and ship, but also our lives."

The Roman officer in charge of the prisoners, of which Paul was one, preferred to listen to the ungodly captain of the ship rather than the godly advice of the apostle Paul.

The ungodly captain knew the dangers involved, but he had no moral constitution upon which to base his decision. However, Paul was far from a skilled seaman, but he knew that God's truth was consistent even when it came to the natural elements. Paul's confidence was secure because of God's promise. The captain depended on self-confidence. The ungodly decision by an ungodly man did not frustrate God's plan for the apostle Paul to go to Rome. Paul gave his advice based on his understanding of God, because God controls the wind and the waves. The ship's captain made the decision based on expediency and utility. What the captain failed to take into account is Paul's concern for the moral dimension and the well being of the entire operation.

This historical narrative shows the characteristics of a godly man looking out for the welfare of the society in which he lives. Sometimes godly ministers are perceived as meddling with the affairs of society when they warn of the dangers that may result from ungodly decisions.

Anyhow the captain proceeded to navigate the ship with confidence in his ungodly decision. The result was disastrous. The ship was eventually destroyed. Before the ship was destroyed by the wind and waves, Paul spoke boldly and said, "you should have listened to me and not have sailed from Crete and incurred this disaster and loss." I do not believe Paul intended to say "I told you so" as much as he still had the interest of the passengers at heart, because he went on to say, "take heart, for there will be no loss of life among you, but only the ship."

Those seasoned sailors were caught in a terrible storm, but they were afraid. With all of their knowledge they were ready to give up the ship. Paul knew very little about ships and storms, but he still said "do not be afraid." Paul's words of encouragement came because he knew God was in control. Paul knew that God had a purpose in sending the storm. Paul had heard of the final words that Jesus spoke just before Jesus ascended into heaven. "I am with you always, even to the end of the age" (Matthew 28:20).

Another example of ungodly confidence is to go against the dictates of common sense. It is unwise to handle poisonous snakes because their bite may cause serious illness or death. Paul was bitten by a viper, but it had no effect on Paul. Although, liberal interpreters conclude it was a non-poisonous snake, the evidence in the text points to the contrary (Acts 28:3-6). God miraculously prevented Paul from harm, but that is no reason to allow ungodly self-confidence to persuade Christians to handle poisonous snakes.

Paul had confidence in God, not in himself. Furthermore, Paul explained why he had confidence in God. Paul knew he belonged to God. For Christians to have confidence in God, they must know God. Paul knew that he served God (Acts 27:23). Paul was not self serving. He did not use his hands and feet for his own benefit. He did not use his tongue and mind for feathering his own nest. He did not crown himself as the center of the universe. Paul's interest was in serving God and that required serving others, even at the peril of his own well being. Paul's confidence was in God and His Word. Paul told the men on the ship, "I believe God that it will be just as it was told me" (Acts 27:25). The Word of God was the rule for Paul's life.

Paul lived during a literal storm on the Mediterranean Sea. It was literally the raging wind and waves that threatened his life and the lives of other on the ship. Christians today may not have to live through that kind of storm, but life is full of storms. Some of them are fierce. During those storms, where do you find confidence and hope? Where is your confidence when personal storms come your way?

When it is time to make a decision, will you trust the counsel of ungodly men, like the captain of the ship, or the counsel of godly men under the authority of God like the apostle Paul? It is common for all men and women, Christians and unbelievers, to face all kinds of storms. Some are storms as a result of private sin such as lust, covetousness and pride. It may be relational storms. It may be a storm of personal fear and the undisclosed consequences of that fear. It be some physical ailment

When the storms come, and they will, where is your confidence? Will you say to yourself "Do not be afraid" and really mean it? You should be able to mean it if you really believe in God, if you know you belong to God, and if you know you serve God.

Where is your confidence when storms blow through the church?

Where is your confidence when civic and social storms disrupt our communities and our nation?

Where is your confidence when political storms threaten you, your family, your community, and your nation?

The Word of God gives the answer to those questions. "And we have such trust through Christ toward God. Not that we are sufficient of ourselves to think of anything as being from ourselves, but our sufficiency is from God, who also made us sufficient as ministers of the new covenant…" (2 Corinthians 3:4-6).

45. Bright Side of a Dark World

Acts 28:1-31

The journey through the book of Acts is an inspired record of "all that Jesus began both to do and teach" (Acts 1:1). From the beginning to the end, Luke emphasizes the kingdom of God. "He presented Himself alive after His sufferings by many infallible proofs, being seen by them during 40 days and speaking of the things pertaining to the kingdom of God" (Acts 1:3). The last verse has Paul, "preaching the kingdom of God and teaching the things which concern the Lord Jesus Christ with all confidence, no one forbidding him" (Acts 28:31).

The book of Acts covers nearly 30 years of church history. Throughout the expansion and development of the church, men like Philip preach the good news about the kingdom of God (Acts 8:12). When Paul went to Ephesus he entered the synagogue and continued speaking out boldly for three months, reasoning and persuading them about the kingdom of God (Acts 19:8). When he met the elders of Ephesus for the last time he said, "I know that you all, among whom I have gone preaching the kingdom of God, will see my face no more." (Acts 20:25)

The apostles expressed a great interest in the kingdom of God. They understood the words of the Lord Jesus Christ when he said, "All authority has been given to Me in heaven and on earth. Go therefore and make disciples of all the nations" (Matthew 28:18). When Jesus used the words "all authority" the reference is to his kingdom regalia. It is an expression of the highest honor that can be given to a king. Psalm 47 is an example of kingdom regalia. It expresses the activities of a particular feast day when God's people gathered to celebrate the coronation of God. The regalia may be found in coronative expressions like:

Clap hands – to welcome the advent of God's reign
Shout – to express the joy of God's awesome power
King over all the earth
God reigns over the nations
Dignity
Honor
Majesty

Paul's preaching of the kingdom of God was a reference to the kingdom regalia concept. Paul believed that King Jesus had all authority. Even though Paul was imprisoned at Rome his expectation was the expansion of the kingdom of God. The logic of the language in the closing words of the book of Acts is not dubious. Paul expected to see the prosperity of the kingdom of God. Paul arrived in Rome as a prisoner. He lived by himself with the exception of one soldier who guarded him. He called the Jews to his quarters so he could declare to them with serious testimony the kingdom of God.

Some believed and some did not believe. Paul's parting admonition was a quotation from Isaiah the Jewish prophet.

So when they did not agree among themselves, they departed after Paul had said one word: "The Holy Spirit spoke rightly through Isaiah the prophet to our fathers, saying, 'Go to this people and say: "Hearing you will hear, and shall not understand; And seeing you will see, and not perceive; For the hearts of this people have grown dull. Their ears are hard of hearing, And their eyes they have closed, Lest they should see with their eyes and hear with their ears, Lest they should understand with their hearts and turn, So that I should heal them.'" "Therefore let it be known to you that the salvation of God has been sent to the Gentiles, and they will hear it!" And when he had said these words, the Jews departed and had a great dispute among themselves. (Acts 28:25-29)

Stop for some solemn reflection on Paul's mission and ministry. Think about all the pain, suffering, and misery in Paul's life as a missionary, teacher, pastor, theologian, and evangelist. He was in prison and the full counsel of God was spurned by the Jews at Rome. The darkness of pagan Rome, the darkness of his cell, and the darkness of the unbelieving Jews all adds up to a dark world. Many would be ready to pitch in the towel and say, "it's a hopeless case; I may as well give up."

Paul did not give up. Quite to the contrary, Paul stayed in Rome two years preaching the kingdom of God. The kingdom of God motif from Paul's perspective was bright. He expected the kingdom of God to prosper and expand, even in the darkness of this world. While we live at the center of turmoil, strife, confusion, and to put it in biblical terms, darkness, we still have a bright side in this dark world. The bright side is the kingdom of God.

Although the kingdom of God has a wide range of implications for every Christian, I want to publish the reasons Paul sacrificed for the sake of the kingdom of God. We must begin our inquiry at the place we best understand the reign of God and that is in our hearts. For instance, when we pray for thy kingdom to come we are asking God to more and more establish his rule in our hearts. When God establishes His rule in our hearts, then the mind, emotions and will become more and more God-centered rather than man-centered.

The reign of the kingdom of God in the heart reveals the sovereignty of God and His will for His people. If the kingdom of God reigns in the heart, the tyranny of Satan will be abolished. The various dimensions of the kingdom of God will become more and more important.

The kingdom of God will rule in the heart of men several different ways. First, the kingdom of God will rule in the heart by way of truth. It may be said that the kingdom of God is the kingdom of truth. When Jesus was on trial before Pontius Pilate, the kingdom of God was the major subject.

> Pilate answered, "Am I a Jew? Your own nation and the chief priests have delivered You to me. What have You done?" Jesus answered, "My kingdom is not of this world. If My kingdom were of this world, My servants would fight, so that I should not be delivered to the Jews; but now My kingdom is not from here." Pilate therefore said to Him, "Are You a king then?" Jesus answered, "You say rightly that I am a king. For this cause I was born, and for this cause I have come into the world, that I should bear witness to the truth. Everyone who is of the truth hears My voice." (John 19:35-37)

God is not confused and He cannot contradict himself. His kingdom is absolutely pure and not mixed with error. The truth begins with an understanding God's nature and character in comparison to man's depraved sinful nature. The holiness of God is in contrast with the sinfulness of man. The power of God is in contrast to the weakness of man. The fullness of God is in contrast to the emptiness of man until God reveals and applies His saving truth to the soul of man. God's truth is delivered to the hearts of men by the preaching of the Word of God and applied to the heart by the Holy Spirit. The kingdom of God is established by God's truth and yet today the majority of professing Christians do not believe there is any such thing as absolute truth.

The kingdom of God will also rule in the heart by way of grace. The kingdom of grace is the establishment of the new nature that brings light to the mind, order to the emotions, and surrender to the will. It is the kingdom of grace that announces to the world that sinners are saved by the perfect atoning sacrifice of Jesus Christ. If the kingdom of grace rules in the heart, it should shine as a bright light. Like the apostle Paul, Christians should expect the kingdom of grace to prosper and expand throughout the family, the church, the nation, and even internationally. The kingdom of God comes by way of grace, so that redemption will be made sure and that the gospel will be heard around the earth.

The kingdom of God will not only rule in the heart by way of truth and grace, the kingdom of God will rule in the kingdom of glory. The kingdom of glory refers to the eternal Sabbath rest where the saints will reign with God and the angels forever. The kingdom of glory will be free from all the imperfections of the human nature and Christians will be endowed with the glorious perfections obtained for them by the Lord Jesus Christ. The kingdom of glory has no more temptations, sorrows, or doubts. The kingdom of glory does have the perfection of divine knowledge and immediate communion with God himself.

The kingdom of God is spiritual, but it has wide reaching implications in day to day secular life. Political, economic, and social life also comes under the authority and rule of King Jesus. The political and social aspects of the kingdom of God take on a new moral code.

Then why is there so much darkness in the secular world? I believe it is the result of many professing Christians, especially leaders, abdicating their responsibility to make disciples of all nations. They are too busy devising church growth strategies and programs to attract people to their religious organization, often referred to as the church.

The result created a vacuum and the prince of darkness filled that vacuum with world views like consumerism, utilitarianism, secularism, et al. Satan's crafty lies duped people into believing that the secular state has no higher authority by which it may be held accountable. Therefore, the state becomes the moral standard by which laws are established. With kingdom regalia out of the way, tyranny prevails.

I don't know how your personal life looks, but if it resembles the world in which we live, I expect there are some dark places that need to come under the rule of God's kingdom. The expulsion of darkness will be replaced with the bright light of God's kingdom.

46. The Church Growth Movement

     The church growth movement, the mega-church concept, and various other exciting religious inventions charm professing Christians with frills, thrills, and entertainment. These religious charms have captured the attention of churchmen around the world. "Marketing the church" has replaced the biblical concept of "making disciples." The Mega-church has replaced the biblical concept of a shepherd and the flock. It is important to realize that the church growth movement finds its most faithful followers referring to "contemporary worship" or talking about the "emerging church." These recent inventions spring forth from the church growth movement. This chapter is the result of my observation, research, and inquiry into the church growth movement. This is my critique of the movement and if correct, it is contrary to the doctrine and practice of the first thirty years of the church. My purpose in this chapter is to explain how modernity is inseparably related to the church growth movement.

     The decline of the evangelical church may be attributed to any number of factors. However, two factors have significantly contributed to the decline. They are modernity and the church growth movement. The argument set forth is that although modernity has shaped the character of the evangelical church, the church growth movement is the driving force to implement the tools of modernity in the evangelical church.

Part One:

Children of Modernity

Modernity has been described as "the character and system of the world produced by the forces of modernization and development."[1] "Modernization is the process that requires that our society be organized around cities for the purpose of manufacturing and commerce."[2] Modernization and Modernity are related, but different. David Wells explains the term modernization.

> A process driven by capitalism and fueled by technological innovation. These forces have reshaped our social landscape and, in turn, have reshaped our inner lives as we have been drawn into the vortex they have created. And it is this vortex that I am calling modernity.[3]

The children of modernity are the ideologies and world views that influence the public sector. Secularism, pragmatism, consumerism, relativism, individualism, and managerialism are a few of the children of modernity. The offspring that comes from these ideologies and world views produce still more offspring. The Enlightenment project gave birth to modernity and modernity has served as an agent to expand the influence of secularism. The focus of secularism as a world and life view is on the present age. Unfortunately the focus on the secular drives Christians to become the progeny of that secular philosophy. The dilemma leads us to the sad fact that "secularized Christians rather than secular

---

[1] Os Guinness, *The American Hour*, (New York: The Free Press, 1993) p. 26.
[2] David Wells, *No Place for Truth*, (William B. Eerdmans Publishing Co.,, 1993) p. 26.
[3] Ibid, p. 7.

humanists...must account for the disintegration of religious vitality"[4] in the evangelical church.

The relationship between modernity and the Enlightenment project has more to do with the expression of ideas than with dogmatic philosophy. When Alasdair MacIntyre, a contemporary moral philosopher, argued that the "Enlightenment project...failed by its own standards"[5], he went on to describe the mass of destruction it left in its path. The Enlightenment was the seed for the full development of modernity. The progeny of modernity which comes out of the Enlightenment project will be a powerful and devastating force against the evangelical church.

When liberalism threatened the church at the beginning of last century, J. Gresham Machen responded by writing an apologetic to defend the cultural mandate for Christians. Machen said, "From every point of view, therefore, the problem in question is the most serious concern of the church. What is the relation between Christianity and modern culture; may Christianity be maintained in a scientific age?"[6] Throughout the book Machen refers, at least implicitly, to the cultural mandate in the period of modernity. Christians should be ashamed for allowing culture to be controlled by the children of modernity. It is the duty of the Christian to invade the culture not for the culture to overwhelm the church. The children of modernity are the monsters invading the evangelical church.

The cultural wars in this country have their roots in theological and philosophical ideas. The cultural wars are

---

[4] Michael Horton, *Made in America*, (Grand Rapids: Baker Book House, 1991). P. 16

[5] Alasdair MacIntyre, *After Virtue,* (Notre Dame: University of Notre Dame Press, 1981), p. 77.

[6] J. Gresham Machen, *Christianity and Liberalism*, (Grand Rapids: William B. Eerdmans Publishing Co., 1923). p. 5-6.

children of modernity. James Davison Hunter argued that "The present culture war has evolved...as a struggle to establish new agreements over the character and content of America's public culture."[7] The cultural wars reflect the failure of Christians to engage themselves in the God given cultural mandate. The biblical cultural mandate is "Be fruitful and multiply; fill the earth and subdue it; have dominion...over every living thing" (Genesis 1:28).

Another child of modernity is the therapeutic revolution. New York University professor of psychology, Dr. Paul Vitz, described America as a "psychological society in which there has been a triumph of the therapeutic."[8] Therapy has become the by-word for Americans who believe they are victims of the power and persuasion of other people. This child of modernity affects the church with its explosive appeal to the senses. God's people still have the capacity to sin and sin they do. The temptations and trials of life drive them to look for answers when they feel threatened and victimized. They go to the therapist for help and the vicious cycle continues. It has produced a worldview known as victimizationalism.

Of all the children that modernity has produced, managerial madness is certainly one whose offspring will change the shape of the church. In MacIntyre's evaluation of the moral philosophy of the western world, he believed that "the bureaucratic manager...could mold, influence, and control the social environment."[9] His assessment is accurate "because sound and positive management is essential for the success of

---

[7] James Davidson Hunter, *Culture Wars*, (Basic Books, A Division of Harper Collins Publishers, 1991), p. 63.
[8] Os Guinness and John Seel, *No God But God*, (Chicago: Moody Press, 1992), p. 95.
[9] Alasdair MacIntyre, *After Virtue*, p. 77.

any organization"[10]   according to the managerial theory.
Management has to do with the biblical concept of stewardship. Management is not a new concept, but modernity has
exploited it and made it a tool which works against the
biblical concept of stewardship.

The progeny of modernity will continue to influence
the evangelical church, unless the church learns how to
control the monstrous children of modernity. These children
of modernity are not intrinsically evil, but they may become
instruments of the enemy to bring about evil. Evangelical
Christians should understand the dangers of these children.
Os Guinness quotes Peter Berger to caution the church about
using the children of modernity. "He warns that whoever
sups with the devil of modernity had better have a long
spoon."[11] More must be said about this warning.

> The believer 'who sups with it will find his spoon get-
> ting shorter and shorter - until that last supper in
> which he is left alone at the table, with no spoon at all
> and with an empty plate.' Our challenge, then, is to
> dine at the banquet of modernity - but with long
> spoons.[12]

There is a sense of power flowing forth from the children of modernity. David Wells argues that "what shapes the
modern world is not powerful minds but powerful forces, not
philosophy but urbanization, capitalism and technology."[13]
He is correct and brings attention to the inevitable relationship between the modern and the postmodern. The postmod-

---

[10] Guinness and Seel, *No God But God*, p. 148.
[11] Os Guinness, *Dining With the Devil*, (Grand Rapids: Baker Book
House, 1993), p. 31.
[12] Ibid., p. 31
[13] David Wells, *No Place for Truth*, p. 61.

ern mind is not necessarily empty, but it is not stimulated by an intellectual agenda. In postmodernism the scholar has replaced the intellectual. The modern scholar schooled by an anti-intellectual teacher does not apply the rules of logic into intellectual inquiry. Every aspect of life is reinterpreted by the postmodern so that tradition will not enter the scene. The postmodern world rejects objective rationality in favor of a critical legal theory, education theory, et al. The postmodern hermeneutic has affected evangelicalism in the area of grammatical/historical interpretation more than any other dimension of the postmodern world. The postmodern interpretation requires the deconstruction of the text. It may be said that "postmodernist theories begin with the assumption that language cannot render truths about the world in an objective way."[14] Deconstructionism may be the majority report in the future of literary analysis, but that does not necessarily make it the right choice. Another voice explaining postmodern thought said "The one thing I have learned in hermeneutics which has changed everything is what I can only call 'obedience to the text' - listening to the text itself instead of modern interpreters of it."[15] The postmodern deconstructionist can make no claim for truth because truth cannot be defined except for deconstructing the text. Thomas Oden corrects this error using the intellectual powers to define absolutes. To understand the non-structure and powerlessness of postmodernism will help one understand the structure and power of modernity.

The power of modernity is rooted in the relativism that springs from it. "It is a period whose key general features (moral relativism, narcissistic hedonism, naturalistic

---

[14] Gene Veith Jr, *Postmodern Times*, (Wheaton, Ill.: Crossway Books, 1994), p. 51.
[15] Thomas C. Oden, *After Modernity... What?*, (Grand Rapids: Zondervan Publishing House, 1990), p. 80.

reductionism, and autonomous individualism) have been well described by modern intellectual historians... ."[16] Relativism as a philosophy has stood in front of every part of our society including religion and philosophy. Relativism is powerful, because it cannot be contained in any body of thought. The children of modernity are poised to use relativization to advance their cause and it is a powerful tool. Relativism is inherently dangerous in modern thought.

> Relativization has its own special hazards, and important distinctions must be preserved. Historicism's rejection of transcendence subjects its followers to the same dizzying loss of stability that Einsteinian physics created for categories of time and space... .Everything is relativized because there is nothing transcending the flux that could provide the stability needed to position everything else... .The kind of relativization that can be affirmed, in contrast, is that which places human values under the judgment of the transcendent God... .A society that cannot tolerate a judge beyond history will find that it can learn to tolerate anything else.[17]

The "judge beyond history" has a fixed unchangeable standard for His created order.   If Christians reject His standard, then they have the awful face of relativism which will lead to compromise and confusion.

---

[16] Ibid., p. 46.
[17] Herbert Schlossberg, *Idols For Destruction*, (Washington D. C.: Regnery Gateway, 1990), p. 36-37.

Part Two:

The Influence
of Modernity

Modernity offers variety and change to any who will make their vows to it. The secret to the success of modernity's expansion is rationalism. The sense in which I am referring to rationalism is that the appeal to reason, apart from sense experience, is the only way to solve problems and ultimately to find salvation. There is a distinction between a rationalist, one who uses reason in an attempt to interpret reality and rationalism as I have just described. Rationalism does not answer all the questions of life and reality. The Bible has the answers to reality and life.

Jacques Barzun has pointed out that eighteenth century Liberalism (the cult of self) and eighteenth century Rationalism (the cult of reason) had the effect of making religion seem superfluous. If man is his own master, and reason his only judge, what is man to do with the lingering sense that there is more to life than his reason and the material world can contain?[18]

Rationalism ends up in the world of subjectivity. The quest to understand reality never completes the cycle, so the next step is to try something new or different. The students of modernity have mastered this concept. It is sad but true that the evangelical church has been persuaded by these disciples to become the vehicle to spread the message of modernity.

Modernity has powerful persuasive elements which indicate that "Modernity is not just a time but a set of passions, hopes, and ideas, a mentality that prevails in some circles more than in others, and nowhere more than the university, the primary agent of the ideology of modernity."[19]

---

[18] Kenneth A. Myers, *All God's Children and Blue Suede Shoes*, (Wheaton, Ill.; Crossway Books, 1989), p. 108
[19] Thomas Oden, *After Modernity... What?*, p. 52.

The university is the place theologians go for an education. Many seminaries have university trained professors. The question is: to what extent have they been persuaded by modernity and how much of that persuasion will be passed on to the coming generations? The evangelical church stands on the edge of the precipice of a plunge into a neo-dark age. Should the church be fearful that modernity is standing ready to push her over the edge?

The potential threat of modernity to the evangelical church is probably greater than ever, but the opportunity for reformation is also greater than any time in recent history. The children of modernity have attempted to secularize Christianity. We see this a number of different ways, but primarily as "the pastor seeks to embody what modernity admires and to redefine what pastoral ministry now means in light of this culture's two most admired types, the manager and the psychologist."[20] David Wells attributes the problem to the disappearance of theology. If sound theology disappears then something must replace that theology. I ask you to consider, "The gulf between the truth-centered evangelism of Edwards and Whitefield and the technique-centered variety of industrialized religion...illustrated by Charles Finney... ."[21] Finney's method of evangelism is one of many examples of how modernity threatens the good health of the evangelical church. Although Finney's theology is not well systematized, it is well documented that he believed "methods" were the key to the salvation of a soul. Likewise, the church growth movement believes that methods will fill the pews.

Modernity has produced a progeny by its power and persuasion and now poses a threat to the church. What can we do? We can reject the "myths of power [and] popularity,

---

[20] David Wells, *No Place for Truth*, p. 101.
[21] Michael Scott Horton, *Made in America*, p. 44.

[which] have led to an unhealthy preoccupation with superficial success, methods over message, technique over truth, quantity over quality"[22] The greater question is how can we accomplish this? Mike Horton responds to the question by reminding us of our world and life view.

> The Bible commands, 'Do not conform any longer to the pattern of this world, but be transformed by the renewing of your mind' (Rom. 12:2). While much fuel has been spent on trying to get people to act like Christians, the Bible insists that we must first think like Christians. The transforming of our minds takes place not through magic, superstitious techniques, or superficial devotions, but through serious and sometimes difficult study. It requires that we know something about the Bible and the people to whom it is addressed, and that we know something about ourselves and the culture in which we live. It is dangerous to pretend one is not worldly when one refuses to critically examine the ways in which one has been influenced more by the spirit of the age than by the Spirit of Christ.[23]

The Christian world and life view does not spring forth from the ground like an artesian well. It is formulated by the laborious effort of the individual empowered by the Holy Spirit. Christians do not devote enough time and effort asking the "why" questions of the Christian faith. Why should we use the tools of modernity is the question we must ask? But all too often Christians are asking, "how may I use the tools of modernity?" rather than running from them. Christians often ask the scientific question "how" rather than the

---

[22] Ibid, p. 12.
[23] Ibid.

philosophical question "why." The "why" question will always need to consult the Word of God to find the correct answer. The Christian begins to use the tools of modernity, relativism creeps in and soon methodology becomes their god. "In 1926 the Bible Crusaders of America formed: its special mission was to "combat Modernism, Evolution, Agnosticism and Atheism."[24] Today evangelicals are no longer contending against Modernism, they are embracing it. The most notable example of this can be found in the church growth movement.

---

[24] James Davidson Hunter, *Culture Wars*, p. 138.

Part Three:

Goals of the Church Growth Movement

The church growth movement is a loose confederation of ministers and laymen whose beginning can be traced to Donald McGavran. He was a missionary to India, professor at Fuller Seminary and founder of the Church Growth Institute. The church growth movement does not have the privilege of pointing to any significant theologian in their ranks. When Martin Luther and John Calvin stood in the gap during the early years of the Reformation, it would not be improper to refer to them as part of a movement that sought to be reformed by the Word of God. Although some of the key men in the Reformation had points of disagreement, they were bound together by a common theology. The church growth movement is void of any theological center. The movement may be found in liberal, conservative, fundamental, or evangelical churches. It may be said that proponents of the church growth movement are bound together by a common philosophy. What is the glue that keeps them together?

Leaders of the church growth movement surround themselves with disciples that have the appearance of a personality cult. Win Arn, a noted disciple of Donald McGavran, said "trainees who come out of victorious churches and have been trained by men, who are themselves multipliers of churches, are generally effective."[25] The idea is that success breeds success. It has been suggested that the concept of a "flagship church" be used as a model.

It must be emphasized that the term 'Flagship Church" is a functional definition. Just as the sim-

---

[25] Donald A McGavran, *How to Grow a Church*, (Glendale, CA: Regal Books Division, G/L Publications, 1973), p. 79.

plest definition of a leader is 'a person people follow,' so a flagship church is a functional designation of a church which has a fruitful, pace setting ministry within a given metropolitan area.[26]

The best guide to know how God wants to grow His church is the Bible. The biblical concept for expanding the kingdom of God is: one plants, one waters, and one reaps the harvest, but God alone causes the church to grow. A fundamental error in the church growth movement is when pastors are told they can expect their churches to grow, but "they must be willing to follow a growth leader."[27]

The pastor is expected to assume the Chief Executive Officer position. George Barna, a leader in church growth methodology, boldly critiques the church by saying, "many people do judge the pastor not on his ability to preach, teach, or counsel, but on his capacity to make the church run smoothly and efficiently. In essence he is judged as a businessman. . . ."[28] The evidence is compelling. The church growth movement is an alliance of professing Christian leaders who are committed to the same goal. What is that goal?

Church growth is the goal! Church growth movement advocates define church growth as "that science which investigates the planting, multiplication, function, and health of Christian churches as they relate specifically to the effec-

---

[26] Lee Roy Taylor Jr., *A Flagship Church Planting Strategy for the Presbyterian Church in America*, (Ann Arbor, MI: U.M.I. Dissertation Information Service, 1991), p. 33.

[27] Win Arn, *The Pastor's Church Growth Handbook*, (Pasadena, CA: Church Growth Press, 1982), p. 887.

[28] George Barna, *Marketing the Church*, (Colorado Springs: CO: Navpress, 1989), p.14.

tive implementation of God's commission... ."[29] Another church growth movement guru stated his philosophy a different way.

> One of the basic premises of the church growth movement is that efforts in evangelism can be measured and that the effectiveness of methods can be evaluated and the responses of people and fields can also be gauged. Perhaps the most basic premise is that God intends for his church to grow and the church growth must be pursued out of obedience to Jesus Christ.[30]

The scientific method is useful for measuring, evaluating, and bringing theories to a conclusion. It is not useful if it impinges upon mandates given in Scripture. I cannot find a hint in Scripture that we should measure the effectiveness of God's evangelistic method. What is clear in Scripture is the mandate for Christians to be involved in the evangelistic enterprise. The problem with the church growth movement is not its desire to be involved in evangelism, but rather the method used in evangelism. Methodology is the culprit. The method used by the church growth movement resembles a multi-level marketing scheme. A dynamic, charismatic and persuasive leader looks for other people who are dynamic, charismatic, and persuasive. With these personalities, add transferable concepts and then church growth will follow.

They would argue that church growth is biblical. Since church growth is de facto biblical, they set out to offer Scripture proofs. The fallacy is that no Christian can deny

---

[29] C. Wayne Zunkel, *Church Growth Under Fire*, (Scottdale, PA: Herald Press, 1987), 218.

[30] Foster H. Shannon, *The Growth Crisis in the American Church*, (South Pasadena, CA: William Carey Library, 1977), p. 3.

that church growth is not biblical. The goal of the church growth movement is church growth and that is accomplished by means of evangelism. They seem to forget that evangelism is only one of several duties God requires of Christians. Evangelism is the top priority on their agenda. They almost dismiss the fundamental purpose of the church which is to worship the triune God. Evangelism is not the purpose of the church; it is part of the mission of the church. They also forget the need for a common confession. "Like the deists in 1776, evangelicals today are suspicious of creeds, confessions, and doctrinal systems."[31] This charge by Horton seems to be very much at home in the church growth movement. They have no common theological system and no common doctrinal statement, just a basic common philosophy based on the common goal for church growth.

---

[31] Michael Horton, *Beyond Culture Wars*, (Chicago: Moody Press, 1994), p. 63.

Part Four:

Philosophy of the Church Growth Movement

The basic philosophy of the church growth movement is to use the children of modernity to cause the church to grow. Even so followers still struggle with the church growth movement philosophy.

> J. Randall Petersen...is involved in starting Hope United Methodist Church... .To gather its congregation, Hope Church used a telemarketing campaign to invite community members to its services... .He is still uneasy with some church-growth ideas... .But it worked, he admits...Petersen is not alone in his pragmatic embrace of church-growth thinking.[32]

Pragmatism is one of the basic philosophies of the church growth movement. "If it works, use it captures the spirit of pragmatism.[33] This is demonstrated by the intense effort to meet the "felt needs" of professing Christians. A felt need is described as "the conscious wants and desires of a person."[34] The pragmatic view attempts to see that "sermons are short, simple, uplifting and personally inspiring. Topics are carefully selected to stress the personal over the doctrinal and the relational over the abstract."[35] *Christianity Today* reports that during the growing days of the movement "church growth was soon marked by strong pragmatism."[36] When I discuss biblical evangelism with Christians who use Arminian methods, most of the time they will defend their

---

[32] Ken Sidey, *Church Growth Fine Tunes Its Formulas*, Christianity Today, June 24, 1991, p. 44.

[33] R. C. Sproul, *Lifeviews*, (Old Tappan, NJ: Fleming H. Revell Co., 1986P. p. 77.

[34] C Peter Wagner, *Church Growth State of the Art*, (Wheaton: Tyndale House, 1986), p. 290.

[35] Douglas Webster, *Selling Jesus*, (Downers Grove, IL: Intervarsity Press, 2992), p. 75.

[36] Ken Sidney, *Church Growth Fine Tunes Its Formulas*, p. 45.

method by saying, "but it works." Is it conceivable that Christians believe that pragmatism is the criteria by which we engage in God's kingdom work? Pragmatism has replaced Scripture as the final authority to direct how we may serve God. Pragmatism takes many forms in the church growth movement. One is the idea that target groups will achieve church growth

The pragmatic strategy of the church growth move-ment demands an embrace of the managerial system of modernity. A lengthy quote is necessary to explain how this works.

> Defining goals and objectives, and making them un-derstandable to each member of the church is the most important leadership task before us. It is difficult and it takes discipline Robert Townsend in *Up The Or-ganization* describes the lengthy and difficult process at Avis in setting objectives. One of the important functions of a leader is to make the organization con-centrate on it objectives. In the case of Avis, it took us six months to define one objective - which turned out to be: We want to become the fastest - growing company with the highest profit margin in the busi-ness of renting and leasing vehicles without drivers.[37]

The goal of Avis Rent a Car and the church are en-tirely different. Avis has one purpose and that is to make money to pay the investors and remain in business. The purpose of the church is to glorify the Lord God Almighty, not accumulate the almighty dollar. Then why do these church leaders try to draw an analogy between Avis and the church? The Bible teaches us to be good stewards of all that

---

[37] Terry L. Gyger, Dave B. Calhoun, and E. Walford Thompson, *Handbook for Church Growth,* p. 271.

God has given to us, but our theology must dictate the methods of stewardship. Is it improper to advertise or even use telemarketing? There is nothing wrong with these tools, unless they become gods. Inviting people to worship may not be the right thing to do, because if they are unconverted they are not able to worship God. The unconverted need to be evangelized and then invited to worship. Inviting someone to come to church is a non-sensible idea. As I said before no one can "come to church." The church goes to worship, fellowship, etc.

Pragmatism does not understand the law of God, or the grace of God. The law and the gospel are on the endangered species list, because of the awful abuse in recent years. Martin Luther said, "the difference between the Law and the Gospel is the height of knowledge in Christendom."[38] The reformers did not attempt to replace the law and the gospel with anything, because everything in the Bible came under the law or the gospel. "We divide this Word into two principal parts or kinds: the one is called the 'Law,' the other the 'Gospel.' All the rest can be gathered under the one or the other of these two headings."[39] Pragmatism may accomplish what is perceived as church growth, but the people may be deceived when something else replaces the preaching of the law of God. Without the law of God how can anyone understand God's love? God's law cannot be ignored.

Just because pragmatism causes a church to grow does not give it approval in the sight of God. "According to the pragmatic interpretation of evangelical faith, Christianity has to compete with other self-help programs. It has to promise health, wealth, and happiness. But what happens when something works better."[40]

---

[38] Michael Scott Horton, *Beyond Culture Wars*, p. 109.
[39] Ibid.
[40] Michael Scott Horton, *Made In America*, p. 49.

The church must have a standard so objective goals for church growth meet with reality. The Word of God is the standard for the purpose, mission, and ministry of the church and there is no possibility of finding something better.

The pragmatic agenda works as well for the Jehovah's Witness or Mormons as it does for the evangelical church. For example, the church growth movement theorists use an assessment center to determine whether or not a man (and his wife?) has the qualifications and potential to start a new church. The fundamental theory behind the assessment center would work just as well for the Church of the Latter Day Saints as it would for a Presbyterian Church. That is the reason liberals and conservatives alike may attend the assessment center. The assessment center is a pragmatic utilitarian psychologically man-made program. Church growth movement advocates argue for this method of selecting men to plant new churches because they say it works better than the old programs! Of course, a man-centered assessment will result in a man-centered ministry.

The story of the man of God from Judah in 1 Kings 13 is a good example of how God deals with ungodly pragmatism. The man of God was instructed by God to go to a particular place, execute a particular task, and return home without eating bread or drinking water. A prophet seduced the man of God to eat and drink, which he did, but God punished him for his disobedience. No doubt, it was a matter of prudence and pragmatism to be refreshed before completing the trip, but God had spoken. God's covenant structure is not compromising or pragmatic. There are blessings for those who keep the covenant and cursed is the man who breaks the covenant.

Dr. Guinness is right. If we dine with the god of pragmatism, we should "have a long spoon." The temptations of modernity are tremendous. Pragmatic utility is not necessarily sinful, but pragmatism may become sinful if accepted uncritically. The church growth movement has adopted the god of pragmatism by its "uncritical use of such insights and tools of modernity as management and marketing."[41] The church will come under the judgment of God if she uses a poll to determine the truth. "For the sake of 'seeker sensitivity,' preaching remains superficial, with thousands of confessing Christians fed a weekly diet of entry-level evangelism."[42]

Another basic philosophy of the church growth movement that comes from the modern table is consumerism. This world and life view is not an illusion, although it is connected with the use of modern imagery. Consumerism has been molded by the cast of modernity. The church growth movement has deified consumerism rather than treating it as an omen of modernity. A consumer is one who uses a commodity or service. The consumer integrates pragmatism and utilitarianism to produce consumerism. Christians, especially in this present time, are consumers, but God is not a product. To put that in evangelical terms: "We are not selling a product to a consumer, but proclaiming a Savior to a sinner."[43]

The church growth movement teaches that marketing the church is necessary for church growth. Consider the progression in the following sentences from the church growth movement treatment of the subject:

> The Church is a business.'/'Marketing is essential for a business to operate successfully.'/'The Bible is one of the world's great marketing texts.'/'However, the point is indisputable: the Bible does not warn against the evils of marketing.'/'So it behooves us not to spend time bickering about techniques and process-

---

[41] Os Guinness, *Dining With the Devil*, p. 25
[42] Douglas Webster, *Selling Jesus*, p. 111.
[43] Michael Scott Horton, *Made In America*, p. 71.

es.'/'Think of your church not as a religious meeting place, but as a service agency - an entity that exists to satisfy people's needs.... [44]

The syllogism sounds reasonable, except "meeting needs does not always satisfy needs; it often stokes further needs and raises the pressure of eventual disillusionment. As Immanuel Kant said to the Russian historian Karamzin, 'Give a man everything he desires and yet at this very moment he will feel that everything is not everything.' The outcome is a massive pandering to the pathology of a consumerist age."[45] The gods created by man will never satisfy the deepest yearning of the soul. Across the pages of history hedonism and narcissism were more than world and life views, they became gods in the eyes of pagans and Christians. Even in the church, Tetzel sold indulgences much like television preachers sell the gospel in our time. Likewise, the church growth movement has knuckled under to the pressure from modernity.

The fundamental goal, however sad, but true, is that most Christians want to be "happy" from a secular perspective. All of life is shaped around the desire to be self-fulfilled and happy. The French Revolution certainly had a profound influence on the concept of "happiness." Liberty, equality, and fraternity redefined happiness for every successive generation. The world view we call consumerism suggests that happiness comes from instant gratification.

Selling Jesus is an art for the church growth experts. Evangelism is no longer God-centered, but rather it is consumer-centered. Singers try to dazzle the audience with sensational music. Preachers preach to "felt needs" using

---

[44] Os Guinness, Dining With the Devil, p. 58.
[45] Ibid., p. 65.

popular aphorisms, rarely expounding from the inerrant Word of God or using sound exegetical and hermeneutical skills.

The strategy for marketing the church may very well be a death angel in disguise. A pastor responded to an article written in "Christianity Today" on June 24, 1991 about the church growth movement.

> My concern with the movement is that it prompts the question, "What is the difference between the Christian church and any other business that makes use of telemarketing, demographic, and other mainstream corporate resources?" Are we saying the church is a business just like any other business - only our message is different? If this is so, possibly pastoral training should lean heavier in the direction of marketing, business, and advertising skills and less on theology, biblical scholarship, and pastoral counseling classes.[46]

Obviously the writer of that article, Rev. David Coffin, is not an advocate of the church growth movement and apparently he is aware that many seminaries have moved toward teaching church marketing rather than theology. Seminaries are responding to the "felt needs" of what used to be theological students. But, that is what they want. "Yesterday McDonalds sold only hamburgers and fish; today you can eat breakfast there! In their vocations, our people [church leaders at Bear Valley Baptist Church, Denver, Colo.] have been taught to think, how can we improve, expand our markets, do a better job?"[47] Implied here is the idea that like McDonalds, the church must find out what people want and

---

[46] Rev. David Coffin, "Letters to the Editor", *Christianity Today*, August 19, 1991, p. 5.
[47] Frank R. Tillapaugh, *Unleashing the Church*, (Ventura, CA: Regal Books, 1982), p. 32.

what makes them happy and provide it without considering the theological implications. The church growth movement has compromised and capitulated essential theological standards to the point that their disciples have turned their backs from the marks of the church.

Christians ought to investigate the variety of world views found in the modern world. The Christian world view is fundamentally rooted in the supernaturalism of the triune God. The Christian world view, as previously mentioned, is characterized by a philosophy of absolute truth. What is truth? Theologians and philosophers in all ages wrestle with this question. It is said that truth is that which is in agreement to that which is represented and truth corresponds to reality, so you might say that truth is that which conforms to fact or reality. Christians have the Bible to help them understand the truth relative to the excellencies of God and the sinfulness of man. Jesus manifestly explained how unbelievers do not understand biblical truth (John 8:43-47). The Bible is truth as the inspired Psalmist said, "The sum of Thy word is truth" (Psalm 119:160). Christians must be affected from that truth. "Thou are near, O Lord, and all Thy commandments are truth" (Psalm 119:151). Moral truth will affect every part of the Christian life. Moral truth is rooted in the integrity of God, therefore truth is an attribute of God which God has chosen to share with His rational creatures. The Bible teaches that there is saving power in truth. "But as for me, my prayer is to Thee, O Lord, at an acceptable time; O God, in the greatness of Thy lovingkindness answer me with Thy saving truth" (Psalm 69:13). It is the duty of all Christians to think about God's truth. The Bible tells us to take "every thought captive to the obedience of Christ" (2 Corinthians. 10:5). Today Christians are being lulled to sleep and Satan's deceptive tricks try to convince Christians that truth is relative and there is no difference between truth and error. However we live in a postmodern world that declares all objective real

truth is dead. Modernity believes that truth is discoverable
though investigation based on world views that allegedly lead
to ultimate truth. If modernity is the god of the church
growth movement, how does the movement discover truth?
This question remains to be answered because the church
growth movement has no theological center upon which to
determine truth.

The church growth movement is exactly that, a
movement, but to further clarify it, it is an unbiblical
movement. The church militant has contended with
movements throughout its history. The church growth
movement is not much different than many other movements
founded on human philosophy. Its founder, Donald
McGavran, taught at a liberal seminary, was in a liberal
denomination (The Disciples of Christ) and it is not feasible
to think that his world and life view, theology, and doctrine
was not effected by those people who surrounded him.
McGavran and his movement are the products of modernity.
His disciples have followed in his steps and they drink deeply
from the streams of modernity. They are not committed to
classical Christianity but instead "the religious leadership
withheld its gift and whored after each successive stage of
modernity's profligacy."[48] The danger of the church growth
movement is found in its god - modernity. They have made
no attempt to identify their theology or doctrine. In fact, they
have "attempted not to allow church growth teaching to
identify itself with any particular paradigm of systematic
theology. Church growth principles have intentionally been
kept as atheological as possible... ."[49] Michael Horton
pointed out the danger by reminding the church that "a
rejection of theology is a rejection of Scripture, inasmuch as

---

[48] Thomas C. Oden, *After Modernity... What?*, p. 31.
[49] C Peter Wagner, *Church Growth and the Whole Gospel*, p. 83.

the Bible is filled with propositional statements about the character of God."[50]

Church growth movement advocates do not seem to understand the concept of church growth. If the methodology of the movement is brought under critical analysis using biblical standards, the reply goes something like this: "When church growth is attacked today, it is usually done by persons who, not having had the opportunity to think their way through the morass, are comforting themselves with the old rationalizations of defeat."[51] It is not church growth that suffers this critique, it is the church growth movement's affinity to the god of the movement which is modernity rather than the God of the Bible.

An evaluation of the church growth movement will reveal the preponderance of modernity in their scheme. The "church growth movement is a matter of both ideas that serve ideals and ideas that serve interests."[52] If the ideals and interests were on behalf of the true and living God, then the church growth movement would be a blessing. However, the weight of the evidence is that the church growth movement has self serving ideals and interests.

The church growth movement waves the banner of modernity and there is no indication the church growth movement will inquire of the dangers of modernity and turn from them. However, there is an antithesis.

The Christian mind has sought and found a way to understand life in the light of revelation; the modern mind rejects that light and turns instead to private experience for illumination. The Christian mind accepts

---

[50] Michael Horton, *Beyond Culture Wars*, p. 67.
[51] Donald McGavran and George G. Hunter III, *Church Growth Strategies that Work,* (Nashville: Abingdon, 1980), p. 19.
[52] Os Guinness, *Dining With the Devil*, p. 75.

God's pronouncements concerning the meaning of life as the only true measure in that regard; the modern mind rejects such revelation as the figment of a religious imagination.[53]

The more room we give modernity, the less room we give the true and living God. The church growth movement openly admits to embrace the children of modernity, but remove themselves from doctrine and theology. Our Lord teaches that "No one can serve two masters; for either he will hate the one and love the other, or he will hold to one and despise the other. You cannot serve God and mammon" (Matthew 6:24).

The church growth movement could make a contribution to the health of the church if they will turn from modernity's control and define their nature and purpose biblically and theologically. "Without any authorized definition of a movement's teaching, it cannot span the generations or even assess the validity of potential misinterpretations."[54] We will do well to remember the tensions we face with the concept of church growth.

The sense of helplessness that prevails among our people...is a serious indictment of the crisis in which we find ourselves. Therefore when we speak of the need of the reflective growth of the church, we are speaking of something of critical importance, affecting the future of the cosmos.[55]

---

[53] David Wells, *No Place for Truth*, p. 280.

[54] Thomas C. Oden, *After Modernity... What?*, p. 151.

[55] Jitsuo Moridawa, *Biblical Dimensions of Church Growth*, (Valley Forge, PA: Judson Press, 1979), p. 46.

Although the adoption of a pantheon of gods by the church growth movement is obvious, the most obvious god of the church growth movement is modernity. The compelling evidence is that the church growth movement finds satisfaction with those false gods rather than with the one true and living God.

The growth and success of the church growth movement may be attributed to ill equipped and patronizing ministers. They are more interested in their own private agendas than in the clear teaching of the Word of God.

The future of the church does not depend on the gods of the church growth movement, but in the powerful work of God through the hands of faithful churchmen who are being reformed by the Word of God.

Sylvester Stallone was the protagonist in the movie "Lockup." He was unjustly imprisoned, so he tried to escape. During the escape, his partner told Stallone to turn left, but Stallone argued that he should go right. At his partner's insistence, Stallone turned left and the prison guards captured him. It turned out that his partner betrayed him and was an informer for the prison officials. Making the wrong turn can be very painful or bring death itself. Is it possible that the spirit of this modern/post-modern world has deceived pastors, elders, and church members?

The arguments in favor of the pragmatic methods tend to focus on "stewardship." The advocates tell us that "God requires good stewardship." Therefore, prudence dictates the consultation of management experts to get the most for your money. Biblical stewardship is married to good sound management, but biblical stewardship follows from faithfulness. Faithfulness is what God had in mind when He sent Joshua in the land of Canaan. Joshua didn't have the option of hiring the Egyptian Army to do his fighting. Joshua had to do it God's way and nothing else was acceptable.

The church growth movement has turned from God's regulative principle. Denominational leaders and financiers actively promote the church growth movement through denominational and independent seminaries. The watershed effect finds its way to pastors who are constantly challenged by local church leaders and congregations to grow, grow, grow. The pastor sees the glitter and gold. He needs an increase in salary, so why not employ these church growth movement methods. The pastor probably thinks, "it's not that big of a compromise and who would be against church growth." No Christian can be opposed to church growth, but all Christians must be opposed to church growth methodology that is not in keeping with the Word of God. The wrong turn to the methods of the church growth movement began at the top with church leadership. Sometimes it seems so right to make the wrong turn. "We should therefore heed Origin's ancient principle: Christians are free to plunder the Egyptians, but forbidden to set up a golden calf."[56]

Christians seem to be so easily diverted to the right or to the left. I think it is the spirit of this modern/postmodern world. It does not matter which world you live in, they both have seductive powers that are equally dangerous. The end of each system denies the authority and sovereignty of God. Modernity depends on the inherent ability of rationalism to conquer the world with modernism through industry, technology and telecommunications. Post-modernity reduces intelligent human discourse to an irrational vacuum supported only by the feeling of personal interpretation. It stands to reason that if a church planter uses the right laws of management, understands psychological needs, embraces the pietistic practices of Christianity, and makes a vow to a creed or

---

[56] Os Guinness, *Dining With the Devil*, p. 90.

confession that can be interpreted relative to purpose, then surely he will be successful and please God at the same time. And after all, look at what the church planter has done for God! The temptation to follow the ways of the world is very tempting indeed. So many diversions are before God's people. The dangers of idolatry are ever present. Therefore, I think it is possible for church leaders and laymen to embrace the church growth movement. But I also think it is possible for God to show them the error of their ways.

It does not take a precocious genius to realize that the language of the Bible simply does not square with the language of the church growth movement experts. It doesn't take an intellectual giant to realize that a "user-friendly church" is nothing more than the *argumentum ad populum*. This argument simply appeals to public opinion. God's Word will not change even if 100% of the people vote against Him. You don't have to be a scholar to realize that church growth movement churches keep their sermons brief and humorous. Anecdotal preaching reduces the sermon to a talk that ultimately entertains. You don't have to look very far to see the anti-intellectual agenda in the church growth movement.

The Word of God must be the determining principle for any Christian belief system and the method that follows from that belief system. The church growth movement advocates must meet at the debate table willing to engage in fruitful discussion that will lead to reformation (discovery or rediscovery) of biblical truth.

All the programs, all the man-centered ideas, all the managerial expertise, and all the psychological strategies will never change God's plan for planting churches. The glitter, gold, and glib tongue of the church growth movement may be the popular method to plant churches. However, the God-centered way to plant churches is to understand and follow the biblical mandates for the purpose, mission, and ministry of the church.

About the Author

Martin Murphy has a B.A. in Bible from Columbia International University and a Master of Divinity from Reformed Theological Seminary. He is the author of several books including *The Essence of Christian Doctrine*.

CPSIA information can be obtained at www.ICGtesting.com
Printed in the USA
LVOW06s1550160715

446499LV00017B/641/P